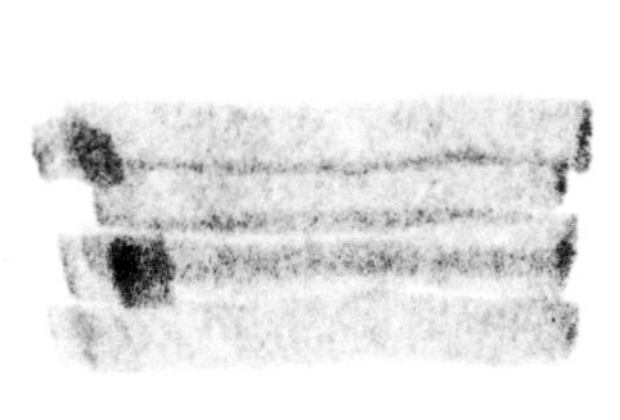

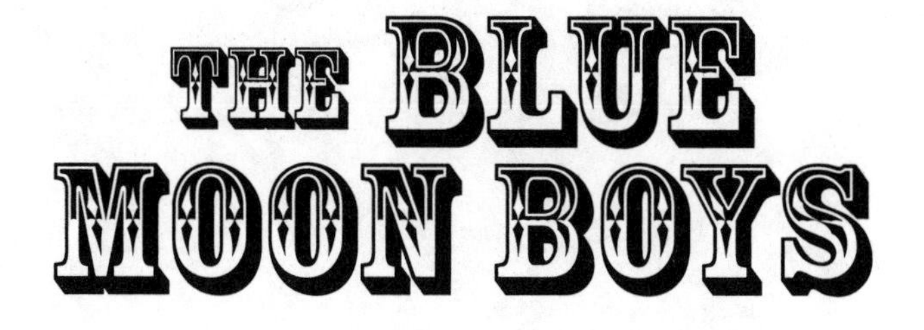
THE BLUE
MOON BOYS

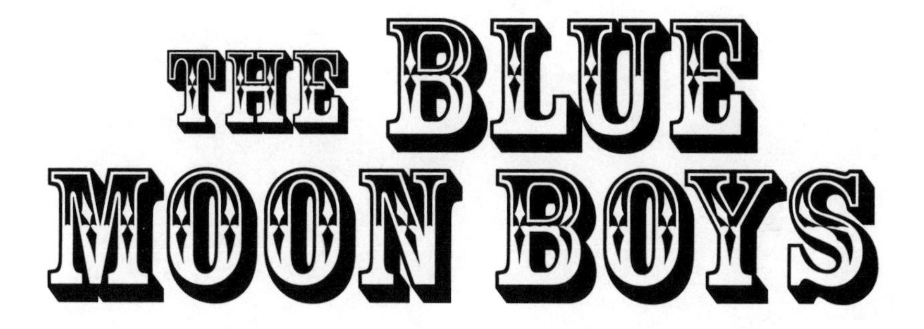

The Story of

Elvis Presley's Band

Ken Burke and Dan Griffin

An A Cappella Book

Library of Congress Cataloging-in-Publication Data
Burke, Ken K.
The Blue Moon Boys : the story of Elvis Presley's band / Ken Burke and Dan Griffin.—1st ed.
p. cm.
Includes index.
ISBN-13: 978-1-55652-614-5
ISBN-10: 1-55652-614-8
1. Blue Moon Boys. 2. Rockabilly music—History and criticism.
I. Griffin, Dan, 1956- II. Title.
ML421.B65B87 2006
781.66092'2—dc22

2006006517

Jacket and interior design: Scott Rattray

First edition
Published by Chicago Review Press, Incorporated
814 North Franklin Street
Chicago, Illinois 60610
ISBN-13: 978-1-55652-614-5
ISBN-10: 1-55652-614-8
Printed in the United States of America
5 4 3 2 1

To Bill Black

The missing piece of the puzzle

CONTENTS

FOREWORD

by Brian Setzer

IN THE BEGINNING, there was Elvis, Scotty, and Bill. And it was good! No, it was sensational! It was a sound no one had ever heard. It was to be called rockabilly and, later, rock 'n' roll. The sound supplied to Elvis Presley via Scotty Moore on guitar, Bill Black on bass, and soon D. J. Fontana on drums was actually the sound of the first rock 'n' roll band, without whom Elvis may have chosen an entirely different path.

Brian Setzer. COURTESY OF SURFDOG RECORDS

To my ears, rockabilly may very well be the first type of music to blend different styles together. Country, blues, hillbilly, jazz, black, and white were all indiscriminately combined with a big heap of sweat and adrenaline—and blended recklessly I might add. For these young guys, just coming home from the service after World War II, where this music came from didn't matter. They just did it.

Scotty Moore has said, "When Elvis first came to visit me in his pink pegged pants and greased-back hair, my wife nearly flew out the back door!" But Scotty knew that crazy lookin' cat from Tupelo had the voice and charisma to start a revolution.

Before he met Elvis, Scotty's guitar playing was still very rooted in country and Merle Travis–style finger picking. Almost immediately after teaming with Elvis, his playing became more electric, more inventive, and more influenced by blues players. He started to take chances, putting heavy helpings of echo on his sound and blending musical styles together much more than he ever had.

Bill Black was a neighbor and friend of Scotty Moore's. It was a bluegrass tradition to sometimes "slap" the bass—alternately plucking and slapping the string back down against the neck—but this was done only occasionally (perhaps during soloing). Bill Black's "slap bass technique" was to dominate the Sun sessions. In bluegrass music, slap bass playing was rarely used, but in this new rockabilly music, it was *always* used. An entirely new sound!

D. J. Fontana actually played a full drum kit. Bluegrass and country bands *never* used drums at all. Now all of a sudden, this music has a beat. A heavy, rockin', hillbilly beat. To my ears, D. J. Fontana added a swing element (almost a Gene Krupa sound) to this new quartet.

So my friends, can you imagine being in the room when this jam session first came down? If you can, close your eyes and picture all these different elements coming together, lighting up the room like a fireball!

Without Scotty, Bill, and D.J., Elvis might have had a band, but who's to say if it could have come close to capturing the magic of those early Sun sessions?

Ladies and gentlemen, introducing the very first rock 'n' roll band . . .

Elvis Presley—vocals/acoustic guitar
Scotty Moore—lead guitar
Bill Black—stand-up bass
D. J. Fontana—drums

ACKNOWLEDGMENTS

KEN BURKE WISHES to thank the following people for their help and encouragement:

A great many people selflessly gave their time and provided contact information to make the completion of this project possible. At the top of the list is our editor, Yuval Taylor, who patiently dealt with two guys attempting to work together for the first time. It was my distinct honor to speak with such legendary figures as Sonny Burgess, Jack Clement, Billy Lee Riley, Barbara Pittman, Gordon Stoker, and the always gracious Tillman Franks.

Many interviews led to other sources. J. M. Van Eaton got me in contact with Roland Janes and Martin Willis. Sonny Burgess made sure that I called Ace Cannon and Jumpin' Gene Simmons. Rockabilly legend Glen Glenn got me in touch with Billy Strange and Kitty Maddox, the wife of the late Fred Maddox. Marc Bristol of *Blue Suede News* hooked us up with the lone surviving Maddox Brother, Don Maddox. Sheree Homer of *Rockabilly Revue* provided literally dozens of contacts. Little Jimmy Dickens's personal manager, Richard Davis, made sure I spoke with Bobby Bare and Jim Ed Brown. Publicist Sandy Brokaw of the Brokaw company provided an introduction to Glen Campbell, who helped me understand Presley's technique better than anyone. Barbara Pittman persuaded Ronnie Smith, a friend of Elvis's from the Lauderdale Courts days, to call me with vital info and perspective. Northwest rockabilly pioneer Bobby Wayne helped set up my interview with Gary Bryant months before Bryant passed away. Larry Rogers got me in touch with Bob Tucker, who led me to Joe Lee. Rebecca Shapiro at Shore Fire Media and Niels Schroeter at Surfdog Records brought the very knowledgeable Brian Setzer onboard. Martha Moore of So Much Moore publicity got Jerry Reed on the phone for me. Cris Busam at Ron Rainey Management lined up Alvin Lee's interview. Bob Timmers at the Rockabilly Hall of Fame—the single most worthwhile music site on the Internet—first got me in touch with D. J. Fontana. My dear pen pal Tommie Wix started the whole thing when she hooked me up with Billy Swan, Billy Lee Riley, Sonny Burgess, and Stan Kesler. Susan Graham of Night Glare Films, in association with Dornasus Productions, diligently transcribed filmed interviews that were conducted by Dan Griffin and Bob Santelli.

Without Dan Griffin, I never would have tackled this project, nor would I have had a chance to meet Scotty Moore, D. J. Fontana, Louis Black, Nancy Black-Shockley, the king of Nashville bass players Bob Moore, the Jordanaires' Gordon Stoker and Ray Walker, or the great Boots Randolph. Thanks, Dan.

I'd like to extend a very special thanks to two people who came to my rescue when things were looking darkest. Canadian entertainer, music writer, and hardcore telephone addict Johnny Vallis not only supplied contact information for Glen Glenn, Tommy Sands, and Tom Tall, but freely shared rare recordings from his personal archives. My old pal Gary Hatch offered support above and beyond the call of duty—and all he wants in exchange is for me to write his life story. Seemed like a fair deal at the time.

Most of all, I want to thank my wife Lorraine and my daughter Emily for all the sacrifices they have made so I could pursue my dream. I love you both.

Thank you one and all.

Dan Griffin wishes to thank the following people for their help and encouragement:

First and foremost, I want to thank Ken Burke and Susan Rod Graham for keeping two wonderful projects about three worthy individuals alive when I would have long given up. I would also like to thank these friends and family members, who have given support in many ways during my life and career: Randy Amos, Joe Arena, Bill Ayres, Barry Barksdale, Sonny Burgess, Paul Burlison, Gary Burke, Jeff Campbell, Dr. Virginia Spencer Carr, Alex Chilton, Lance Cowan, Marshall Crenshaw, Dr. Cynthia Denham, Dr. Carlos Dews, Steve J. Dubner, Pat Duncan, Mitch Easter, Horst Fascher, Doug Ford, Jeffrey Dean Foster, Jon Fried and Deana Shoshkes, Jeffrey Gaskill, Jeri Goldstein, Ben and Shirley Griffin, Sally Grossman, George and Olivia Harrison, Mary Harron and John C. Walsh, Diane Haas, Tameron Hedge, Faye Hunter, Ian and Helen Kimmet, Eric Krohel, Susan, Jackie, Chris, and Adam Leamy, Michael Lesser, Peter Lippman, John Lombardo, Bill Lloyd, Dr. Mary Mercer,

Natalie Merchant, Carson and Reeves McCullers, John Porter, Mary Ramsey, Keith Richards, Ira Rogers, Robert Salvatore, Robert Santelli, Rees Shad, Bruce Sinofsky, Dr. Ray Stonicher, Syd Straw, Ron Swartz, Garry W. and Tammy Tallent, Suzanne Vega, Michael and Brenda Visceglia, Dr. Christopher Wang, Rex Welch, John Williams, Ron Wood, John Zeigler, and, especially, Captain Patrick J. Leamy (1944–2005), NYSP, my brother.

INTRODUCTION

by Ken Burke

"In later years Sam Phillips would say it was Scotty more than anyone who provided and/or influenced much of the 'Elvis Presley sound,' that Scotty was the Great Unsung Hero in Elvis Presley's life."

—Jerry Hopkins, *Elvis—A Biography* (1971)

SINCE JERRY HOPKINS first wrote those words more than 30 years ago, hundreds of Elvis Presley–related books have reached the marketplace. Canny publishers seeking to fill the void created by the 1977 death of rock's first true superstar have issued everything from cookbooks and spiritual guides to collections of movie trivia, "still alive" hoaxes, tell-all confessionals from ex-lovers (both real and imagined), and stories about the controversial life and times of Colonel Tom Parker.

There is a good reason why all these books are printed.

Elvis Presley still matters.

During this modern age, when hip-hop has supplanted rock music as the number-one radio force and the average country star is a thinly disguised pop singer in a "wife beater" T-shirt and cowboy hat, Presley still clearly embodies the most thrilling musical creation of the twentieth century—rock 'n' roll.

Of course the genre was in full swing before Presley truly emerged. RCA's *50th Anniversary of Rock 'n' Roll* promotional campaign, based on the release of "That's All Right (Mama)," is pure hogwash. Bill Haley, Fats Domino, and Bo Diddley had already made hit rock 'n' roll records. But Presley created the most resonant image of what a rock 'n' roll performer should be. Sexy, outrageous, and blessed with a playful sense of self-mockery, he daringly blended

R & B with up-tempo country, perfecting a potent new musical strain in the process. Indeed, even though the mainstream record industry now flees in terror whenever it hears the word, the fact remains that our collective image of a true original rocker is that of the greasy, sneering rockabilly.

More importantly, Presley's personal rags-to-riches transformation reinforced the myth of the American Dream, a time-tested fable that ends with the moral that if you work hard and never stop believing, you, too, can become rich and famous. Why, just look at Elvis! Writers of every stripe have fleshed out Presley's rendition of that legend, each summoning variations of the following themes:

"Elvis was born poor white trash, but his God-given talent made him a millionaire."

"Elvis was a good boy. He *loved* his mother."

"Elvis was hypnotized by the Colonel."

"Elvis was so generous that he gave Cadillacs to perfect strangers."

"Elvis was deeply religious. He sang gospel songs all night long."

"Elvis slept around . . . *a lot*!"

"Elvis was patriotic! He went in the army—not like that Cassius Clay!"

"Elvis could have been the next James Dean, but Colonel Parker wouldn't let him."

"Elvis was betrayed by his closest friends."

"Elvis tricked his doctors into giving him too many pills."

"Elvis and Priscilla still loved each other. After he died, she came to his defense, saved Graceland, and resurrected his reputation."

Each book has its relative merits. For humor's sake, I like the one that claims that Presley actually died during military training, the army covered it up, and the Presley discharged from the army in 1960 was an imposter. (Yup, I've bought and read my fair share of these things.) Yet, whether the Presley phenomenon inspires scholarly treatise or inane schlock, most writers miss what Hopkins initially pointed out. The Hillbilly Cat would probably never have made it out of Memphis without the exhaustive efforts of the Blue Moon Boys: guitarist Scotty Moore, bassist Bill Black, and, later, drummer D. J. Fontana.

Given their importance to the development of rock 'n' roll, it is utterly surprising that Moore, Black, and Fontana—while often feted by nostalgia buffs and rockabilly revivalists—are for the most part forgotten by American music fans. Whole commemorative books and documentaries about Presley have been issued wherein these historically important figures are barely mentioned.

One could reasonably blame Presley himself. He was the show, and a damned good one at that. Once his career blossomed, it's doubtful that anyone ever came away from a Presley stage show commenting on the band. Yet, for a performer who was surprisingly articulate in interviews, he never said much to journalists or disc jockeys about the guys in his band other than the obligatory, "I'm lucky to have them." In fact, what little he did say about his early career was usually inaccurate. Yet there are other reasons for the relative anonymity of his bandmates.

Moore, modest and more than a little bitter, ducked the limelight for a great many years and still seems uncomfortable talking about those early days. Black, the real heart and soul of the Blue Moon Boys, died in 1965, before pop culture embraced the art of rock journalism. Fontana, who has never been able to communicate his highly enjoyable private wit to mass audiences, suffers from the Ringo Starr-oh-he's-just-a-drummer syndrome. It also didn't help that, compared to Elvis Presley's movie-star beauty, his fellow musicians resembled a drugstore clerk, a bowling alley bartender, and a barber playing an outdoor picnic.

Appearances aside, it's unquestionable that Scotty Moore, Bill Black, and D. J. Fontana were pivotal figures in Presley's life and career. In fact, it might be argued that Moore played an even more important role in the aspiring performer's career than did Sun Records chief Sam Phillips. Think about how history would have been different if, when Phillips asked Moore to audition the shy singer, Moore had refused, or if he'd flat-out told Phillips that the kid had nothing worth pursuing. Fortunately, that didn't happen. Although Moore believed that Presley possessed a merely adequate voice, he was amazed at the youngster's knowledge of songs from every genre. Subsequently, after asking Phillips to book studio time, it was Moore—aided by friend Black—who set everything in motion. A frustrating night spent looking for a sound to build on brought about the Coca Cola–break clowning that resulted in "That's All Right (Mama)."

Upon forming an official band, Moore gave young Presley his record collection and instructed him to choose songs for their upcoming recordings and stage shows. Onstage, the inexperienced vocalist was so nervous that his leg began to shake, eliciting screams from some female patrons. Any other bandleader would've told the kid to cool it and act like a professional, for crying out loud. But Moore told Presley to *keep shaking that leg*. Further, at the suggestion of Sam Phillips, Moore was quickly pressed into service as band manager, tour manager, and driver. Moore introduced the new King of Western Bop to the hardscrabble life of the music business, and Presley loved it.

And what about bass player Bill Black? What would have happened had Bill Black decided that the youngster he dubbed a "snotty-nosed kid" in all those "wild clothes" wasn't worth his time? Who would have egged Presley on when he was "acting the fool" (according to Moore) while banging on the guitar during an impromptu belting out of "That's All Right (Mama)"? During those early stage shows, when the Memphis Flash simply wasn't connecting with the audience, who would have lit a fire under his insecure ass with crowd-pleasing jokes and screams, if not Bill Black? Never a virtuoso on the bass the way Moore was on his guitar, Black nonetheless played with a percussive vigor that eliminated the need for drums on those early Sun singles. The interplay and groove he forged with Presley, Moore, and, later, Fontana, was simply irreplaceable.

Without D. J. Fontana, who would have inspired Presley to transform his stage moves from daring-for-the-times leg wiggling into the semi-choreographed displays of sexual bravado that shocked and delighted a nation? In the studio, Fontana's work on Presley's early RCA Victor recordings was nothing short of phenomenal. Alternating strip-club blues with New Orleans shuffles and rapid-fire big band rolls (check out his work on "Hound Dog"), the drummer made Presley's records almost as exciting to hear as the young phenom was to see. What other rim-shot jockey could have done that?

Certainly not the ham-fisted Johnny Bernero, who played on "I Forgot to Remember to Forget." And jazz and big band players abhorred Presley. Earl Palmer, who played on records by Fats Domino, Lloyd Price, and Little Richard, was strictly a New Orleans commodity at the time. J. M. Van Eaton, who would eventually play on all of Jerry Lee Lewis's great Sun hits, was still in high school. Buddy Harman, the greatest of all Nashville drummers, would never have given up lucrative session work to tour. So, it had to be Fontana, whose youthful drive and humor kept him on Presley's wavelength every bit as much as his talent did.

In 1954 Presley, Moore, and Black began their relationship as a band, and on those early Sun singles their names appeared as "Elvis Presley" in big type with "Scotty and Bill" just below that, in slightly smaller type. On early concert posters they were most often billed as Elvis Presley and the Blue Moon Boys. Drummer D. J. Fontana entered the picture nearly six months after their formation and beefed up their live sound with professionalism and flair. It wasn't long before Fontana became so important to the band that he became their highest paid member.

Together, Moore, Black, and Fontana enabled Presley to realize his most grandiose dreams—making hit records, high-profile television appearances, movies, and riches galore. Further, when his career needed rescuing after a decade of formulaic, drive-in-quality movies, Presley called upon Moore and Fontana (Black had passed away by this time) to help reignite his rapidly fading star on the Singer Company–sponsored television special *Elvis* (also known as the *'68 Comeback Special).* Once his career's heat was reestablished, though, Presley promptly turned his back on them.

To our knowledge, this is the first book to attempt a biography of Elvis's band. While Scotty Moore's autobiography (as told to James Dickerson), *That's Alright, Elvis*, and D. J. Fontana's quasi-autobiographical picture book, *The Beat Behind the King*, are both useful, what they don't provide are insights into the life and death of Bill Black, information about his hit-making instrumental group the Bill Black Combo, or a solid discussion of what the men who were the Blue Moon Boys have been doing since Presley simply left them behind.

It is our aim to fill that void.

This book has a circuitous history. It began with Dan Griffin, a former sponsor's liaison man for the Rolling Stones and award-winning concert promoter in Woodstock, New York, writing a memoir about his years as booker, manager, and producer for Scotty Moore and D. J. Fontana. Unfortunately, in a cost-cutting move, the publishers who initially signed on dropped the project. Fighting leukemia, Griffin was forced to allow his manuscript to lay dormant while he concentrated on his health. I learned about Griffin from Sun rockabilly legend Sonny Burgess, and we began phoning each other regularly.

As a contributor to the *Contemporary Musicians* series of books and to such small-press publications as *Blue Suede News*, *Brutarian Quarterly*, *Original Cool*, and *Roctober*, I interviewed every original rockabilly that came within my purview. Whenever the subject of Elvis Presley came up, I invariably asked, "What can you tell me about Bill Black?" Some had stories. Most did not. As Griffin and I began talking we discovered that we both had a strong interest in finding out more about Presley's bass player. Griffin had already laid much of the groundwork with the intermittent filming of his documentary about Moore's and Fontana's comeback years, but we both knew more had to be gotten.

We approached Chicago Review Press editor Yuval Taylor with the idea of doing a biography about Bill Black, thinking it would be a unique twist on the typical Presley-connected publication. Taylor, who had hired me to write my first book (*Country Music Changed My Life*), felt that the story of a dead bass player might be a bit too esoteric for mass audiences. As we groaned with disappointment, he quickly countered, "How about a book on Elvis's original band? I don't think that's ever been done before." We jumped at the chance. (Taylor, a gravely serious individual, provoked big laughs with his deadpan criticism of the project's initial title, *The Power Behind the Throne*. "It sounds like someone is lurking behind a toilet.")

Dan Griffin has generously allowed me to draw from his unpublished memoirs and to view many hours of interview footage with Moore, Fontana, and various members of the Bill Black Combo. Much of this footage, which includes several rare, star-studded performances, will appear in the upcoming documentary *The Return of the Blue Moon Boys* by Night Glare Films in association with Dornasus Productions. We both conducted fresh interviews with various friends and associates of the band, but many revelations in this book come from Griffin himself. Traveling from gig to gig with Moore and Fontana, he was told honest, unvarnished versions of the band's stories from the Golden Age of Rock 'n' Roll.

Despite the fact that we criticize some of his actions, neither author has set out to disparage the King. Both of us are in this because Elvis Presley still matters to us, too. We dig the music, we admire the people who helped create it, and we want to present stories told by the actual participants whenever possible, before it is too late.

Myself, I was looking for more information about a genre that I prize with all my heart—rockabilly. Presley's was the first music I remember hearing. My sister had 45s of "Hound Dog," "I Gotta Know," "Trouble," and many others. An intense six-year-old, I played only the fast stuff over and over again. Years later, my fascination with Jerry Lee Lewis and Sun Records led me back to the recordings of Elvis, Scotty, and Bill. These seductive, invigorating performances renewed my appreciation of how great a rocker Presley truly was. Today, I champion "Baby, Let's Play House" as the gold standard of rockabilly music. For me, no other recording even comes close.

Until he met Moore and Fontana, Griffin was more of a fan of Presley's comeback period ("Don't Cry, Daddy," "Kentucky Rain," "Suspicious Minds") than he was of the seminal 1950s hits. Being with the surviving Blue Moon Boys hipped him to the residual power of those early sounds and, through sheer dint of personal exposure, he became a rather knowledgeable rockabilly buff—only in his case, he didn't read about the genre in books and CD notes; he met the people who played the music firsthand. Griffin traveled with the Sun Rhythm Section, roomed with Paul Burlison (the legendary Johnny Burnette & the Rock 'n' Roll Trio guitarist) and was befriended by none other than Sam Phillips.

Like any management figure, Griffin has endured many personal and professional conflicts with Moore and Fontana. That said, he still cares about these men more than even he would like to admit. If you ask Griffin for his favorite piece of trivia, he'll invariably respond, "Did you know that the Blue Moon Boys are the only band to have played with Elvis, three Beatles, the Stones, and Led Zeppelin?" He knows, because he helped make much of that happen.

So, we banded together—me, a blue-collar rockabilly aficionado, and Griffin, the experienced industry professional—to tell you the true story of three of rock 'n' roll's greatest unsung heroes: Scotty Moore, Bill Black, and D. J. Fontana: the Blue Moon Boys.

Black Canyon City, Arizona

Scotty Moore

"Had we not been very patient and very persistent, we would not have had the influence, quote unquote, that we have been given credit for."

—Sam Phillips, at the Hard Rock Café awards ceremony honoring Scotty Moore, 1997

THE PATIENCE Sam Phillips spoke of was very much in evidence at his Memphis Recording Service on July 5, 1954. Scotty Moore, Bill Black, and an eighteen-year-old singer named Elvis Presley were trying to make some sort of music that would show off the kid's potential. Once the singer passed this, the audition phase, *maybe* they'd all get together with a larger band, and *maybe* they'd cut something for Phillips's little Sun Records label. No promises, mind you. Phillips has often said that this initial process occurred over four to six months; Moore believes it happened within a few days of their first official meeting. Regardless, both agree that it was an unusually tough and unpromising experience.

"I can't tell you how many songs we worked through," Moore says today. Presley seemed committed to ballads, a few of which ("Blue Moon," "I Love You Because," and "Harbor Lights") were committed to tape. Years later historians would heap praise upon these overly sincere attempts at R & B crooning, but at the time, none of them were what Phillips wanted. God only knows what the singer himself was looking for that night. "I knew it just wasn't coming off," he later explained to Gordon Stoker of the Jordanaires.

Sometimes the Sun Records owner would simply call a halt to the proceedings, taking great pains to assure the boys that it wasn't a full-out dismissal. On the night in question, a tired Phillips again felt like the trio was going nowhere and he wanted them to get hot or go home. "Scotty put his ax in the case and Billy Black set down his bass," he told VH1's Sonicnet.com decades later. "Elvis, I think, was a little disappointed. He had his guitar around his neck. He had always played guitar real hard, beating hell out of it, and he started on 'That's All Right (Mama).'"

Black, picking up on the kid's manic, nearly comedic chanting, grabbed his bass and began slapping away in time. For the hell of it, Moore picked up his guitar and added some little fills that punctuated each exclamation Presley made. "That's all right mama! (DEE-dee) That's all right for you! (DEE-dee) That's all right mama anyway you do, that's all right."

The delighted Phillips had no inkling that Arthur "Big Boy" Crudup's 1951 blues hit was even in Presley's repertoire. Only this version was different; it was simple yet full, fast yet in the groove, and most of all, totally unique.

Scotty Moore and Elvis Presley onstage, 1957. Courtesy of Belle Meade Records

They may not have invented the form, but that night Elvis, Scotty, and Bill perfected what would come to be known as rockabilly.

After telling the boys to back up, find a place to start, and do it again, Phillips mockingly hollered out from the control room to the singer, "You've been putting us through this damn torment and this is what I've been looking for for *six months*."

If you ask Scotty Moore what it was like to be present at rock 'n' roll's "big bang," he will look at you as if you're crazy, and he might even call an abrupt halt to the interview. Normally a stoic and kindly figure, he has little tolerance for hyperbole and overstatement.

It's not hard to guess why.

How would you like to be a talented, creative individual in your own right, yet inevitably be asked every day, "What was Elvis Presley really like?"

How would you like to put your marriage and family life at risk for your job and then be denied the back-end payoff by a high-pressure, cutthroat manager and his passive-aggressive superstar?

How would you like to be denied the opportunity to capitalize on your talents and associations, but still be kept around in a lesser capacity, and then read how loyal and good-hearted the guy that you helped make famous was?

Then, after years of having your role downplayed or omitted in biographies and documentaries, how would you like to be told by hard-line revisionist historians that both you and the superstar in question stole your music from black artists?

You wouldn't like it, would you?

Well, neither does Scotty Moore.

So, if he occasionally breaks away from his trademark southern gentleman demeanor and lashes out, Moore can be forgiven. After all, even when he's had reason not to be, the Tennessee-born guitarist has been enduringly loyal to the late Elvis Presley.

Oh sure, when the libations are flowing among friends, he might put an amusing edge on stories about the girls the band met during those early road trips, or about Presley's childish temper tantrums and lack of manners. Yet, in public and even in his autobiography *That's Alright, Elvis*, Moore has observed that most sacred of covenants: what happens in the band stays in the band.

After all, that's what it initially was; a band. *Scotty Moore's band.*

Born Winfield Scott Moore III on December 27, 1931, Scotty Moore's first exposure to music came from his father, Winfield Scott Moore, Jr., and his three older brothers, Carney, Edwin, and Ralph. (His sister, Mildred, died of pneumonia at age fifteen.) The elder Moore picked some banjo, fiddle, and a bit of guitar, and Scotty's three brothers played, too. The family farm was situated five miles from the Tennessee towns of Alamo, Gadsden, and Humboldt. "We had a few hogs, cows for milk and butter, horses and mules for cultivating," Moore would remember later. "It was bigger than what we call truck farming, where people take stuff to the side of the road and stuff; it was bigger than that, but smaller than those massive, big, big farms."

Like many farm dwellers, the Moore family didn't own a record player or any records. They relied on a radio to tune in the wonders of gospel, R & B, and pop, but for the most part they listened to the string-heavy sounds of prewar country music. "Yeah, on a good, clear Saturday night we could pick up the *Opry*. But it's a strange thing. My dad or any of my brothers weren't really country fans. I remember my dad taking me to a little theater in Humboldt, Tennessee. I couldn't have been over nine, ten years old. Uncle Dave Macon and his son, they appeared at this theater, and he took me, mainly 'cause he played a little banjo. But when you start saying Ernest Tubb and all these different acts—they weren't really fans of them. I don't know why. My older brother, he was into more pop things, pop songs, like 'Mr. Saturday Night.'"

Moore recalls being exposed to country gospel, but he doesn't believe it influenced him. "I was raised Church of Christ, which had no instruments in the church itself. I think if there had been instruments it might have had more bearing. But I liked the quartets and such like that. In fact, in Humboldt at the courthouse, usually about once a month, one of the traveling quartets would come through, like the old Statesmen, and they'd have singing in the courtroom. I remember going to a few of those with my dad way back in the early days."

There was a fourteen-year age difference between young Scotty and his next eldest brother. As a result, by the time he became interested in making music with the family, his siblings were either getting married or living their adult lives elsewhere. Departing brother Ralph gave the youngster his first guitar, which Moore remembers with a rueful chuckle. "The very first one, that my brother gave me, was a Kalamazoo, which was later bought by Gibson. It wasn't a real beautiful guitar, but *now* I know, it was a very good guitar. The brother next to me was headed to the South Pacific. He had a beautiful, shiny knock-your-eyes-out Silvertone Gene Autry. It was really pretty. And I'll never let him forget it, either. He said, 'Well, let's trade guitars, 'cause I don't want to take this real nice thing over there and get it full of saltwater and everything. Let me just have yours; it's not in that good a shape.' 'Cause it wasn't a new one. And dummy me, I traded with him."

With no brothers left on the farm, it seemed only natural that the boy's father would teach the aspiring guitarist. However, says Moore, "My dad was at an age he really didn't care anything about it anymore." Moore ascribes his decision to play guitar as "hardheadedness if nothing else," and he dug into his instrument with youthful zeal. In fact, very little else mattered to him. "When I was fourteen or fifteen I dropped out of school, and my dad said, 'You don't want to go to school, you've gotta work.'"

Moore's father wasn't a stereotypical redneck hard-ass. He just wanted his youngest son to make the connection between hard work and reward. "He gave me an acre of cotton, and I sold whatever the amount of cotton I made that year and bought a big black jumbo Gibson guitar," Moore crows today. "So that was one of the first real—I guess—professional guitars I had."

A year of full-time farm labor convinced Moore to return to high school, but partway through the year he changed his mind again and asked to join the navy. "I wasn't getting into any trouble or anything like that. I just had ants in my pants, I guess. So I decided I wanted to join. My two brothers had been in the navy. So I was only sixteen—in fact, I was going to be sixteen in December—and I went into the navy in January. My mom was raising holy Cain. My dad just went and told her, 'He ain't gonna be worth a flip around here, so we might as well let him go.' So he went into the family Bible and wrote in he lied about my age one year. You could go in with your parents' permission at seventeen then. It was probably the only time my father told a lie."

Moore's father reckoned the kid could use the discipline, but he underestimated just how important playing music was to his boy. Scotty Moore played anywhere, anytime, for as long as he could get away with it. Sometimes his obsession with the guitar proved embarrassing to others.

"Now, a boy that I grew up with, James Lewis, he was four years older than I was, and just before I went into the navy, we were playing some together. In fact, he got married just before I went into the service, and his wife, 'til this day, every time I see her she says, 'You ruined our wedding night! You came over and wanted to play all night.'"

An outsider might reasonably conclude that Moore was trying to create the nurturing aspects of family life that he'd missed out on with his brothers and father. The camaraderie of like-minded musicians is a close, unspoken bond that certainly mirrors the more harmonious aspects of family life. Moore's distant placement in the familial pecking order made the musical interplay of equals impossible. The navy, however, with its routines every bit as humdrum as the farm's, and its aircraft carrier denizens kept in close order, seemed the solution.

Shortly after his 1948 induction, Moore began playing with other servicemen. They played all styles of music, including jazz, which Moore was exposed to for the first time. "Now I'm talking about the old-style jazz where you can still hear the melody once in a while," he quickly amends. "We had a black piano player, and when he was working we'd go down to the rec hall that had a piano in it. There were a couple of other guys that played guitar that were very, very good. I can't remember [the piano player's] name, it's been so long. But he was kind of, I wouldn't say jazz, but more of a dance band–type player. I was very impressed by him, too."

To this day, Moore claims that he never wanted to be a singer, "not even in the shower." "I wanted to be the guy behind the rest of the guys." That said, he got quite a kick out of organizing the jam sessions that served to refine his chops. As with many armed-service musicians, he quickly discovered opportunities to whet his feet at a professional level. "I got on the aircraft carrier and there were quite a few people on there that played quite a few instruments, and I formed a couple of little groups. One was on an LST [landing ship tank], which they put out of commission in Bremerton, Washington, which was a three- to five-month job. [We] actually had a radio show on Saturday—fifteen minutes, thirty minutes. Steel, rhythm guitar, and me. It was live, Bremerton, Washington. KBRO, I think."

While on leave, Moore married Mary Durkee before shipping out again. (Eventually, the guitarist would be married and divorced three times. Coauthor Dan Griffin admiringly observes, "Scotty's on good terms with *all* of his ex-wives.") Initially he'd hoped to serve only three years, and he refused to take the chief petty officer exam because that rank would have been a determining factor in whether the government would ship him out for active duty. Nevertheless, once the Korean War broke out, his service was extended an extra year, and he saw the world, playing music when he could.

"When I got on the aircraft carrier I started meeting different guys from different divisions. In fact, we had one little group. We couldn't play until four in the morning because there were a couple of guys who worked in ordnance, loading the planes for sorties to Korea, and we had to wait until they got through with their shift. The rest of us worked daytime, and we didn't get much sleep sometimes."

Traveling to China, Korea, and other foreign locales not only allowed Moore to deepen his experience as a guitar player, but it also helped him to mature as a person. As a result, his 1952 discharge unveiled a vastly different person than the kid who'd married and fathered two children—Linda and Donald—with a girl he'd met on leave. Stoic to the point of being downright cold, Moore demanded military-style regimentation in his home, and he brooked no disagreement with his methods, especially after moving his budding family to Tennessee. Mary Moore hated farm life and the Moore family's oppressive Church of Christ beliefs. Eventually, after much interpersonal hardship and culture shock, the couple divorced.

Music remained deep in Moore's mind, but he had no earthly idea whether he would be able to play professionally or would play just as a tension reliever during slack hours. Working in the hat department of his brother Carney's dry-cleaning establishment in Memphis, he bought his first record player and began studying the works of Chet Atkins and Merle Travis. Of course, there is nothing surprising there; most country-born pickers delight in Atkins's and Travis's exploits with the six-string guitar. A more unusual influence was jazz guitarist Tal Farlow.

Another Gibson guitar wielder, the South Carolina–born Farlow rose to fame with the Red Norvo Trio, which featured the great Charlie Mingus on bass, during the late 1940s and early 1950s. By the time Moore was out of the service, Farlow's remarkably long fingers were laying down rapid-fire improvisational runs and tasteful, expressive leads for his own recordings on the Blue Note and Verve labels. "These were instrumental records," says Moore of the 78 rpm records he studied. "They weren't playing behind somebody, the ones that I was hearing. And I was trying to figure out how they were doing this stuff. I started playing some weekend gigs, and maybe some of the stuff that was popular then, I'd go buy a record to learn it. Not necessarily the guitar, but just the overall song."

Cautiously, Moore began easing himself into the Memphis music scene. Stan Kesler, then a steel player for Clyde Leoppard & His Snearly Ranch Boys, clearly recalls Moore sitting in with the band and admiringly adds, "Pretty good straight country picker." In time, other musicians began to take notice of the guitar player. One of them was Paul Burlison, who is known to generations of rockabilly fans as the lead guitarist for Johnny Burnette & the Rock 'n' Roll Trio.

"Scotty Moore had such an unusual style," Burlison told Dan Griffin. "You could walk into a building somewhere and not even know he was there and tell it was him. He had his own style. He played with all his fingers. Us two-string guitar pickers who played with a pick would sit around and watch him make chords. He'd make those big old crab chords and we'd say, 'What's he doing?' He had the sound that just knocked you out."

By the early 1950s, the Memphis music scene had been elevated by local disc jockey Dewey Phillips and Sun Records owner Sam Phillips (no relation). Almost overnight, bands and artists sprang up on the bustling Beale Street scene like never before. Competition was heavy between bands, which all played an audience-savvy mix of covers, original songs, and hillbilly-flavored interpretations of blues numbers.

The best of these early performers sporting the new hybrid sound were Johnny and Dorsey Burnette, two navy veterans and Golden Glove champions who loved to play music, chase women, and pick fights. With fists as quick as their respective tempers, the Burnettes would often slug it out with each other when no one else was available. One of these nights remained vivid in Burlison's memory. He had booked a series of dance-hall gigs in honky-tonks in and around Memphis. Wanting to avoid canceling a date due to the flu, Burlison called Scotty Moore in as his replacement for a couple of the gigs.

During one dance, a fight broke out. Dorsey Burnette later told Burlison of looking around for Moore during the fight and seeing only his backside: with his guitar and amp in hand, the substitute guitarist was heading for the back door. Never ones to run away from a fight, the Burnettes jumped right in with the rolling and tumbling crowd. The melee grew violent, and a participant stabbed Dorsey Burnette with a broken beer bottle. Burlison recalled the Burnettes' father waking him in the night, telling him the story, and requesting his help in tracking down the perpetrator. "Dorsey's been stabbed, boy! They gotta go get the guy that did it," yelled Burnette's dad. Wanting to know the location of the fight, Burlison asked, "Where, Mr. Burnette?" Misunderstanding, the father replied, "In the *ass* boy, he stabbed Dorsey in the ass!"

Although there were plenty of bloody buckets and chicken wire–protected bandstands in the Memphis area, the local music scene wasn't always as violent as the old-timers often claim. And group lineups weren't set in stone.

According to Moore, the gigs he took part in during those days were largely casual affairs. "I started nosing around town, meeting guys [and finding out] who's playing here, who's that, and started working maybe a Friday and Saturday night with different groups. There weren't any groups that were together. We had some of the darndest combinations you'd have seen. I could go out and get a club or something and they never asked you what instrumentation you had or anything. You could play trumpet; you could go ahead and jump in with a couple of fiddles and whatever, 'cause everyone was playing these same songs all over town. You could show up with a piccolo and, you name it. As long as you could play, say, the top eight or ten songs from country, pop, R & B. They didn't care what instruments you had, as long as people could dance. There wasn't any rehearsal, because it's just the way things were. When a new song hit the charts, somehow everyone would listen to it and became familiar with that song. Then maybe the first time they played it in a club it would be raggy, but they'd adapt real quick."

Performing in local beer joints four hours a night on weekends, playing (or faking his way through) everything from Hank Williams and R & B to "In the Mood" and "The Bunny Hop," Moore met most of the area's local pickers. One of the guys he occasionally met up with at gigs was Bill Black, and they immediately hit it off. Both were frustrated with the local scene's ever-changing band lineups and lack of professional focus. On a good night, one of these ragtag aggregations would net about twenty dollars a man. There had to be a better way, Moore thought. He decided to organize his own group.

Keen observation and gut instinct told the guitarist that he would have an easier road to success with country music than with pop music. He began asking around for interested musicians, telling everyone the ground rules in advance. "I said the only restriction would be if I don't have a booking for the full band, and you'll know at least a week ahead, you're free to do anything you want to that weekend, but the band comes first. And everyone agreed to that."

Early in 1954, Moore formed the Starlite Wranglers, which featured himself on guitar, Bill Black on stand-up bass, Clyde Rush on rhythm guitar, Tommy Seals on steel guitar, and fiddler Millard Yeow. Their chosen singer, Doug Poindexter, came from the Hank Williams–Lefty Frizzell school of honky-tonk. Moore made the group wear cowboy hats, and everyone except Poindexter wore western wear. Soon, the group began taking any gig that didn't interfere with their respective days jobs.

Despite the obvious country overtones of their stage costumes, the band still played the usual mix of whatever was popular at the time, as well as instrumentals for dancing. When a pop tune proved too much for Poindexter's reedy nasal twang, Bill Black would step up and sing it. The bass man also filled a traditional role in country music as the group's comedian. Scotty Moore recalls, "I can't tell you why; it seemed like every country group in the country, the bass man was always a comedian. Told jokes with the leader or whatever. We'd go out to the VA hospital and do things like that, and he'd dress up in his old outfit and do a lot of crazy things."

Armed with a reliable band and a good floor show, Moore began thinking ahead. "I knew we had to get a radio show or get a record out and get it played on the radio to get more publicity to get better pay. They might not like you any better, but you could say, 'But we're on the radio,' so you could ask for a little bit more. And we did a few radio things on KWEM in West Memphis, Arkansas. Saturdays they had usually black artists and blues artists and country artists—seemed like all day long. Fifteen to thirty minutes, one right after another at a time, all day long. We weren't getting paid; it was just advertising for where we were playing at night. Then I heard about Sam Phillips."

Poindexter has been quoted (in Colin Escott's and Martin Hawkins's 1980 book *Sun Records: The Brief History of the Legendary Label*) as saying that he sought an audition with Sun Records on the advice of local record distributer Bill Fitzgerald. However, according to Moore, it was he who, in his capacity as the band's official manager, took the initiative and talked Phillips into letting the group audition for Sun. "I didn't even know there was a recording studio in town," says Moore today. "But I found out that he had a studio, plus he had a record label.

"I took 'em in—I'm sure it was on a Saturday, 'cause most of the guys had day jobs, you know—and he liked the group. He said, 'You guys been rehearsing? You sound good, pretty tight. I can't see you recording somebody else's material unless you can make it sound completely different. Have you got any originals?'"

Encouraged, Moore huddled with Poindexter and wrote two songs: the slow ballad "Now She Cares No More for Me" and the bouncy hillbilly ditty "My Kinda Carryin' On." (Moore says the latter was inspired by a catchphrase that television host Jack Paar regularly uttered at the time: "Let's have a hand for the Jose Melis Orchestra. My goodness, fellas, that's my kinda carryin' on.")

Billed as Doug Poindexter & the Starlite Wranglers—Moore wanted to remain in the background—the coupling was released as Sun Records #202 in May 1954. Stamped with a red "hillbilly" insignia, it was typical country music with a twist. Black's bass work seemed to drive the recordings more rhythmically than would have been allowed on other country records, and the addition of reverb (or slapback) resulted in the suggestion of something more manic happening within the song.

Although the record sold a mere 330 copies (Poindexter received a royalty check for $8.06) the Starlite Wranglers were able to line up a few better-paying gigs at both rough roadhouses and classier places like the Bon Aire Club. However, it became apparent that they weren't going to break out of the local circuit anytime soon, and plans for the band began to disintegrate just as their leader learned of a new singing prospect: Elvis Presley.

After the failure of his group's record, Moore began casting about for something else that might click. The opportunity for the historic meeting of Elvis Presley and Scotty Moore materialized simply because Moore had fallen into the habit of dropping by the Sun studio every day after work.

"I would get through with my job usually about two in the afternoon, and this was after we had already done the Starlite Wranglers [record]. We were working on weekends and stuff and sold our twelve records," Moore chuckles. "But Sam and I became real good friends through this whole process, and the cleaning plant wasn't that far. It only took fifteen, twenty minutes to where his studio was at."

Phillips and Moore met often at Taylor's, the tiny diner in the same small building as the studio. (It now serves as the ultra-cramped Sun Records museum gift shop.) The two would drink coffee and engage in sensible little chats about what was being played on the radio and about current music trends. Called by some a master psychologist, Phillips was taking stock of Moore and trying to determine how effective a worker the younger man might make. Owning both a recording service and a record label and working full time as a radio engineer, Phillips had little time on his hands. Stretched to his limit—he had suffered a nervous breakdown caused by exhaustion a few years earlier—the Alabama-born entrepreneur needed to find help in the form of people who shared his level of commitment, who understood talent, and—equally important—who would work for, more or less, nothing.

The young Presley had been in and out of Phillips's studio for nearly a year since he'd cut "My Happiness," that famous first acetate, as a gift for his mother. During that time he'd cut and paid for two other discs as well, and they couldn't have been intended as mere presents. In Presley's own shy way, his paying for three acetates was his roundabout method of auditioning for the label. The experience gave him an excuse to hang around the studio and chat with the office receptionist, secretary, and unofficial talent scout, Marion Keisker. Sold on the greasy young cat with the sideburns, Keisker kept mentioning him to Sam Phillips. Her persistence caused Moore to take note of the singer.

Moore certainly respected Keisker's opinion. The receptionist and radio personality was truly the heart of Phillips's early operation. But it was the guitarist's hunger to earn a steady position with Phillips—which would allow him to quit his day job and pick guitar for a living—that inspired him to pester Phillips about the kid with the sideburns.

"So finally again, Marion was having coffee with us," says Moore, "and I asked the question and [Phillips] turned to Marion, looking almost like [irritated expression], 'Marion, go get that guy's name and phone number out of the file.' And he turned to me and said, 'Scotty, you call him and get him to come over to your house and you tell me what you think about his voice.' 'OK,' I said, 'cause I was anxious."

Phillips recalled, in a 1997 speech given at the Hard Rock Café in Memphis, that he had initially considered pairing Presley with a sixteen-year-old black guitarist named Floyd Murphy, but that Moore's ability to "adapt to what you felt" tipped the decision in his favor. (There are no listings of work by Murphy in the current Sun files. Where he is and what he did with his life remains a mystery.) This is how Sun's founder told the story: "I called Scotty, and he was working at his brother's dry-cleaning establishment between his gigs with the Starlite Wranglers. I said, 'Scotty, pick out who you think would be good to work with you to help out on the rhythm.' He picked out Bill Black, and I said, 'Scotty, that is a perfect selection.' Bill was on one end of the pole and Scotty was on this end of the pole, and Elvis was all out here for us to try and get out of him, basically, what he had."

Moore's version is a bit different. He recalls picking Bill Black without any input from Phillips, and that there wasn't much discussion about it. Regardless, once he was given the official go-ahead, Moore called Presley, representing himself as Sam Phillips's talent scout. "I kinda stretched it a little bit 'cause I didn't know what the hell he was looking for," admits Moore today. "I invited him to come over the house the next day, and he came over and we spent a couple of hours. Bill Black, his full-time job was at the Firestone tire plant, which was just a few blocks down from us. Bill just lived down the street from me, and he came down and listened for a little while. Elvis seemed like he knew every song in the world. He didn't know how to play 'em all on the guitar, but he really knew them from memory."

Moore remembers with a laugh that somebody dropped Presley off and that the kid, probably hoping to make an impression, was dressed garishly. "He either had black pants with a white stripe or pink slacks with a black stripe. But I do remember he had on, for sure, he had on a kind of a see-through lace shirt, with his hair all slicked back."

At the time, the guitarist was married to his second wife, Bobbie, and she was equally bemused by Presley's appearance. "The first time I saw Elvis, I remember thinking that he looked like a punk with his long hair slicked back in a ducktail. It seemed kind of strange to me that he would sing country songs with that look."

Of course, the word *punk* wasn't a compliment during that era. Today the word conjures up a young rebel who rages against social convention with raw and outrageous music. (In that context, Presley was indeed a punk.) During the 1950s, however, a punk was a junior-league criminal with a smart-ass demeanor. When screamed from a neighbor's doorstep ("Hey you young punks, get outta here!"), the word was used as a synonym for hooligan, delinquent, and shiftless troublemaker.

Based on what she heard of his music then, Bobbie Moore felt the flashily dressed kid wasn't that impressive. "I don't know if I had that much of a reaction," she explained to Dan Griffin. "He just looked odd with his hair so long. He had a good voice, and if he had played something real fast or speedy, it would have been something different. But he just sat around and played slow songs. I guess that's what he thought Scotty and Bill wanted to hear."

Bobbie got tired of listening to the punk kid singing lackluster country ballads and slipped out the back door to visit her close friend Evelyn, Black's wife, who lived down the street. For his part, Black thought Presley was a "snotty-nosed kid" with little out of the ordinary to offer.

Despite his partner's downbeat take on Presley, Moore's report to Sam Phillips was complete and professional. "I called Sam at home that afternoon—this was on Sunday—and I told him what I thought. I said, 'Boy's got real good timing. It seems like he knows every song in the world. He's young; his voice is still a little high pitched.'" Then, remembering what Phillips had wanted from the Starlite Wranglers, he quickly added, "'He doesn't have any new material.'"

Phillips then surprised his nascent talent-scout guitarist by saying, "Well, maybe we can find him some material. Come on. Just you and Bill; don't bring in the whole band. I just want a little noise." The whole idea was to have Presley audition in the Sun studios with just a basic rhythm section and see what came of it. Phillips kept no logs of the rehearsal/audition process, and, as was mentioned earlier, his memories about how long it took to get something worthwhile out of the shy but ambitious singer differ from Moore's. Ostensibly, Phillips had a song in mind for Presley: an R & B ballad titled "Without You." Having never heard the song before, Presley had a tough time mastering it, and they just stopped work on the number rather than get bogged down in it. After all, even though Phillips's suggestion of the song showed that he was ready to move to the next step rather quickly, it was still just an audition.

"We went in at night 'cause Bill had the daytime job," recalls Moore. "I can't tell you how many different songs we worked through. I do know that 'Blue Moon' was one. There were some others. Sam recorded each one of them, and we'd listen to them, and then we'd move on and kind of run through another one. I didn't know any of them, so it didn't matter what key any of them were in at that time.

"Sam's story, which I have no reason to disbelieve—Sam said, 'Well, I was figuring to say, "Wrap it up for the night, boys, and come back maybe another day or something." But the control room door was open, and Sam's fiddling around with the tape machine or something, and I had a cup of coffee, I think, and Bill had a Coke. All of a sudden Elvis started playing the guitar and singing 'That's All Right (Mama).' Just nervous energy. Bill was standing holding his bass, and he started slappin' and just beatin' the hell out of it. My guitar was laying down and I picked it up—found what key they were playin' in—and started making some rhythm thing with 'em.

"Sam came 'round the corner of the door and said, 'What are you guys doing?' 'Just goofin' off.' 'Well, goof off a little bit more,' he said. 'Round the door it sounded pretty good. Elvis, get back on the mike and let's see what it sounds like.' I don't know how many times we went through it. It wasn't that many times."

Remarkably, neither Moore nor Black had ever heard "That's All Right (Mama)" before that night. But all at once, the trio jelled. Phillips reset the microphone positions—he was a master at that—and instructed Presley to move in and out so his vocals wouldn't pop into the AllTech M11 piano mic. Simultaneously adapting to and supporting Presley's impromptu chanting, Moore's guitar glittered in all the right spaces and Black's bass smartly alternated clean boogie with percussive tic-tac slapping. Before the night was finished, they had one damned fine little rocker in the can.

Had that been the unspoken wish of the Sun Records founder all along?

Years later, Phillips would tell Eric P. Olsen of *The World & I* Web site, "Elvis cut a ballad, which was excellent. I can tell you, both Elvis and Roy Orbison could tear a ballad to pieces. But I said to myself, 'You can't do that, Sam.' If I had released a ballad I don't think you would have ever heard of Elvis Presley."

Bill Black

"I want you to give Bill Black the credit. I want to emphasize the fact that Bill Black was such a big part of Elvis making it. Bill Black, the way he hit his bass fiddle, he sounded like a band all by himself. He could hit the bass like nobody in the world. Like I hit a downbeat or a slap beat on the bass like a drum, well, he could hit a double lick on that bass fiddle. He did that on 'That's All Right (Mama)' and 'Blue Moon of Kentucky.' Elvis sang the way Bill Black played bass. That helped Elvis start jumping around."

—Tillman Franks, *Louisiana Hayride*

A FEW DAYS LATER, Scotty Moore, Bill Black, and Elvis Presley recorded the B-side to "That's All Right (Mama)." Since Sam Phillips's label didn't keep accurate session records until 1958, we will probably never know the exact date that this occurred. However, two points are agreed upon by all parties concerned: First, that the quick production of a B-side was made absolutely necessary by the zealousness of Memphis disc jockey Dewey Phillips; second, that Bill Black was vital to the creation of Presley's incendiary redraft of Bill Monroe's "Blue Moon of Kentucky."

Sam Phillips had cut an acetate of "That's All Right (Mama)" and taken it to WHBQ for Dewey Phillips's appraisal. On his *Red, Hot, & Blue* show, the motormouthed disc jockey played unfiltered R & B that every local teenager listened to when their parents thought they were asleep. Disc jockeys were the original kings of rock 'n' roll, so naturally there were others who played the good jive (notably Big John R and Hoss Allen at WLAC in Nashville), but Dewey Phillips had the ear of thrill-crazy listeners like no other local personality before or since. (The 1995 Memphis Archives release *Dewey Phillips: Live Radio Broadcasts 1952–1964* includes some gloriously entertaining air checks.)

George Klein, who'd gone to Humes High School with Presley, also spun records on WHBQ, where he learned Dewey Phillips's methods firsthand. "Dewey had a great ear for music. I was on in the afternoon and Dewey was on at night at that time. The music was changing. We were getting away from the Doris Days and the Perry Comos and getting into the Drifters, the Clovers, the Platters, Chuck Berry, James Brown, and all that stuff.

"Back in those days there was no music director, and that was part of the secret of your success: picking the right records. Of course, the promo man would bring you the records, but by the same token, if you went to the distributor you could get the new records before the other stations did. It was very important to play a new record first. Let's say a new Chuck Berry or a new Jerry Lee Lewis record came out; if you were the first disc jockey to play it, the kids thought you were real hip. So they knew you were really into the music. You just didn't go on the air and start playing records and have fun. You had to be pretty program wise to what you were doing. And you had to be selective. You had to play [the records the kids wanted to hear] because if [you] played the wrong records you'd lose the kids real fast."

Dewey Phillips seldom lost the kids.

According to Klein, who would eventually become a mainstay in Presley's entourage, the best indication of a DJ's impact came via phone calls and letters. "I would go up to Dewey's show some nights and see what kind of requests he was getting. Sometimes he would tell me, 'George, you ought to jump on this record. I'm getting a lot of requests for it. I think it's a smash hit.' So, the next afternoon I would play it, because Dewey was playing it and we were getting mail for it. Back in those days, the kids would write you letters. It was unbelievable. I was getting 50 to 75 letters a day. I was also getting telegrams that had requests. Whenever you got a telegram, you multiplied that by 10; because it cost money to send a telegram, that would be worth 10 letters."

The night Dewey Phillips broadcast the acetate of "That's All Right (Mama)," WHBQ's phones rang off the hook, a surprising number of telegrams came in. It seemed that everyone was requesting Presley's record.

Sensing a true radio audience event, Dewey Phillips had Presley dragged to the station for an interview. During the interview the DJ subtly brought out the fact that the singer, who many assumed was black, had gone to an all-white high school, and to the delight of his young bop-cat listeners, he played the acetate over and over again. The unintended consequence of this spontaneous blast of publicity was that it forced the hand of everyone involved—Sam Phillips, Scotty Moore, Bill Black, and even Elvis Presley.

Before it was even released, local fans were clamoring for "That's All Right (Mama)," and advance orders for five thousand copies filled the tiny office of the Memphis Recording Service. But there were some problems that needed to be immediately addressed. First and foremost was getting Presley officially signed to the label. Had he been a more experienced performer, the young singer might have demanded more than Sun's paltry three-cents-a-record royalty rate. But the kid was too humble, and way too hungry for a break, to even consider dickering over money.

A potentially bigger problem was Moore and Black. They weren't officially Presley's band; they were just two guys helping him through an audition. Sure, the three had clicked once, but there wasn't any guarantee that the two musicians could pull another good performance from the kid. Further, being seasoned pros, they could have demanded that Presley be made part of *their* group and be paid only a nominal employee salary. Other bandleaders had signed singers on the cusp of fame to disadvantageous contracts before (Cleveland Orchestra leader Sammy Watkins's deal with Dean Martin is a good example). That didn't happen with Presley because Moore and Black were fair-minded men. They took it on faith that the money issues could be worked out to everyone's mutual advantage and threw in with the youngster.

The largest obstacle was the creation of a flip side for "That's All Right (Mama)." Although he knew "every song in the world," finding one that worked for Presley took some doing. Moore remembers the emergency recording session quite well.

"[Sam Phillips] obviously had to call us and say, 'Well, guys, if we're gonna put this out, we gotta cut a B-side.' Now we're going in to do 'a session.' It's not an audition anymore. 'Cause we done gone through I don't know *how* many different songs looking for something. We all of us knew then we needed something. You know most things back then, you get a ballad on one side and maybe something a little up-tempo on the other side. But Sam, he wanted to find something more in the same kind of groove."

Once again, things seemed hopeless. Yet Moore recalls that, by lightening the mood, his bass-playing partner saved the session. "Bill is the one who came up with 'Blue Moon of Kentucky.' Same deal. We're taking a little break and he starts beating on the bass and singing 'Blue Moon of Kentucky,' mocking Bill Monroe, singing the high falsetto voice. Elvis joins in with him, starts playing and singing along with him."

The result was sensational. The transformation of Bill Monroe's bluegrass standard into an R & B–fed rocker is one of the undisputed highlights of Elvis Presley's recording career. Oozing low-register sex appeal on the tension-building hooks ("Blue moon! Blue moon! Blue moon! Keep a-shinin' bright") and yelping in joyous release on the verses, Monroe's mournful waltz-tempo ditty was reinvented into an R & B–tinged country rocker. It was paired with "That's All Right (Mama)," and the record became the first of many two-sided hits the singer would enjoy throughout his career. It even provided the still nameless band their official sobriquet, as disc jockeys and promoters, struggling to identify the singer with the odd name for the public, worked the song's title into their introductions, saying thing like, "Here they are now—Elvis Presley and those Blue Moon Boys."

Born William Patton Black, Jr., on September 17, 1926, in Memphis, Tennessee, Bill Black was the son of a motorman for the Memphis Street Railway. He was the oldest of ten children—five from his father's first marriage, five more from his second. (One child, a twin, died at birth.) According to Johnny Black, one of Bill's younger brothers, their father's second marriage was the quintessential May-December relationship. "Mama had twins when daddy was seventy years old. Daddy was fifty-five [when] he married mother; she was twenty. See, back in that era—she had just lost her mother and father. She was stayin' with her uncle, and I guess from a security standpoint, he was still workin', Daddy was, making good money at the time and everybody liked him."

Families who are rich in children are often poor in luxuries. As a result, the burgeoning Black household made its own entertainment. "They used to get together at the houses—this was probably before I was born—and Daddy would play the banjo and the fiddle," Johnny Black recalls. "A hoedown, 'Old Joe Clark,' 'Sally Good'n,' whatever was popular then. We grew up with what he played."

In later years, Bill Black would tell his son, Louis, about his first musical instrument. "He said when he first wanted to play some music, or learn to play, Grandpa—his daddy—fixed a cigar box, nailed a board to it, put strings on it, and keyed it for him. He learned to play on that."

Bill Black, who was fourteen or fifteen years old at the time, proved a natural on the homemade instrument. "It wasn't something that he had to sit down and really learn," his son, Louis, explains. "He loved to play music, and it came natural to him. He didn't know how to read a note of music . . . but he could play anything he wanted to. He could even play it on the piano."

Johnny Black also recalls that Bill played guitar with his next-youngest brother, Louis, and that he may have been ambidextrous. "I know when Bill started school he was left-handed, but [back then] they changed you around. He could write either way, but not the best of writings, you know. So when he had themes or a thesis in school he would pay us to write 'em out for him."

A rumor that often follows Black's legend is circulated by his friend and former neighbor Ace Cannon, who claims, "Bill is three-quarters Cherokee Indian, and that's why he couldn't hold his liquor." Black's daughter Nancy has heard that rumor, too. "That's what [paternal aunts] Linda and Carolyn have told me, too, but I don't know that for a fact." Louis Black, Bill's oldest child, never heard his father speak of having Native American ancestors. At any rate, although Black did take a drink now and then, he never seemed to let the habit get the better of him.

Details surrounding Black's early life are hard to come by. His wife Evelyn passed away in 2003. Surviving siblings aren't comfortable being interviewed, and some are uncooperative due to the belief that the late bass player's widow didn't allow them to share in what they mistakenly perceived as Bill's vast fortune. It is a controversy that has, sadly, divided the family to this very day.

Family rifts aside, some reliable information has dribbled out. Johnny Black, who concedes that he has concocted some real whoppers during his drinking days, recalls with sober clarity that his eldest brother began playing in bars and small clubs at the age of sixteen. Most of the musicians interviewed for this project started their careers as teenagers who played in places that served liquor. The patrons seldom complained, and the authorities hardly ever checked up on them. Most of these places were beyond the notice of polite middle-class society. They were musty, sawdust-on-the-floor barrooms where men felt free to wear their greasy work clothes, drink, and start fights. During that pre-television era, live music was a big attraction, and there were plenty of places a kid could go to jam in front of people and rationalize it as entertainment. Louis Black heard his dad speak of those days. "You'd have these guys who could play music, and one of them would hear that somebody wanted a band to play here, and they'd run over yonder and get two, three guys. They knew people who played the guitar, banjo, or whatever they needed. And that's the way they did it."

Black, usually playing acoustic guitar, strummed along with several different barroom-inspired contingents. He preferred country music but, according to his son, "He would perform with anybody." As a result, he learned his way around danceable pop, country standards, and jump blues. Years later he would simply refer to the mixture of sounds as "honky-tonk music."

Although he could—and would—fight his way out of any bust-out joint in town, Black developed a nice little knack for joshing drunken hotheads back to their tables. He was also pretty good at getting a bartender or club manager to furnish free beers to the band. "He had a way about him, *unreal,*" chuckled his brother Johnny. "Really, he knew just the right thing to say."

Mary Anne Kennedy, one of Black's sisters, told Peter Butler of the Rockabilly Hall of Fame that her eldest brother went into the army during the "mid-forties." The best guess is probably 1945, when the war was winding down, because he only served a two-year stint. Black's son, Louis, recalls his dad talking about playing music with other soldiers while stationed in Fort Lee, Virginia. It was there he met the woman he would eventually marry, Evelyn.

Louis Black recalls that his mother's side of the family was especially musically inclined. "She played the guitar and my grandfather played the banjo. He played with a bunch of the older people—Grandpa Jones, Stringbean and his wife—and my grandmother played the zither. There was a bunch of 'em that played; cousins, nephews.

"My mother's been in [the music business since] she couldn't even hold the guitar. They'd put her on a stool and held the guitar for her so she could play. Her and her brother would sing. Most of the time they were in a gymnasium or some building like that. People would come from everywhere . . . they were just little kids who would sing and play. At the end they would say, 'If you really enjoyed us and you want to hear some more, let us hear you roar.' The people would all roar and give 'em a standing ovation, so they'd play some more.

"They used to all just get together and play. So, my mother and daddy met playing music because my grandfather played music too."

The couple married in 1946.

Black's children feel their parents' marriage was held together by their mutual humor and background in music. Black was also very clear about wanting a career in music. "That's just the way it was," explains son Louis. "He loved music. My mother, whether she liked it or not, she understood it because she had been in it."

After his army discharge, Black came back to Memphis with Evelyn in tow and started a family. He worked at Ace Appliance and the local Firestone plant—a major postwar employer in the area—and tried to find time to play music. No one can say with certainty when he began playing the bass, but one can reasonably surmise why he did. The least respected yet most necessary instrument in any combo (the bass provides both percussion and a sonic bottom to the rhythm section), it didn't take a lot of skill to play. Anyone with a good sense of timing could whack on a few root notes and provide low-register fill on the bandstand. The smart players, like Black, learned to vary basic runs and alternate their instrumental attack. A good practitioner of the bass fiddle makes it all look deceptively easy, but slapping the upright was more dangerous than people thought.

Arkansas rockabilly Sonny Burgess, a contemporary of Moore's and Black's, recalls one particular bass-related incident with his band the Pacers that ended badly for an overzealous audience member. "Everybody wants to play the upright bass. I don't know why. We'd have college kids get up there; they'd get drunk and want to play the upright bass. So Dorsey Wilmette, he still lives in Newport, he hopped up onstage and talked Johnny Ray Hubbard into letting him play his bass. Well, he started beating and a-bangin' on that upright, and all of a sudden blood starts flyin' everywhere. I looked up and said, 'Where's that blood comin' from?' We looked around and he held those fingers up to us. He was tearing it up there for a little bit—but he ended up tearing all the hide off his fingers. Johnny Ray always taped his."

Black seldom taped his fingers. Through simple repetitive hard work he developed enough of a proper technique and thick-enough calluses on his hands and fingers to avoid serious injury. Of course, even when using proper mechanics and a well-miked instrument, playing the upright bass eventually takes a visible toll on its practitioners.

The authors spoke with legendary Nashville bassist Bob Moore, who eventually replaced Black in Presley's studio band and who has played on more country hits than any other musician. No bassist keeps better time or holds a truer note than Moore has during his 50-plus-year career. When asked about the physical consequences of his chosen instrument, Moore, who has played both upright and electric bass, simply grinned and held out his fret hand palm up. His powerful, nearly muscle-bound hands sported equally tough-looking digits ending in fingertips that resembled small hidebound shovels. Moreover, each fingertip had the groove of a thick bass string worn into it at a cross angle. Since Black played much harder than most bass players to achieve his striking rockabilly tone, we can only imagine the condition of his hands and fingers.

Today the preferred model of neo-rockabillies worldwide, Black's Kay bass was originally deemed little more than a budget item that was built more for endurance than for tone. Certainly he tested the instrument's limits, plucking hard double-lick shuffle rhythms and smacking the living music out of boogie-woogie riffs. One of Black's better tricks was loosening the top string of the bass so it made a tic-tac sound as he slapped out rhythm patterns on the second and third strings. On fast numbers, this created the vibrant illusion of added percussion, and it was used to good effect on Elvis's early Sun records, which did not feature drums. Sam Phillips admired Black's tone and drive on the instrument more than he did the musician's technical skill, but Paul Burlison thought differently, telling Dan Griffin, "I don't think there was anybody at that time who could've played any better than Bill." Burlison also felt that Black was a better bass man than his old boss Dorsey Burnette.

In 1973 *Rockville International*'s Adriaan Zeuw asked Scotty Moore how important Black's "wart's 'n' all" style was to the rockabilly sound. "Very, very important," Moore replied, "because the things we were doing was mostly rhythm. It wasn't a thing where he had to hit the correct note; it was just a blending, an overall sound, you know."

Yet, with modern digital technology able to clean the sonic mud off of old master tapes, we can hear just how good Black was on his instrument. Indeed, if the plethora of outtakes released by RCA over the years is any indication, Black was the cause of far fewer false starts and botched takes than were Presley, Moore, or Fontana. Playing an instrument that demanded such physical vigor dictated that he get it right the first time. Another oft-repeated comment about Black is that his brother Johnny, who did some session work at Sun and who temporarily replaced Dorsey Burnette in the Rock 'n' Roll Trio, was technically the better bassist. There are few available recorded works by Johnny Black, which makes it difficult to judge if this is true. But the advent of modern digital remastering shows his older brother to be an engaging stylist who played with spotlight-grabbing zeal.

Of course, the biggest reason Black took up the bass is obvious. In the days before rock 'n' roll, the upright bass was the ultimate showcase instrument.

The biggest handheld piece on the bandstand, it naturally attracted the eye of the audience. As a result, it was also the perfect comedy prop. Although the "bass player as comedian" dated back to the days of Bob Willis and his Texas Playboys, it was the *Grand Ole Opry* radio broadcasts and touring shows that popularized the role for post–World War II audiences. In the pantheon of early rock 'n' roll, Marshall Lytle (of Bill Haley's original lineup of the Comets) enlivened instrumentals and finales with his bag of tricks—riding the bass like a horse, playing it while lying on his back, standing on it, and gesturing with it as if it were a guitar.

Initially Black's stage persona was that of the jokester country bumpkin. When he began playing with Moore, he blacked out his teeth, wore a straw hat and overalls, mercilessly needled the band leader, and played a malaprop-spouting hick for laughs. "Daddy loved to make people laugh," his son, Louis, recalls. "He said, 'We all got enough problems out here. Everybody's struggling trying to make a living. If I can give 'em a few moments of entertainment and maybe a little bit of humor that'll tickle 'em for a while, they can forget all their mess for a little bit.'" Later, Black used his instrument to add to the excitement of a budding rockabilly show.

According to California rockabilly pioneer Glen Glenn, Black modeled himself after Fred Maddox of the famed Maddox Brothers and Rose. Glenn, who recorded the cult classics "One Cup of Coffee" and "Everybody's Movin'" for Era Records in 1957, met Black through Maddox when the former came to Los Angeles to film movies with Presley. The two bassists knew each other from several *Louisiana Hayride* tours.

"Bill Black just idolized Fred Maddox," recalls Glenn. "He said he learned everything, how to play the bass and to be a good showman, because of Fred." Fred Maddox died in 1992, but his widow, Kitty, confirms Glenn's recollection. She adds that her late husband was somewhat taken aback by Black's open admiration. "Well, Fred didn't know what to think when people said things like that. He liked it, of course."

Dubbed the World's Most Colorful Hillbilly Band, the Maddox Brothers and Rose put on a crowd-pleasing show that made them superstars on the West Coast. The Alabama group had fled to California during the dust bowl era, and they started a family band when farm work proved too exhausting for the lousy pay. "As each [of the six children in the family] got older, they just started playing the next instrument that they needed in the band," says Kitty. Sister Rose briefly served as the bass player, but once matriarch Mama Maddox saw the impact her daughter's vocals had on an audience, Fred was drafted to play the instrument instead. It would prove to be a wise decision.

The group blended feisty barn-dance country with elements of small-combo boogie-woogie and western swing. In the process, they may have invented the rockabilly genre. "Maybe we did," chuckles Don Maddox, the lone surviving original band member. "But back then we didn't call it rockabilly music. We were just straight hillbilly, but we did all kinds of songs and Fred did that rockabilly bass. It wasn't called rockabilly bass at that time. It was just something that he done." Today Fred Maddox's bass is displayed at the Experience Music Project museum in Seattle. Says Kitty, "They wanted his bass because they believe he might have hit the first note of rock 'n' roll on it."

The Maddox Brothers and Rose may very well have paved the way for rock 'n' roll, but that's not why their original fans loved them. People packed dance

"The world's most colorful hillbilly band": The Maddox Brothers and Rose. Left to right: Henry, Don, Rose, Cal, and Fred. Courtesy of Arhoolie Records and K. C. "Don Juan" Maddox

halls to see them because they put on a wildly energetic show. "We didn't drink, smoke, or do drugs," explains brother Don, "but we had so much energy a lot of people thought we were on drugs." Decked out in colorful western outfits designed by Nathan Turk—whose work with embroidery and rhinestone predated Nudie's—they grabbed the audience's attention and wouldn't let it wane. At the core of their nightly shows were the scene-stealing visual antics of brother Fred. "He wanted to be in the limelight," Kitty Maddox laughs today. "He would kick his bass and holler and ride his bass across the stage. He'd do most anything, and it was funny."

Ironically, rock 'n' roll more or less split up the Maddox Brothers and Rose. By 1957 bookings were getting thin, and very few of their later Columbia recordings sold well. Eventually Mama Maddox decided to cut her losses and moved her daughter to Nashville so that Rose could make regular appearances on the *Grand Ole Opry*. The siblings would not get over their anger about the split until after their controlling mother died.

Although in reality their relationships with each other were often strained to the point of animosity, onstage the Maddox siblings presented the perfect image of a close-knit family whose bond was sealed in good times, hot rhythms, and bust-out anything-for-a-laugh joviality. It was an image that appealed to Bill Black on a very deep level. When he began jamming with Scotty Moore in 1952, his likely intention was to be part of a show in which he could have his turn in the spotlight, just as Fred Maddox's group did. Little did he suspect that his first band association would end just as bitterly as his spiritual mentor's had.

Working at Firestone, where he inserted the webbed belts that held the tread on tires, Black made a good enough living to move to a better neighborhood, just down the street from his new friend Scotty Moore. On most nights he left his bulky Kay bass at Moore's house and picked it up only for rehearsals and gigs.

While Bill Black was getting on with his adult life, his brothers and sisters were still existing close enough to the poverty level to qualify for low-income public housing at the Lauderdale Courts. Located in North Memphis, the neighborhood was a delinquent-infested area that just happened to provide a fertile breeding ground for some top-notch musical talent, including fight-loving brothers Johnny and Dorsey Burnette.

Dorsey Burnette's future wife also grew up in North Memphis. "She says Elvis was just a regular kid," states Billy Burnette, her son. "The stories I heard were that he used to come over to the Lauderdale Courts to the laundromat all the time," says Billy. There, his dad and uncle would be playing their guitars. "My dad would kind of run him off, you know? Lee [Denson] told me that one time my dad said, 'If you don't get out of here, I'm going to break this sled over your head,' meaning the guitar. But later on they were nice to him. But he was just hanging out all the time. Everybody that was there tells me the same thing. Elvis kind of wanted to be in their deal. That was the first kind of rock band he had ever heard that was doing that type of music."

Young Elvis did not make many friends among the local toughs. Johnny Black, who was three years older, took pity on him. "He lived in the same place that I did and [he] would sit outside on the stoop of his apartment and would play the guitar," he told Dan Griffin. "I remember back when we would play, I would feel sorry for him sometimes because nobody would talk to him, and I'd go over there and we'd talk. No one would've ever imagined what he would turn out to be. He was a nice guy, very humble to any adult. He must have been about fourteen then, maybe fifteen. As time went by, we began to play together on the guitars and started playing parties on the playground or at people's houses. Elvis was real shy; you had to practically beg him to sing at the parties. And I say party—it was just a gathering where people would get together and hang out."

Many rock writers have reasonably concluded that by hanging out with Johnny Black, Elvis Presley must have at least caught a glimpse of his brother Bill at one time or another. Certainly it was possible, but both Bill Black and Scotty Moore were already married adults when Presley was still a young teen, and there was no reason for them to have taken special notice of the young outcast. At that time, Presley's casual friendship with Johnny Black provided the future King a major step up in his little corner of the universe. It likely gave Presley an in with the Burnette Brothers crowd; at the very least, it kept him from getting beaten up on a regular basis.

"Some of the guys were very jealous and very negative about Elvis," explains Johnny Black. "The reason being their girlfriends liked him, and they would say derogatory things to me. 'Why don't you get rid of your singer up there?' They had a nice little sarcastic name for him, because he was different and he appealed to the girls. Back then sports was king; all the boys played sports in the late forties, early fifties. Elvis didn't play sports until, I guess, maybe when they moved to Graceland."

One of Johnny Black's most controversial assertions is that he and Presley played "That's All Right (Mama)" in the style in which it would be recorded a full year later, at Sun. Both Moore and Phillips have said repeatedly that the Sun performance came spontaneously, and that the full arrangement was hammered out through a great many retakes. That said, it is worth noting the younger Black's recollection. If true, it provides a glimpse of Presley's budding musical vision.

Black recalls, "We were out, just [Elvis] and I, bass and guitar, out on the football ground, and he kicks off 'That's All Right (Mama),' and I said, 'Man, where did you get that?' He told me, 'off a radio show,' and I started whackin' that bass like a drum, 'cause when you don't have a lot of equipment you gotta make do with what you have. I don't know if I heard him play it anywhere else. That's the only time I ever heard him play it, just he and I that day. But he had to sing it to me 'cause I had never heard it."

Like many Presley man-behind-the-man myths, it's hard to swallow. But Ronnie Smith, who knew both Black and Presley, felt that it could have happened. "We all listened to WDIA at night and the *Grand Ole Opry*—Elvis and I did—running around in this old Lincoln that I'd end up pushing to a gas station. The point is, we all ping-ponged around to all the radio stations. Memphis was so diversified with music. So, that song by Arthur 'Big Boy' Crudup had a jump to it or a groove that we all liked. So yeah, I'm sure [Black] did [play the song that night]."

If Johnny Black did playfully jam out "That's All Right (Mama)" with Presley, he didn't tell his brother about it. Both Moore and Bill Black have said they had never heard the song before that auspicious night in 1954, and if the elder Black knew young Elvis at all, it was only in passing.

Scotty Moore, who admits his memory may be fading, doesn't clearly recall whether Johnny Black was present during the famed get-acquainted rehearsal held for Presley at Moore's house, and Bobbie Moore doesn't remember the younger Black being there at all (although she concedes that he could have arrived after she left), but Black claims he was, indeed, on-hand to witness the event. He recalls, "Bill, Scotty and I lived in separate homes, all married but on the same street. Elvis came over that Sunday afternoon, and he was dressed for goin' out! Pink shirt, white pants; he'd painted his shoes green! Wore the loudest clothes that he could afford. That was his formal attire. Bobbie, Scotty's wife, had never seen anything like that. It was funny! She left and stayed with Evelyn—Bill's wife—until they were through. Bill didn't think a whole lot of

[Presley] because they didn't come up with anything out of the ordinary. What was Bill's comment? 'The boy knows a lot of songs.'"

It's true that Bill Black bluntly proclaimed: "Well, he didn't impress me too goddamned much." Evidently, these comments got back to Presley, whose feelings were understandably hurt. According to Peter Butler's article "Blackie," on the Rockabilly Hall of Fame Web site, Phillips assuaged the youngster's pride by assuring him that it was just Black's way to say things like that, and that he didn't mean anything by it.

Although there was a nine-year age difference between them, Black and Presley shared a rather puckish sense of humor. Both loved practical jokes, and both were absolutely turned on by the musical style they forged together. They also got big laughs from all those screaming girls. "Daddy and Scotty used to play around with Elvis and stuff, getting him to do things just to see the girls' reactions," chuckles Louis Black. "He said they'd sit around sometimes and talk about it: 'Let's see what they do about this. Let's see what they do about that.' It got to be a joke. 'Let's see what you can make the girls do tonight.'" Occasionally Presley would try to stand still long enough to actually sing, and Black—noticing the calm audience reaction—would needle him by saying, "Hey man, move, *move*! Them girls want to see you *wiggle*."

And Presley would.

There's no question that Black got Presley out of his shell, which made the singer a star. However, there is no escaping the fact that the two had a rather prickly relationship at times. Barbara Pittman, who knew both Presley and Black, speculated that Presley, a frequently picked-on only child, sometimes viewed Black as yet another in a long line of tactless bullies he'd encountered in his short life. He'd let the flashes of temper go for the sake of the group, but he never really forgave or forgot. At the Hard Rock Café awards ceremony Sam Phillips dredged up this memory, seemingly out of the blue: "Bill Black was an absolute riot, but sometimes he was the quietest riot you ever heard in your life. I'll never forget the time when him and Elvis got at each other, and I don't know who would've whipped the other one's ass. But this type of thing would go on in the studio when we were together. There was just something being done that we knew about and we felt . . . every one of us."

At times, even Moore and Black would get into a violent quarrel. Gordon Stoker reports one particular outburst, during which the relatively diminutive Moore pretty much kicked his bass player's ass. D. J. Fontana concurred, adding with a laugh, "[Scotty] can get feisty when he wants to. Yeah, he'd fight you. You might beat him, but he'd stand up to you." The difference between Presley and Moore was that Moore loved Black like one of his big brothers, with whom he had always longed for closer relationships. After a few jokes ("I hope my face didn't hurt your fist, Scotty"), Black and Moore would put their dispute behind them and go back to being friends.

The Sun Days

"Way before there was such a thing as rock 'n' roll, there was a group of guys who had a dream. All of us who came after can relate to that. And it wasn't easy, and they really didn't know what they were creating. There was country music floating around and there was blues music floating around, and these guys—and Mr. Phillips—loved all of it. They started jamming and practicing and jamming some more. And, they didn't know it, but they were inventing rock 'n' roll. Anyway, these people invented something that's still here, and for my money they're still the best. Everybody who came after is just sort of an imitation. They walked that road first."

—John Fogerty, honoring the Blue Moon Boys
at the 1997 Hard Rock Café Awards

"Never ceases to amaze *me, baby."*

—Elvis Presley in the Singer Company–sponsored
television special *Elvis* (1968), in response to a girl
screaming rapturously over receiving a shred
of Kleenex that had stuck to his face

Young women didn't always scream for Elvis Presley, but the phenomenon started remarkably early for a performer with such little experience.

Roughly a week after creating a sensation on Memphis radio, Presley's father signed his son to a one-year management contract with Scotty Moore. "It was actually Sam's idea," remembers Moore. "As soon as they started playing that on the radio, there were a couple of guys there—promoters, bookers, et cetera—who started calling Elvis saying, 'Have you got a manager?' And he didn't know what to say to them. All of us were there in the studio one day and we were talking about it and Sam said, 'Why don't you sign a contract with him for a year, give us all time to find somebody we can trust?' That's what that was all about. I mean, I hadn't even thought about being manager or anything. Of course, during all that time I was trying to book things and look after stuff."

Although the dismal showing of the Starlite Wranglers was Moore's only music business reference, it was assumed that a formal contract would keep unscrupulous promoters and management types from preying on the young singer. It also formalized each member's split of the nightly take: 50 percent for Presley and 25 percent each for Moore and Black. The guitarist proved handy when it came to booking local gigs, but for anything larger, Phillips was still running the show, and he usually called on disc jockey/promoter Bob Neal.

First on everyone's agenda was to get Presley some exposure so that they could eventually book better-paying gigs, sell some records, and possibly quit their day jobs. Moore, lacking a genuine rehearsal space, brought Bill Black and Presley up to a room above his dry-cleaning establishment. These after-work sessions were serious business, for even though their singer kept good time on his acoustic guitar, they didn't know if this nervous kid could remember his songs. They decided to ease him into live performance with a guest appearance at the Bon Aire Club with the Starlite Wranglers.

"We took Elvis out, and I think Sam came out, too," says Moore. "And, during the intermission, me and Bill and Elvis got up [and performed]. After a couple of intermissions Bill made the point that 'this ain't gonna work. I ain't getting enough time to drink no beer, here.'"

Performing both sides of his first Sun release, Presley received only courtesy applause. Most of the patrons were there either to drink or dance to the Wranglers. The Wranglers themselves didn't particularly care for the loudly dressed kid with the sideburns, and they were insulted that they weren't asked to play on his record. Worse, they felt that they were due a piece of Presley's contract. The trio played one more gig with the Wranglers before the situation became untenable.

"They were kind of mixed. We broke up shortly down the line, but everybody understood," Moore said years later. "There wasn't any big fallout. They'd seen what was happening and it was like a 'go for it' type of thing."

Poindexter's own comments in Colin Escott and Martin Hawkins's book *Sun Records: The Brief History of the Legendary Label* reveals an undercurrent of resentment. "At the time, the record business was in a funny state, and I wasn't sure that I wanted to go with it. Scotty and Bill had the chance to go to Shreveport with Elvis and they wanted to go ahead with it, but I stayed in Memphis. Sam forgot about me, and I guess it was for the best. There was no way of knowing that success was coming to Presley. Frankly, I thought the boy would starve to death."

In September 1954 Poindexter played guitar on Presley's rockabilly remake of the Shelton Brothers' "Just Because," which wouldn't be released until 1956, after the singer's contract had been sold to RCA. "He put paper up through the strings," says Moore, remembering how Poindexter achieved his sound during the recording, "so it was just kind of a 'chik-a-chik-a-chik-a' type thing." The technique (Johnny Cash also used it on his Sun recordings) created a percussive fill that sounded similar to a wire brush on a snare drum. Soon after the song was recorded Poindexter left the music world. According to Moore's Web site, Poindexter went on to work for the Continental Baking Company (the makers of Wonder Bread) and later owned a business called Southern Statistical Computer Consultants. He died on October 1, 2004. Former Sun artist Barbara Pittman commented that Poindexter was one of the "bitterest men I've ever known."

With their record getting bigger every day in Memphis, audiences began to respond more warmly to Presley. The played intermission sets at the Eagle's Nest club for local disc jockey Sleepy Eyed John, as well as a few roadhouse gigs on the outskirts of town. The money wasn't important; they were trying to build up an act. At that time, though, the only reliable element they had to work with was the knockabout comedy of Bill Black. "After we started with Elvis, [Bill] didn't dress up anymore, but then we worked up stuff where he and Elvis would do a lot of little jokes and stuff," remembers Moore. "Not dirty stuff, but kinda on the risqué side. Clean stuff if you compare it to stuff today."

Years later, Moore told Louis Black just how important his dad had been to the early act. "He'd say, 'You know, everybody thinks that Elvis just popped right up and went on. That ain't the way it happened. Elvis used to just stand up there and not move, and Bill would jump around on the bass. Your daddy would come down through there and get everybody to laughing and loosen them up.'"

Then came the August 10, 1954, performance at the Overton Park Shell.

Booked for the two-show gig alongside such established country music stars as Slim Whitman, Billy Walker, and the Louvin Brothers, the trio was getting its first taste of the big time. During the first show, which was held in the afternoon, Presley tried to fit in with these great stars and sing nothing but ballads. He flopped, which greatly increased his nervousness. Taking the stage for the second show that evening, Presley began singing his local hit. Then, as he often did in the studio, the novice entertainer started to move his leg in time to the music. Wracked by stage fright, his balance became a bit unsteady, and that leg began shaking more visibly. "In those big-legged pants he looked like he was doing three times what he really was," Moore told Bruce Feiler of the *New York Times*.

The females in attendance began to scream appreciatively.

According to legend, Presley had recently entertained notions of quitting "the blues" and going back to gospel. Now he had stolen the spotlight in a show that starred other entertainers who could buy and sell his whole family. "What did I do? Why are they screaming?" he asked Moore. The guitarist/manager told him that the crowd was responding to his wiggling and that he ought to keep it up. A few years later Presley told *TV Guide*, "So I did a little more, and the more I did, the more [screaming] I got."

Naturally, people couldn't hear that leg shaking while listening to "That's All Right (Mama)" and "Blue Moon of Kentucky" on their record players and radios, but the disc's slapback echo provided the perfect sonic correlative. Overnight, musicians from Carl Perkins and Jerry Lee Lewis recognized Presley's sound as kindred to their own, and they made plans to come to Memphis.

In contrast, Arkansas-born Sonny Burgess had to see the band live to believe it, but when he did, it changed the course of his career. "There's not that many good-paying gigs in Memphis," the singer explained. "So, some of the biggest stars in the world played at places like the Silver Moon here in Arkansas. A lot of us played smaller places, honky-tonks like Bob King's place or Porky's Rooftop, which they made those movies about. They served liquor and had gambling—it was supposed to be illegal, but everybody knew about it."

The shy Burgess had reluctantly fronted a generic country band named the Rocky Road Ramblers until early 1955. The band had just changed its name to the Moonlighters when Elvis, Scotty, and Bill blew into Newport, Arkansas. The trio shared a bill with the Moonlighters twice, and Burgess and his group were deeply impressed. "Scotty had that great sound on that guitar, and Elvis could really sing. He was just the best we had ever seen. We knew he'd be big. Of course, we didn't know he'd become the star of *all* stars."

Presley liked the Moonlighters as well. In fact, after viewing their show-stopper—a cover of Smiley Lewis's "One Night of Sin"—he decided to cover the song himself. He eventually recorded it at RCA and later reworked the tune into his 1958 hit "One Night." Burgess didn't mind. "He was a nice guy, and he still was the last time I talked to him in '58, when he was in the army. Still the same, as far as we could tell, and he was *big* time by then."

More important to Burgess was the way in which Presley, Black, and Moore had inspired his own band. The group changed their name to the Pacers (after the Pacer high-speed airplane) and began to rock the local scene with utter abandon. "We wanted to be on Sun Records after that, man. That's all we could think about. All we wanted was to get that little yellow record in our hands. That was it. That was the big time to us."

Presley and his band went from ground zero to regional fame in just a few short weeks. Oftentimes they would drive Bobbie Moore's BelAir to their increasingly far-off roadhouse gigs. Contrary to popular belief, the guys didn't run the car ragged until it burned up on the side of the road in some dank southern town. (That would be the fate of one of Presley's own cars later in his career.) "It went up and down a lot of little country roads," Moore says of treasured BelAir, "but it was all right." So what happened to the first car that Elvis Presley ever toured in? After trading it in for a '56 DeSoto, which featured punch buttons for the gears, says Bobbie, "Next thing I knew, the dealer sold it to Johnny Cash. I liked Johnny; he was real down to earth."

Presley's climb to national stardom would take a full fifteen months—a very short time by show-business standards. However, although the public would quickly dub the singer the King of Rock 'n' Roll, neither Presley nor Sam Phillips invented the genre. Phillips did not even cut the first rock hit, as has often been suggested. If you narrow your definition to the post–World War II tunes that became famous as rock songs during the mid-50s, then Fats Domino's 1949 recording of "The Fat Man"—a number-one R & B hit in 1950, was the first true rock hit. Certainly it predates the 1951 Phillips-produced "Rocket 88" by Jackie Brenston.

Presley did not even popularize rock 'n' roll, although he led the charge of great second-wave performers. By the time the Tupelo, Mississippi-born singer had walked into the Memphis Recording Service, disc jockey Alan Freed had already applied the phrase "rock 'n' roll" to the music of black vocal groups. While Elvis was making inroads into the mid-south and southwest, records by Bill Haley, Pat Boone, and Bobby Charles were scaling the pop charts and also being identified as rock 'n' roll. Haley and his Comets in particular enjoyed a top-ten national hit with their cover of Big Joe Turner's "Shake, Rattle and Roll." (Turner, who had been belting blues and boogie since the 1930s, is rock 'n' roll's true spiritual godfather.) Haley's amalgamation of hillbilly, pop, and rhythm sounds dated and contrived today, but he was rock 'n' roll's first breakthrough white performer.

What Phillips, Presley, and the Blue Moon Boys did, however, was redefine rock 'n' roll as guitar-based music that highlighted the performer. That redefinition had a tremendous impact on the genre. Before that point, piano and sax players provided the key rock ingredients. The setup at the tiny Sun studio dictated that recordings there had to be done less expensively and with more basic rhythm instruments upfront. It was a trick that only Phillips would have attempted, and he succeeded.

"He had two or three things going for him," says Moore of Phillips's studio technique. "The Sun room had a real live sound, and then the slapback, or delay, gave it a different brightness. I don't think he even had an equalizer in the console at all, best I can remember. Another thing he did, that I don't think Sam knew that he was doing it, he only knew that he was doing things that sounded good to him—if you remember back in the early fifties, all your pop and country things, the vocal was always way out front when we were recording. The music was way in the background. Because there was just three of us, and I guess because he thought it sounded kind of empty, he pushed Elvis's voice back down close. You could understand it, not like later on in the fad where you couldn't understand what the singer was singing. He brought his voice back down to all the instruments, and to me, he actually used the voice as an instrument. That, to me, was one of the biggest parts to the sound."

As Moore alluded, slapback echo was an important tool for Phillips, who had perfected the technique on his early blues sessions. Legendary engineer/producer/songwriter Jack Clement, who used slapback quite well on many Johnny Cash and Jerry Lee Lewis recordings for Sun, describes the

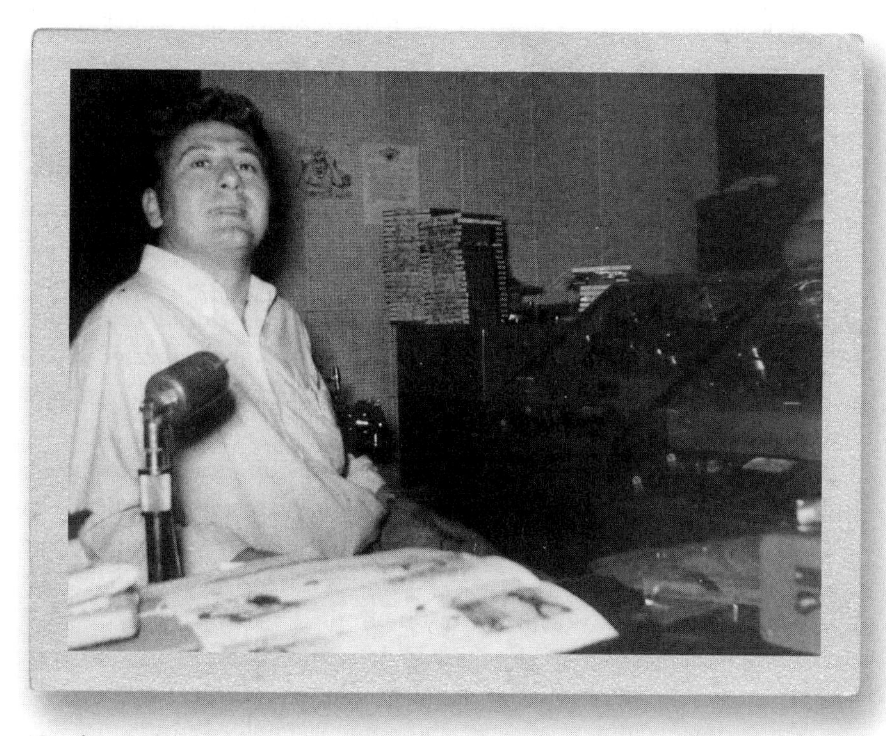

Cowboy Jack Clement in the Sun studio, 1958. COURTESY OF MARTIN WILLIS

process. "There's two heads; one records, and one plays back. The sound comes along and it's recorded on this head, and a split second later, it goes to the playback head. But you can take that and loop it to where it plays a split second after it was recorded and it flips right back into the record head. Or, you can have a separate machine and do that. If you do it on one machine, you have to echo everything."

The use of slapback, in addition to Phillips's creative use of room acoustics and microphone placement, conjured the illusion of a sound so full and thick that promoters often were disgruntled when they saw that Presley and crew were only a trio. "I thought I was getting the full band that played on the records," they'd gripe.

Recording rock 'n' roll in a blues-sonic environment, Phillips and the trio transformed mere dance music into a statement of personal expression that could easily be interpreted as cultural rebellion. Popular music had been increasingly mixing R & B and country—albeit in a sugary fashion—since the boys had come home from World War II. Presley made the raw, harder-edged music a cathartic mainstay of rock 'n' roll. That was his and Phillips's real contribution, and it was a mighty one. Everything else, from the fashion to the youth culture rebellion, was largely symbolic in nature.

Ultimately, we are left with Sam Phillips as Presley's greatest single influence. "Sam was the genius that blended it all together," says George Klein, Presley's former classmate. "You know the story about how Sam heard Elvis singing 'That's All Right (Mama)' during a break. Well, Sam had the genius to hear that. With Sam blending those two guys together with Elvis, and the way he put that record together and followed up with those other records, that was just a stroke of genius. I don't think anybody else but Sam could have captured that sound."

The authors believe Phillips's contributions to American culture went even deeper. Consider what Phillips did in the context of the Eisenhower fifties. He openly welcomed black talent (from Howlin' Wolf, B. B. King, and Roscoe Gordon to Rufus Thomas, Ike Turner, and others) into his studio and created opportunities for them with either with his or others' labels. He also encouraged interracial appreciation by having his white artists publicly sing and play in a black style. Further, he formed the first "all girl" radio station, WHER, long before women's lib was an acceptable concept. Phillips's private life was also rather unorthodox for the times. After Marion Keisker, with whom Phillips had been having an affair, left in a jealous huff and joined the air force, he lived openly with his new girlfriend, Sally Wilbourn, while he was still married to his wife and the mother of his children, Becky. Dan Griffin (who, like Phillips, is a native Alabaman), said it best: "By the Southern standards of the fifties, Sam Phillips probably should have been lynched."

But Phillips was persuasive, perceptive, and far better educated than most of the people he dealt with, black or white. He was also a pretty fair studio psychologist. Jack Clement observed Phillips's technique in the studio. "Well, he was pretty easygoing and paternal, you might say. Sam had a real knack for making people want to please him. I think that was his real ace in the hole. He did that. *I* wanted to please him. It was real fun when you pleased him, because he'd make you feel like gangbusters."

Phillips's paternalistic attitude was key to young Presley's artistic development. In his heart of hearts, Elvis Presley envisioned himself as a Dean Martin–type pop crooner. He felt that a respectable show-business career could only be achieved in gospel music. During his initial burst of fame, he sincerely told interviewers that such vanilla singers as Pat Boone and Kay Starr were "two of the finest voices out right now."

But, because Sam Phillips was interested in what he called "the Negro sound and Negro feel," Presley gave vent to all those juicy sounds he surreptitiously heard on Dewey Phillips's radio show. Initially, he attempted to do it through R & B ballads performed in a plaintive country style. Once he stumbled onto faster material, Phillips began to show interest. The producer's eyes lit up, and Presley basked in that fatherly approval.

Scotty Moore and Bill Black were not exempt from Phillips's sway—they, too, ached for his acceptance. All those chats over coffee allowed Phillips to impress his will upon the young guitarist. And, once he realized that Black's energetic bass playing and occasionally blunt manner were both catalysts for Presley's best rhythm performances and necessary counterpoints to Moore's sometimes taciturn silence, he made sure the three stayed together as a group.

Although every session was a trial, Elvis, Scotty, and Bill enjoyed a great deal of freedom in the studio. They made up arrangements on the spot, and they were allowed to experiment as much or as little as they wanted. The fact that Phillips kept very few alternate takes has often been ascribed to his penny-pinching ways. Indeed, during Presley's time at Sun, the cash-strapped producer reportedly rewound and taped over anything he didn't believe was fit for release on a single. However, the few alternate takes that do survive from that era allow us to hear the interpersonal dynamics that took place among the four men in the Sun studio.

Today's rockabilly audience clamors to hear the outtakes of songs recorded during the 1950s more than it does the commercial hits of the era. This rankles Moore, who chides, "What an invasion of privacy for anybody's record company to put out the outtakes! You're working your fanny off, trying to get to a master cut that the boss inside likes, and now, forty years later, they bring it out and you've got to listen to it again without getting paid for it." What Moore doesn't address is the fact that neo-rockabillies are so in love with the fabled Sun sound that they want to hear *everything*—including every dropped chord and changed lyric—by the original masters of rockabilly. Further, without having access to the snippets of studio chatter that have surfaced in outtakes, how could one hear Sam Phillips practicing his distinctive brand of studio psychology on his famous acts?

On RCA's two-disc compilation *Sunrise*, an early version of "Blue Moon of Kentucky" can be heard. In the recording, Phillips can be heard offering joyful congratulations to his band on finding part of their approach to the remake of Bill Monroe's waltz-tempo hit: "Fine, man. Hell, that's different. That's a pop song now, nearly 'bout." The chuckles from the trio, and from Elvis in particular, play out like nervous sighs of relief. Sonny Burgess, who recorded his best early sides for Sun, understands the men's emotion. "We were all there trying to impress Sam Phillips. His liking or not liking what you did meant everything."

It certainly meant a great deal to Presley, and he worked tirelessly on take after take to get that approval. Phillips understood the dynamic, and he created an atmosphere of unconditional acceptance in which his singer, an only child, could take his accustomed place as the center of attention. To the lonely, sideburn-sporting outcast, Phillips's attentions were exhilarating, and he responded with performances that were the equivalent of, "Hey Daddy, look at me! Look at me! Look at what else I can do!"

Another snippet of conversation heard on *Sunrise*, placed just before an alternate take of Jimmy Wakely's "I'll Never Let You Go (Little Darlin')," demonstrates just how cognizant the trio was of making black-oriented music. As Phillips calls a halt to a band take, we hear Moore make the laughing pronouncement, "Too much Vaseline!" Presley just chuckles. "I had it, too," says Moore. "You ain't just a woofin'," counters Presley in his best impersonation of black disc jockey Hoss Allen. Quickly, Bill Black pipes in with an R & B reference: "Please, please, please!" Moore is confused "What?" "*Damn*, nigger," responds the impressed bassist, mimicking street dialect, "Whoa nigger!" Not the least bit insulted by the racial epithet, Presley is cheerful and enthusiastic: "Man, we was hittin' it that time." Someone begins snapping their fingers in jive time. Black, still talking in dialect, agrees, "We *hit* that song! It jammed like *crazy*, boy!"

Black, who enjoyed jamming with musicians of all colors, was definitely no racist. Being the oldest member of the group and the one who'd lived in Memphis the longest, he knew about the area's racial tensions. Moore was well aware of the prevailing local attitude as well. Both had known and loved elements of black music all their lives, but the culture in that area at the time kept them from incorporating those elements into their music. But Phillips wanted that sound. Keen on currying his favor as both a record producer and a man, they gave him what he wanted and felt good about it in the bargain.

Phillips employed a different strategy for each of his label's famous acts. Presley needed to be babied and reassured. Jerry Lee Lewis had to be challenged. Carl Perkins needed coaxing. With Johnny Cash, Phillips played the wise colleague. Billy Lee Riley felt that Phillips smooth-talked good performances out of him. Each performer felt safe with him. More importantly, each artist thought he was running his own session, although in reality Phillips was simply providing the illusion of control. In the process, he taught them to be confident in their natural gifts and instincts.

It was emotionally exhausting for Phillips, and he could focus that type of attention on only one act at a time. When his gaze shifted to another performer, the previous artist often became jealous and resentful. After Presley left Sun, Phillips switched off behind-the-glass duties with engineer Jack Clement, who would produce and write some of the label's biggest hits. "My technique was to just tire 'em out until they gave up," recalls Clement. "Wear 'em down, you know. Or make 'em mad. There's all kinds of tricks. In the case of Johnny Cash, I'd say, 'Whatever you do—don't relax!'" Then, to comically illustrate his point, Clement would scream at the top of his lungs, "RELAX!"

This, too, pleased Sam Phillips.

Remarkably, Phillips nearly went too far with his bluesification of Elvis, Scotty, and Bill. The genre-blurring charm of "That's All Right (Mama)" and "Blue Moon of Kentucky" was that both songs could be played on country radio stations. After all, when the trio worked clubs, they were billed as a country music act. Their first record sold over 20,000 copies, which was damned good for an independent label with virtually no clout in the white-music world.

The authentic R & B strain in their music made it unique, but it was the country element in their sound that got the group an audition gig with the *Grand Ole Opry* in late 1954. "Everybody says, 'Oh, what a bad time we had at the *Opry*,'" comments Moore. "It just wasn't so. They always had a full house there, just about, and we were just different. They were used to their regular artists coming out there and singing, and whatever, and the applause was nice, but they didn't jump up and pull their hair out like they did later on. And we were only there to do the one song, and that's what we did and we left. Elvis was kind of disappointed, of course."

There exists the legendary story that *Opry* manager Jim Denny told Presley to go back to driving a truck. Most country music insiders insist that Denny never said it, including his friend and rival the *Louisiana Hayride* musician Tillman Franks. "I don't think that Jim Denny said that to him, but once the word gets out, everybody believes that. Elvis might have been told that. But they don't talk like that up there."

Still, Moore believes the story is true. "I didn't hear that with my own ears, but he told me about it, and Sam told me about it, so I have no reason to say that it didn't happen. Like I said, that kind of knocked the blocks out from under him for a little while."

If Denny did reject Presley, it was because of that strong black feeling in the singer's music, which went hand in hand with his greasy juvenile delinquent look. Many country music old-timers were under the impression that the group's melding of country with such a vigorous strain of blues was an indication that Presley didn't really like country music. "Elvis didn't much like country music," says Tillman Franks. "He was making fun of it when he first sang 'Blue Moon of Kentucky' and 'That's All Right (Mama)' with Scotty and Bill." Jack Clement disagrees. "Oh, no, Elvis loved country music. He liked Hank Snow and Eddy Arnold. There was nothing irreverent toward country music in his records."

But Franks's impression remained a strong one within the country music community. When Elvis, Scotty, and Bill recast the Roy Brown–Wynonie Harris R & B hit "Good Rockin' Tonight" as a flat-out rocker (replete with one of Moore's most exciting solos), [country] radio programmers blanched, and older audiences were somewhat mystified.

A good example of listeners' indifference to the trio's rendition can be found on an early live-show broadcast from Houston disc jockey Biff Collie's club and released on the 1979 LP *Elvis, Scotty, & Bill: The First Year.* Presley, Moore, and Black rave through a rendition of "Good Rockin' Tonight" that very nearly outshines the record. Oddly, at song's end, the crowd barely responds. As the set nears conclusion, the trio strikes up "Blue Moon of Kentucky" and the fans go stark raving nuts with joy. Sure, part of their rapture was due to their recognition of a hit record, but the fact is that the style that Phillips had persuaded his artist to incorporate on "Good Rockin' Tonight" sounded too "black" for the comfort of country audiences. Subsequently, one of the best records ever cut at Sun was largely unappreciated in its time.

The flip side, a remake of "I Don't Care If the Sun Don't Shine," a song featured in the 1953 Dean Martin–Jerry Lewis vehicle *Scared Stiff,* did not provide country fans a comfort zone either. Bongo-type percussion (singer Buddy Cunningham beating on a cardboard box) kicks the record off. "Sam hated drums because he didn't know how to control them," explains Moore. The guitar fills are jaunty and the bass syncopates neatly with the percussion, but Presley is overly coy. Conscious of being cute, the singer indulges in his first recorded instance of outright cheese. Like most Sun-era recordings, the song is somewhat redeemed by its catchy tune and by the chemistry exhibited by the band and singer, but both it and "Good Rockin' Tonight" stiffed.

Their next single, "Milkcow Blues Boogie" (a remake of the blues standard "Milkcow Blues"), sports a slow intro that seemingly mocks Presley's blues leanings. The singer stops cold and acts the hepcat as he commands, "Hold it, fellas. That don't move me. Let's get real, real gone for a change." One of the coolest, yet most contrived, moments on record, it paved the way for a triple-tempo rendition of the song, complete with the emergence of Presley's sexy lower register and some remarkable cow-milking solos from Moore.

If Phillips thought the barnyard double entendres of "Milkcow Blues Boogie" were going to win back country fans, he was mistaken. One of the most original records in the rockabilly canon, the song was just too damned weird for country or blues programmers. It was released with the B-side song "You're a Heartbreaker," a punchy ditty that has often been overlooked. The sentiments are country and so is the guitar, but Black plays modified boogie on the bass, and Presley's vocal approach is as pop as he ever got at Sun.

Sun's release of the "Milkcow Blues Boogie"–"You're a Heartbreaker" record sold even fewer copies than "Good Rockin' Tonight"–"I Don't Care If the Sun Don't Shine." As of this writing, no live versions of either song have surfaced. Chances are good that the trio, sensing that the record was an unredeemable flop, abandoned both songs pretty early in the game. Presley would not get a foothold in the national charts until he gave country radio something they could play right alongside Webb Pierce's and Faron Young's offerings.

The trio's exposure on the *Louisiana Hayride* radio broadcasts from 1954 through 1955, with a belated final appearance in 1956, paved the way for their national breakthrough. Elvis, Scotty, and Bill offered up a rockabilly version of Arthur "Hardrock" Gunter's "Baby, Let's Play House" (the original 1954 rendition was closer to ragtime-flavored folk than R & B) that overflowed with sexy humor. Hiccupping passionately through the intro ("B-baby, baby, baby, baby, baby, buh-buh-buh-buh-buh-baby, baby, baby"), Presley playfully alternates between begging his woman to come back and ominously declaring, "I'd rather see you dead, little girl, than to be with another man." (John Lennon would later alter the line slightly for the Beatles' "Run for Your Life.") Equally important was the obvious in-studio chemistry between the bandmates. Elvis, Scotty, and Bill never played together better in their lives. Backed by the hardest-driving slap bass Bill Black could muster, Moore's glittering Delta blues fills

Elvis Presley, San Diego, April 4, 1956. COURTESY OF GLEN GLENN

were the calm before the storm created by his two solos on the recording. Years later, he recalled using "a combination finger-picking and trying to do a sliding of blues notes in the thing." Describing the solos, which sound like big-band brass being fed through an electric guitar, Moore offers the following: "The first solo in it, I tried the blues thing, and for some reason—I can't tell you why—I did an all-out Chinese feel for the second solo. But it worked!"

The flip side of the record, "I'm Left, You're Right, She's Gone," is significant in that a slower, alternate take of that song, called "My Baby's Gone," was briefly made available to disc jockeys before the record was released. Stammering, stuttering and moaning in the alternate take, Presley offers up a tantalizing serving of Mississippi blues that comes off more as a measured threat than as a song of triumphing over lost love. It provides a captivating glimpse into the trio's interpretive brilliance, but one could easily understand why country radio would back away from that version. The song's countryish hook and story line is put to best use on the officially released version, which features Jimmie Lott's rather clunky drumming.

Stan Kesler recalls that he and Bill Taylor composed the song when they were both members of Clyde Leppard's Snearly Ranch Boys. "We were working at the Cotton Club that time, and I think [Bill Taylor] had a girlfriend, and somehow we got to talking about how he had broken up with her. I said, 'Well, has she left?' He said, 'Yeah, you're right, she's gone, and I'm left.' I think it sprang from that. Now I've heard other writers that interviewed Bill who said it came from a Campbell's soup commercial. But I don't ever remember a Campbell's soup commercial having that in it at all."

Billboard, which had always been supportive of the trio's work, deemed both sides of the disc "country," which was a good-enough recommendation for some stations. However, it was the impact of all the screaming girls heard during Presley's appearances on the *Louisiana Hayride* that made record buyers curious. Subsequently, "Baby, Let's Play House" rose to number five on the national country charts in July 1955. "I'm Left, You're Right, She's Gone" got strong airplay too (usually by DJs who were too chicken to program the innuendo-filled A-side) and skimmed the top ten. (Years later, Moore's guitar work on both tunes would prove especially influential to Creedence Clearwater Revival, who would employ his techniques in such late-1960s classics as "Born on the Bayou" and "Bad Moon Rising." In 1997 Fogerty admitted as much, saying to Moore at the Hard Rock Café Awards, "Man, it took me years to figure out that you used a thumb pick sometimes." Then, to the audience, "That was the whole secret. Other times he didn't.")

Even more successful with country audiences was the coupling of the Stan Kesler–Charlie Feathers composition "I Forgot to Remember to Forget" and a redrafting of Herman "Little Junior" Parker's 1953 song "Mystery Train." Despite some intrusive, ham-fisted percussion by Johnny Bernero (a part-time drummer who made his living selling insurance) "I Forgot to Remember to Forget" was the closest the trio came to doing traditional country music at Sun. Moore's guitar aped the twangy sound of a Nashville steel guitar, and Black's bass clip-clopped like an *Opry* veteran's. Although the recording has not aged well, thanks to its lovelorn lyric and Presley's brooding vocal, it became the first number-one record of Elvis's career, and it spent 39 weeks on the country charts.

Clearly, of the two songs, the enduring classic is "Mystery Train." Originally the tune was conceived as a sensual shuffle with locomotive allusions by one of Sun's early blues acts, Little Junior Parker and the Blue Flames. Phillips, who held the publishing rights to the song, hoped that, with "Mystery Train," the trio could earn some badly needed extra coin for him. (It wouldn't be the last time he trotted out one of Parker's songs for a white act. Hayden Thompson cut a remarkable version of "Love My Baby" in 1956. Both Jerry Lee Lewis and Sonny Burgess recorded renditions of Parker's hit "Feel So Good." "I think Sam played that record for everybody who came in the door," chuckles Burgess today.)

Besides some smartly executed Merle Travis–styled train rhythm, Scotty Moore brought something new to the session: an EchoSonic amplifier custom built by Ray Butts. Moore had first heard it used by his idol, Chet Atkins. Moore recalls, "I heard the sound that Chet was getting, and I said, 'OK, that's basically the same sound Sam is getting on the whole record.' 'Cause I'd already run into the [experience of] getting out and playing with the public and, even though we were playing all the same notes, it didn't sound the same as it did coming off the record. And when I heard that I thought if I could get that amp, that would at least give it some semblance of the same kind of sound. Not his voice, but at least with the guitar. Chet used a different kind of setting than I did, but it was still the same amp."

Moore had to finance the five-hundred-dollar amp through a local music store, but as a tool it proved invaluable. With it, not only could he replicate the Sun guitar sound onstage, but he would also be able to re-create it in other studios. Other Sun artists, such as Roy Orbison and Carl Perkins, would eventually purchase the same model amp, and Moore himself would use his until he stopped playing with Elvis Presley.

Spurred on by the guitarist's echo-laden rhythm, Presley transformed "Mystery Train" into a defiant cross between folk, blues, and Rosetta Tharpe–style gospel. Every sonic element—Black's tic-tac bass, the singer's hard-scrubbing acoustic rhythm, and Moore's country lead break—came together to lay the foundation for a remarkably confident and mature vocal. So rich is this recording that one has to listen hard to realize that it features no drums at all. A number-eleven country hit for the band in December 1955, "Mystery Train" would remain, on and off, in Elvis Presley's stage repertoire until his death.

By November 1954, disc jockey/promoter Bob Neal had taken the reins of the band's management from Moore. Today this arrangement would be viewed as a classic broadcast industry conflict of interest. "He had an early morning radio show," says Moore of Neal. "It came on like at five in the morning—WMPS, I believe. Boomed right down to the Delta, Mississippi, and over in Arkansas. And he started booking us on stuff that we could make on the weekends, at first. We could leave early Saturday morning or could get there in a couple of hours—by eight Friday night—and do a gig here and so forth. And then it got to the point that he was getting more and more calls, and then that's when we all quit our day jobs and took a chance on the whole thing."

The first thing Neal felt compelled to do was remind country fans why Presley, Moore, and Black were famous. So he officially dubbed them Elvis Presley and the Blue Moon Boys. The band didn't particularly care for the idea, but they had quit their day jobs after signing a deal with the *Louisiana Hayride*, and they needed someone and something to ensure bigger and better-paying bookings outside the relatively low-paying *Hayride* promotions.

Moore, who says he was never really interested in being a full-time manager, continued to serve, in effect, as the trio's unpaid road manager. "I was calling the shots for me and Bill, mainly. Elvis, whatever he wanted to wear was fine with me. But being an old navy guy, I wanted the band to be all alike, at least." Initially, all Moore had to worry about was getting the boys to the gigs on time. As Presley's female followers got more grabby, however, he became concerned with security. As fans became more vocal, he also fretted about the band's suffering musicianship. A solid percussionist of Fontana's caliber could be heard above the frenzied screams, which would help Black and Moore keep better time and create a better groove for their singer. It was a hard sell—Moore and Black had to agree to pay for it out of their shares of the band's take—but Elvis Presley and the Blue Moon Boys were finally going to get a full-time drummer.

D. J. Fontana

"This was about the best band I'd heard up to that time. D. J. Fontana planted those drums down and started stacking verses against one another with his fills, building up to the solo, riding the solos in and riding them out again. He had incredible technique and fast hands, so he could employ those Buddy Rich press rolls whenever he wanted to. He played like a big-band drummer—full throttle. Now Elvis had a real foundation, some architecture, and he made the most of it. D.J. set Elvis free."

—Levon Helm, *This Wheel's on Fire: Levon Helm and the Story of the Band*

To EXPAND UPON what fellow drummer, the Band's Levon Helm, saw during those early years, it's necessary to skip ahead a year to one of early commercial television's most notorious moments—a moment for which D. J. Fontana served as the catalyst.

The time: June 5, 1956. The place: the set of *The Milton Berle Show.*

"Elvis Presley," shouts the host before he whistles appreciation through his pinky and index fingers. "How 'bout my boy!"

What were Elvis Presley, Scotty Moore, Bill Black, and D. J. Fontana doing on the stage of Berle's NBC variety hour in the first place? Sure the kid had been on the show once before, but wasn't this rock 'n' roll thing over yet? Milton Berle knew that, in fact, it was just taking off, and he was playing to the country's ongoing furor over the music for all it was worth. He had to. He needed the ratings. Further, he had a score to settle with his rival at CBS, Jackie Gleason.

Berle's popularity, which had been phenomenal up until that time, was petering out. The glory days of *Texaco Star Theater*, when the ham-and-egg vaudevillian's energetic, anything-for-a-laugh style made the ownership of those newfangled television sets de rigueur, had already ended. The previous year, Berle's new sponsor, Buick Motors, had convinced him to stop being the comic protagonist and play for sympathy as the butt-of-the-joke straight man. Sensing he needed to change something to help reverse his sliding momentum, Berle had acquiesced. The result was a disaster. Longtime fans were bored by the "new Berle" and critics didn't know what to make of the changed format. To add insult to injury, Buick dropped his show and switched their allegiance to Gleason. Berle's show improved during the next year, but it was expensive to produce and the ratings never really recovered; they'd only spiked upward when Presley had been on in April.

Compared to his show-business cronies, Milton Berle was an odd duck. He liked rock 'n' roll. Not for its music, but because it followed the first rule of showbiz: give 'em something to see. (Just a year later Berle would advise Steve Allen, "When that Jerry Lee Lewis kid kicks the piano stool, kick it back at him. It'll look great on camera.") The comic knew in his gut that Presley, with his good looks, wild music, and shaky hips, was every showman's dream. All you had to do was get out of his way and let him do his thing.

For both of the young rocker's appearances on his show, Berle had played ball all the way with NBC, a partner of RCA Victor. He referred to Presley as "*our* new RCA artist," presented him gold-record awards on the show, and gave little introductory speeches along the lines of, "Incidentally, ladies and gentleman, I don't think I'm revealing any secrets when I say that Elvis Presley is the fastest-rising young singer in the entertainment industry today." Despite such supplicant acts of loyalty, NBC had decided to cancel Mr. Television's prime-time hour after this final show of the season. He knew it, too.

In an interview before his death, Berle claimed he told Presley to leave his guitar backstage when he sang "Hound Dog," during his second appearance on the show. "Let 'em see you, son," advised Uncle Miltie. The comic knew in advance what the singer was going to do when drummer D. J. Fontana slowed the tempo. Any other television star of that era would have said, "Whoa, you can't do that on my show." Not Berle. Not now. Earlier that year,

Gleason, who produced Tommy and Jimmy Dorsey's *Stage Show* series (on which Presley made his television debut), proclaimed of Elvis, "He can't last. I tell you flatly, he can't last." Then, when he learned that Berle's series was in trouble, Gleason callously taunted the elder comic about it in public.

Berle needed to go out with a bang, and Presley and his boys were his key piece of ammo.

Upon their introduction, Presley and the band lit into a punchy, up-tempo version of "Hound Dog." Although the song was originally belted out by Big Mama Thornton as a snarling repudiation of a gigolo, the guys had learned their version of it from a white group, during their ill-fated Las Vegas gig earlier in the year. Sharing a bill with bandleader Freddie Martin at the New Frontier Hotel, the group had received mostly polite applause from the gamblers in attendance. During off-stage hours, Presley had attended other casino shows and was impressed by Freddie Bell & the Bell Boys' show-stopping rendition of "Hound Dog" at the Sands. He quickly added it to his own repertoire.

By the time of the Berle appearance, the Blue Moon Boys put a twist on the song. Moore took a guitar solo (one that actually made him grin as he played), and Fontana added a hot drum roll between verses. "Elvis would let you do something," Fontana explains modestly. "He let me add that bit to 'Hound Dog.' I guess it worked out."

With every machine-gunned drum roll, Presley's legs and hips shook in time, harder and harder as the song played out. The younger girls in the studio audience screamed as if on cue. Suddenly, Presley threw his arm back; the band stopped, then began to vamp at half tempo as the singer raved accusingly, "You ain't-a nuthin' but a hound dog, hound dog, cuh-crying all the time."

Writhing and sliding around the mic stand, Presley performed a jaw-dropping bump and grind to the salacious strip-club beat that Fontana laid down. The only things missing were tassels twirling from his nipples. Loud mumbling, scattered laughter, and delighted female shrieks rose from the studio audience. Black and Moore laughed at the reaction as they got set for one final salvo of burlesque action.

"You ain't never caught a rabbit . . . ." A final wave signaled the band to stop. Presley then pointed threateningly at the audience and belted out, "You ain't no friend of mine." Excited, the rocker nearly jumped the gun, but managed to suggestively thrust his hips in synch with Fontana's last propulsive drum roll and cymbal crash. The studio audience was applauding before Presley could even get out the deep-voiced tag, "You ain't nuthin' but a hound."

A delighted Berle hit the stage clapping, whistling, and shouting, "How 'bout my boy! How 'bout my boy! I *love* him!" Then, as the show prepared to go to a commercial, Berle sang a few goofy bars of "Hound Dog" with his new brother-in-arms.

That performance shocked every adult in America. Newspapers published columns denouncing the singer and his moves. Preachers railed about the performance from the pulpit. Politicians and others had a field day debating the morality of Presley and his impact on modern teens. Although some now say the appearance nearly killed his television career, the controversy actually propelled Presley's star even higher.

Berle reveled in the notoriety. Suddenly, no one was talking about Jackie Gleason. People across the country began conversations with, "Did you see what happened on the Berle show?" When Presley appeared on Steve Allen's show weeks later, he was dressed in a tux and tails and was told not to move. Afterward, disappointed fans rebuked the bespectacled host, saying, in effect, "We want the Elvis Presley that Milton Berle gave us."

Years later, a cigar-chomping Berle would sport a twinkle in his eyes as he told a television host, "I tried to take Elvis under my wing. He was a nice young man. He was just dancing to the beat."

That beat, of course, was supplied by Dominic Joseph Fontana.

Compared to his future bandmates, Fontana was a well-to-do city boy. The son of a local grocer, he was born on March 15, 1931, in Shreveport, Louisiana. While the family wasn't exactly rich, he never went hungry. Early on, Fontana heard western swing bands led by Hank Thompson, Tex Williams, and Bob Wills, but it was the wide-open sound of big-band jazz that first grabbed his ear.

Growing up during the peak of the big-band era, the youngster was exposed to the sounds of Woody Herman and Stan Kenton. He also liked the Dorseys, Charlie Ventura's small combos, and any band that spotlighted a drummer. Big-band drummers were the breakout stars of the music world. Beat-crazed kids followed the comings and goings of top percussionists the way teens in the 1960s would keep up with guitarists. Young D.J.'s particular favorite was fast-handed Buddy Rich. "Buddy was a genius," Fontana exclaims with awe. "Nobody played like Buddy Rich. I've never seen anything like him. I've never seen him in person, but just watching some of the films and the TV shows he did, I don't know how he played some of that stuff, and I don't know if anybody else does, either."

What about that other demon of the drum kit, pulse-pounding Gene Krupa? "He wasn't the technician Buddy was, but he was very good too," explains Fontana. "Krupa, Rich, Louis Bellson—all the old-timers could really play, and it all made *sense* when they played. I used to listen to 'em when I was a kid growing up, and I learned a little bit from each one, actually."

At the age of fourteen Fontana began playing drums in high school, where a teacher named J. B. Mullens provided the youngster's only formal musical training. "He was just a great drum teacher," says Fontana. "Of course he taught all the instruments, but drums were his thing. His hands! I don't know how he did it. I used to watch him; he'd drop his hands and they'd move—he didn't move anything else, hardly. He used the finger technique I guess, and his hands would do anything he wanted them to do."

When he wasn't playing in the high school's marching band or concert orchestra or in the ROTC Drum and Bugle Corps, Fontana would sneak over to cousin A. J. "Ace" Lewis's house to dig the copacetic jive of popular jazz. The drummer recalls, "He was the only guy in town who had a set of drums that I knew of. So, I'd go over to his house. He was always playing along with records and he was really good at it. I'd go over there and watch him. When he'd play a little bit, I'd play a little bit. That's how I got started, listening to the music of other artists."

Fontana, who has never held a regular day job other than one at his father's grocery, turned pro early. "I was playing in these little old bars and clubs when I was sixteen. I had to join a union then. Back then you had to have your parents' permission to work some of them bars. They'd check from time to time to see if any young people were working in those clubs. They had to have a note in case anybody came in."

The drummer's early work experience was similar to that of Moore's and Black's. He played the hits of the day, such as "Stardust" and "Moonglow," and even though he didn't read music, he was able to adapt to the style that each hastily put-together band attempted. "Yeah, we'd play 'How High the Moon' and semi-jazz things. I was playing brushes mostly. Those cocktail lounges were small, but we also did a lot of weddings and stuff where you could play a little bit harder. Then I worked with a couple of seven-piece Dixieland bands. It was just a mixture of, like, three horns, three saxophones, a couple trumpets, piano, bass, and drums. It was kind of fun. They had good musicians and we'd work from like eight till twelve, or maybe nine till one, so it wasn't working hard. We'd take a break every forty-five minutes, take off fifteen or twenty, you know. You pick a little from each band you work for and you just put that in the back of your mind, hoping you remember it."

It was a good life for a young guy. He could play music, meet like-minded musicians, impress the girls, and even earn a few dollars. However, Fontana didn't really consider drumming for a living until after he got home from his uneventful army hitch during the Korean War. Playing the bar scene in Shreveport again, he was now old enough to work at a local burlesque club. The strippers and comics would bring in their sheet music, "But how are you going to read a big chart when you only have four pieces?" The musicians, who had memorized a staggering amount of popular tunes, usually simplified the arrangements in order to play the piece with only the four instruments they had.

Fontana remembers his days in local burlesque fondly. "I worked that bar off and on," he chuckles. "It was actually kind of an after-hours bar. When all the other bars in town closed down, everyone would show up at this one club. Like I say, we had comedians and singers too, and they had a circuit they all worked. It was fun to play because all the musicians, artists, and strippers were doing something different, so you had to watch 'em close. They wanted you to do the bumps and grinds for 'em, so that's where I learned the bumps and grinds I used with Elvis."

Although he had played many kinds of music in widely disparate settings, Fontana proclaims, "I never played country in my life until I went to the *Hayride*."

In the country music world, KWKH's broadcasts of the weekly *Louisiana Hayride* were second in importance only to WSM's airings of the *Grand Ole Opry*. Beamed across the South over two fifty-thousand-watt clear channel networks, played on vinyl transcription discs, or "V-discs," over Armed Forces Radio, and picked up for an hour each week by the CBS network, the radio show made the likes of Webb Pierce, Faron Young, Johnny Horton, and Hank Williams very big stars. Fontana remembers the popular host, Horace "Hoss" Logan, well. "Well, he had the cowboy suit, he had the two guns—pistols on both sides, like a cowboy—and he had the big wide hat, just like a country artist would. And he had a heck of a voice; he was great at emceeing. So was [announcer] Frank Page. Frank was really good."

Many touring performers brought their own accompanists with them to do the show. Those who couldn't used whomever they could get from the *Hayride*'s pool of musicians. Because Shreveport was a relatively small town, Fontana knew most of the area pickers, as well as some of the folks who booked the show. The *Hayride* was always further ahead of the curve, musically speaking, than was the *Opry*, and in mid-1954 it decided to break with country music tradition and put drums on its stage.

"But," recalls Fontana with a laugh, "they said, 'We don't want to throw the drums on there all of a sudden.' So they put 'em behind this little thin curtain at first. I played a couple weeks back there. I could still hear." Bit by bit, they allowed the staff drummers to bring out the snare, then try the cymbals, until finally management directed, "Well, just bring all your drums one night. We'll see how it works."

Fontana taught himself how to play this new form of music by listening to country records. Soon he was backing the region's biggest stars, including Pierce, Young, Horton, Nat Stuckey, David Houston, George Jones, Claude King, Jimmie C. Newman, and many others. "You gotta remember, in the early days, the country guys didn't like drums. If they wanted me to, I'd play behind 'em. That's what I was there for. Like I said, some of 'em didn't like drums, so I didn't always play. Which was OK; I didn't mind. They paid me anyway."

As a staff drummer with the *Hayride* band, Fontana's first recording experience was garnered with Merle Kilgore in KWKH's basement studios. One of the first noteworthy discs he played on was the Tom Tall–Ginny Wright duet "Are You Mine," which became a number-two country hit in January 1955. The drummer liked freelancing, although it wasn't particularly lucrative.

"I really like him," Tillman Franks laughs as he reminisces about Fontana. "D.J. likes to tell of the time I hired him to play a date in Carlsbad, New Mexico. I couldn't get a drummer. I got [Hank Williams's widow] Billie Jean ready to go and Elvis. D.J. tells everybody that I booked him for fifteen dollars in Carlsbad but he had to take his own car and buy the gas!"

Despite the lousy dough, moving from artist to artist and style to style suited Fontana's temperament. He wasn't really looking to join up full time with the wild young cat who took the *Hayride* by storm.

Elvis, Scotty, and Bill were brought to the *Hayride* by house booker Pappy Covington and promoter/manager/musician Tillman Franks. Presley had already failed at the *Opry*. Was the *Hayride*—who had lost so many name performers to the Nashville-based show—trying to one-up Jim Denny and company by picking up their leavings? "I didn't even know the *Opry* had turned him down," says Franks, who still lives in Shreveport. "The reason I had called him up was because Sam Phillips had gotten a record to [disc jockey] T. Tommy Cutrer on KCIJ in Shreveport and one to Biff Collie in Houston. I think he carried it to him—I don't think he mailed it to him; that's what T. Tommy told me. Both 'em, when they started playing it, that was the hottest record they were playing. That's two big markets there, and Shreveport and the *Hayride* had so many listeners back then, like in San Angelo, Big Springs, Odessa, and all them towns in west Texas—Corpus Christi—and down south in Del Rio. After sundown KWKH would beam the signal real strong to the southwest, and Elvis really got hot in Texas because the *Hayride* really had some listeners back then."

Fontana picks up the story from there. "Pappy was booking acts, and at that time nobody knew anything about booking acts at *Hayride*s or anything

D. J. Fontana and Elvis Presley at the *Louisiana Hayride*.
COURTESY OF D. J. FONTANA

else. [Pappy] and Tillman came into the office of the old KWKH building downtown and said, 'Hey, why don't you listen to this record.' It was Elvis, Scotty, and Bill. I said, 'Damn, that's a good record! Sounds like five or six musicians.' You know, with the echo and everything. They said 'Oh no, it's only three guys.' 'Well, we're gonna try and bring him in and see how he does.'

"Well, they brought him in and he got a lukewarm response. They didn't tear the house down. The reason for that was, they were used to seeing Webb Pierce, Faron Young, and Johnny Horton—guys who just stood and sang. They didn't jump or move around. They didn't do nothin'. They just sang all their hit songs. Just like a statue, like they always had. They've gotten better now, of course, all these new guys. But when they saw [Elvis] coming out there running all over the damn stage, they said, 'What *is* this?'"

It's Fontana's feeling that parents—who generally liked straight country music better than their children did—went home and told their kids about Presley. "Evidently, a few kids came, and then next week a few more came. Then the next week, the parents didn't come. Their kids came! So, it was all mostly young people. That's kind of how we got started on that little deal there."

The drummer sees his invitation to play with the Blue Moon Boys as an act of necessity. "[Elvis] just needed somebody. Scotty said, 'Well, you want to work with us tonight at the *Hayride*?' I said. 'Yeah, that's why I'm here.' So we went out and did a couple of tunes. Back then you only did about one or two tunes, then you're off and you come back at ten-thirty and do another one."

Even though he and his drum kit were now in front of the curtain with the rest of the band, Fontana was still worried about overpowering the other musicians—especially Elvis, Scotty, and Bill. "It's just a point of not getting in the way of what they were doing, you know. You learn that as you go as a musician. And that's the first thing I thought of: 'Man, I'm not getting in their way. I'll be cluttering up what they're doing,' so I just didn't do it." It was a good strategy. After a few more *Hayride* appearances, Presley reassured the drummer, "It's OK. I don't care what you play—just make some noise."

The Blue Moon Boys had been looking, on and off, to expand their ranks since the group had formed. In addition to using local drummers Johnny Bernero and Jimmie Lott, the trio latched onto other *Hayride* musicians for their live shows. Rhythm guitarist Sonny Trammell, future piano king Floyd Cramer, and steel guitarist Jimmy Day can all be heard on some of the scratchy, early live-broadcast transcriptions. When Presley hit the big time, he asked

Cramer and Day to officially join the group. Hoping to latch on as house musicians at the *Grand Ole Opry*, they refused. In 1997 Day told an interviewer for *No Depression* magazine that, had the two joined up with Presley, "It would have changed rock 'n' roll forever. Rock 'n' roll would have had a steel guitar." (It might also have resulted in Presley being forever identified as a country artist, thereby effectively cutting his record sales to a fraction of what they ultimately were.)

Another early candidate for the band was Kern Kennedy, who played piano with Sonny Burgess and the Pacers. Recalls Kennedy, "We were playing at the Silver Moon Club in Newport, Arkansas; myself, Punky Caldwell, and Sonny. If I remember correctly, we had opened for Elvis that night. He asked me to come up and sit in with his group, and I did. Then he asked if I would care to join him. At the time, I thought Elvis was going to be big, but I never, ever thought he was going to be as big as he was. And really, he never impressed me. I'll be honest with you; to me he always appeared to be a three-chord musician and that was about it. In fact, I always thought that Sonny was five times the showman that Elvis was. Elvis was just this phenomenon to come along, and maybe the first guy in that particular field to step out there and do all the shakin' and wigglin'."

Presley's consideration of Kennedy—a solid, Moon Mullican–style piano boogie man who enjoyed pop standards as much as western swing—for his own band showed that the singer was looking to branch out from his blues-drenched rockabilly, at his live shows if nowhere else. During their earliest days, Presley and the Blue Moon Boys struggled to build up their stage repertoire. "Most of it we learned from listening to the radio," explains Scotty Moore. "We'd find a song—Little Richard's or somebody's song on the radio—and then, when we got to where we were going, if we had time, while it was fresh on our minds, we'd try to work it up. And a lot of this happened when we went to the *Hayride*, until we cut the next record. We only had two songs and we had to do something! They wanted at least fifteen to twenty minutes onstage."

Most of the new songs, including LaVern Baker's "Tweedle Dee," the Charms' "Heart of Stone," and Ray Charles's "I've Got a Woman," fit the trio's style like a glove. In order to perform tunes that had trickier arrangements, such as Chuck Berry's "Maybellene" or the Drifters' "Money Honey," they required the steadying influence of a good drummer. Fontana's presence immediately took pressure off each of the individual band members.

"Yeah, it did," affirms Moore. "I wouldn't have to necessarily drive a note this hard as maybe I would have or did on some of the early stuff because he would be there to help me." Fontana also helped to support Bill Black's hard-slappin' bass work. "Oh yes. On stage, [Black] didn't care whether he was hitting the right notes or not. You know, this is showtime. And Elvis would break three or four strings, he'd play so hard, and it was up to me and D.J. to keep the thing going."

However, the drummer's biggest impact was made on Elvis Presley. On *The Complete Hayride Recordings*, KWKH announcer Frank Page's narration stresses the fact that Presley's wiggling became increasingly exaggerated as he became more famous. That was instigated in no small way by Fontana, who began mischievously accenting the singer's onstage moves. "I'd throw a cymbal crash here, a tom-tom fill there, give him a little beat with the kick drum. He loved it. It was fun. A lot of the guys who work today, they don't have no fun up there." The two men's shared sense of humor allowed them to build a reliable stable of strip-club allusions, which in turn allowed Presley to work up some crowd-pleasing bits of business. "You know, Elvis weren't no dummy," Fontana would later report. "If he saw something that worked, he kept it."

Their relationship outside the confines of the weekly radio show began slowly at first. "Yeah, we probably did two or three shows on the *Hayride*," remembers Fontana. "And then one weekend they came up and said, 'Well, we're going to go here to east Texas,' Longview, Tyler, Kilgore—about a hundred miles away—and they said, 'Do you want to go?" I said, 'Yeah, I'll go.'" That sort of "day-to-day, week-to-week thing" went on for nearly six months before Fontana was officially asked to join the band on August 8, 1955.

"They had tried some different guys up and around Memphis," recalls Fontana. "Somehow, they just didn't work out for them. Some people you can put together and the band just won't work. Other people you just fall in with and it works. There's no rhyme or reason for it, but it just happens, it jells."

The addition of Fontana was so vital to the Blue Moon Boys' sound that the drummer was initially paid more than either Moore or Black: a whopping one hundred dollars a week plus expenses. "It came out of everybody's pocket," says Fontana. "Because they were splitting it, see. Scotty and Bill were getting 25 percent each and Elvis was getting 50 percent. So they would all split expenses, which I was one of them, and the rooms and the car and the gas and what all, so they didn't have a whole lot left." Moore and Black had to work hard to convince Presley to accept that arrangement.

The Blue Moon Boys and Elvis Presley nearing their early rockin' peak. COURTESY OF D. J. FONTANA

Not only was Fontana good for them musically, but he also provided the band a much-needed extra driver on long car trips, and he shared the individual band members' musical tastes. Moore, who marveled at artists ranging from Wes Montgomery to Django Reinhart, remembers that he, Black, and D.J. had to listen to jazz surreptitiously, because young Presley's tastes ran more toward pop and R & B. "If Elvis wasn't with us, or if he was asleep, we would always listen to a disc jockey named Moonglow McMartin in New Orleans; [his radio program] came on at midnight on WWL at the Roosevelt Hotel. And he played jazz all night long. And we could pick it up all the way out in Arizona and everywhere, late night. [Bill] liked all kinds of stuff. D.J., from being a big-band addict, you know, he loved the stuff."

Moreover, Fontana got along well with the young superstar-in-training. "Elvis liked him," observes Tillman Franks. "He liked him as a friend. He was buddies with him. See, D.J. was funny, really. Elvis really dug him, and Elvis didn't get that close to anyone, but he liked D.J. as well as anybody he'd ever met."

"D.J.'s got a lot of funny expressions," Gordon Stoker laughs. "I'll call him up and say 'Hey D.J., what's happenin'?' He'll answer, 'Nothin', every minute.'"

Former Sun artist and Presley friend Barbara Pittman observed, "D.J. says funny things all the time without really knowing it. At least I don't think that he knows it." Pittman illustrated her point by recounting the following. "I ran into D.J. backstage at a CBS Elvis tribute special. I think it was in 1981. I hadn't seen him since 1957 at the Cotton Club. Well, I walked up to him and said, 'Hi D.J., do you remember me?' He said, 'Yes, I do. You've been in love with me your whole life.' I just fell out and couldn't stop laughing."

Humor was an important pressure release for Presley. As his career got hotter, there were more demands on his time, energy, and pocketbook. The country music old-timers kept telling him he was a flash in the pan; adults decried him as a symptom of juvenile delinquency; and damn it, the road was tiring. Fontana's non sequiturs, one-liners, and mock insults reminded the Memphis Flash that this whole music thing was supposed to be fun. As time went on, Presley would work some of Fontana's spontaneous remarks into his stage patter—not that anyone really heard them amid all the screams. But the jokes allowed the singer just enough distance to enjoy the spectacle of the moment. Presley's self-mocking humor and irreverent ridicule of his own impact proved to be a big part of his early charm.

The well-liked Fontana was also Presley's connection with the *Hayride* crowd. Because of the long distances they had to drive from gig to gig, the boys seldom had time to mingle with the other stars. When they did have time and opportunity to socialize, both the reticent Moore and the shy singer were often perceived as "standoffish." Singer Tom Tall, who actually roomed with the guitarist, recalls, "He was a lot like I was. Quiet and, if I may say so, pretty decent." Gary Bryant remembered that the group mainly kept to themselves, "But D.J. and I were best friends. I met him when he was playing drums for Lefty Frizzell. We ran around a lot together, and one thing I remember about D.J. was, one Christmas, I was all by myself in this hotel and he come down, grabbed me, and took me out to his house and introduced me to his family. They took me in and treated me like I was part of the family. That was so special to me." Bryant clung to that memory until his death in 2001.

Younger performers like Tommy Sands, Bob Luman, Werley Fairburn, and the Browns were turned on by Presley's music. However, the older, established country musicians didn't approve of what the Hillbilly Cat and his crew were doing to their industry. It wasn't just the rambunctious music they objected to, but Presley's audience as well. Youngsters who came out to see the Memphis Flash didn't want to sit through fiddle tunes, heartbreak ballads, or traditional country music of any kind. They'd sit politely for a brief spell before they began to chant, "We want Elvis! We Want Elvis!" Once Presley hit the stage, the young women would scream themselves hoarse. Worse, once Presley was offstage, they refused to quiet down for the emergence of even the biggest names in country music. Musicians accustomed to headlining, such as Hank Snow, Ferlin Husky, Webb Pierce, and many others, found themselves forced to allow Presley to headline shows lest they face a rapidly emptying auditorium or fans loudly insisting on the young singer's return. As a result, those in country's old guard who didn't insult the rocker to his face (as did Faron Young, although he needled everyone), stewed with self-righteous resentment.

One such performer was George Jones. By birth, the world's greatest honky-tonk singer, he was also a pretty fair rockabilly when he wanted to be. (Jones's late-fifties rockabilly-style hits "White Lightning" and "Who Shot Sam" are superior to the proto-rock recordings he made billed as "Thumper" Jones.). In later interviews he claimed to like Presley and his music, but one *Hayride*-era stunt shows that, at the time, the performer seethed with resentment. Opening for the exciting young act, Jones went onstage and promptly performed all of the Blue Moon Boys' tunes. Afterward he told his friend Gary Bryant, "That oughta show that fella. *Anybody* can do what he does."

Left with few alternatives, Presley hit the stage, performed three gospel numbers, and said, "Let's get out of here." He would go on to much bigger and better things, but he never forgot that slight. Years later, when Jones was sodden with drink, he tried to visit Presley at Graceland and, later, Las Vegas. He wanted to show his friends that he really did know the King of Rock 'n' Roll; that they were buddies from way back. Jones was turned away without comment each time.

If Fontana ever heard the traditional country acts gripe about Presley, he didn't acknowledge it. In fact, the hysterical reaction the singer got from the girls opened up more opportunities for his own humorous escapades. "D.J. and I did a lot of knocking around in Shreveport," Gary Bryant fondly recalled. "Once, we went to the fair, and I was wearing the cat clothes and all this kind of stuff. When I was younger, I kind of looked like Elvis in a way. Anyway, he passed me off as Elvis, and these girls started mobbing me everywhere. They had recognized D right off the bat."

Leaving the *Hayride* for life on the road with Elvis Presley and the Blue Moon Boys was a gamble, but it all worked out—for a while, anyway. "We were like brothers, I guess," reminisces Fontana. "Oh, we'd fuss every now and then about something, but after about two minutes it was over with, so it didn't make any difference. Yeah, it was just like a bunch of family guys, the four of us. We couldn't argue very often because we had to drive to other places."

Back before the days of luxury travel for touring acts, the band had to make do with what they could carry with them. Black's bass was mounted on top of the car, "And everything else [was] inside the car, the trunk," says Fontana. "Bill's bass was the biggest instrument; then we had the little set of drums. Elvis had his guitar. Scotty had his guitar and an amp. That was all we had, really, plus our clothes."

So much driving, especially at night, made occasional car accidents inevitable. Black's son, Louis, recounts a particularly terrifying moment experienced by his father. "When he was with Elvis he had his bass tied on top of his car. I think Daddy was driving. This man pulled out in front of him somewhere down there in Mississippi and he hit him. Well, the bass come flying off and went down in the bushes, and Elvis, Scotty, and D.J. all jumped out and went running to look and see if the man was all right. He was OK. All of a sudden, they couldn't find Daddy. They said, 'Where's Bill?' It was dark and they heard this 'boom-boom-boom-boom-boom-boom' sound coming from down in the bushes there. He was checking that bass out. [Laughs.] That was his bread and butter; he had to have that thing in order to play music."

During those grueling early road trips, the monotony was often relieved by young Elvis's pranks and practical jokes. "He was playful," remarks Bobbie Moore. "He liked to play and pull little tricks on people." Sometimes the Blue Moon Boys would pay him back by pretending to leave him behind, and the prank would invariably instigate a fight. Moore's ex-wife also remembers the band hitting the road for an early Bob Neal–promoted tour with Johnny Cash and the Carter Family. ("Elvis had a crush on Anita Carter, I think.") During the trip, everyone got silly and began throwing firecrackers at the rural mailboxes they were passing. Yet no matter how high spirited or grumpy they became, the group always had business on their mind. "No matter where we were," recalls Scotty Moore, "If we saw a radio tower, we would head right for it." Once there, they would impress the local disc jockey with their polite, friendly demeanor, and they'd do their best to persuade the DJ to play their latest record.

Elvis Presley, Glen Glenn, and D. J. Fontana, San Diego, April 4, 1956. Courtesy of Glen Glenn

Fontana felt they had something pretty snappy, musically speaking, for a small combo. Like the teammates in a good ball club, each member executed his role perfectly. "You gotta remember, we only had three pieces—four including Elvis playing rhythm guitar, and he played excellent rhythm guitar. You can hear it on those records, some of that early stuff; boy, he was right on top of it. He'd play really *good* rhythm guitar; he didn't miss a beat.

"Scotty was shy but played great guitar and handled business things. Bill was a boisterous, rambunctious type of guy. He didn't care what happened. Bill sold Elvis's pictures, and he sold more in pictures than he was making playing for Elvis. He did! But he'd get out there and holler and scream at the folks and cut up. They loved him! Bill was almost like a comedian. He saved our lives a lot of times onstage, when Elvis was just bombing out in some of these little old towns. He'd sing one or two songs and look over at us and say. 'I don't know, I just can't get 'em on my side. I don't know what we're going to do here.' Next thing you know, Bill'd be up there hollerin' and screamin', riding on his bass, cuttin' up and havin' a good time. All of a sudden them people would be having a good time. So, he saved us a lot of days when we would've just been mediocre out there. He got the fans on our side."

As the number of screaming girls grew and their volume increased, it became difficult for the guys to hear each other onstage. Fontana recalls, "We didn't have any monitors. They had one speaker for the whole building, maybe. We didn't have these twenty-thousand-dollar monitor systems or anything, equipment like that, like they do now. All we had was what was in the house. If they only had one mic, that was what we used. Everybody just bled into that one mic, and the kids were all hollering and screaming anyhow, so it didn't make a difference. They'd hear the first two or three bars of each and every song and that was it. They'd start screaming and hollering again. We were playing it right, but they didn't know that. We tried to keep up and hear everybody, but it was hard."

Asked how they managed to stay on track with their singer during all that vocal adulation, Fontana explains in detail. "Well, you didn't hear him. We'd watch his legs, watch his arms, watch his feet, watch his head. If you turned your head a minute, you lost him. You didn't know where he was. But he had a knack; you couldn't really lose him if you wanted to. He could hear what nobody else could. Every so often, he'd back up into the band, and get a clue where he was. 'Where we at guys?' 'Well, get back in, we'll find out.' We just played it straight ahead; we didn't vary it or change anything. Then we'd watch his arms. Like, I could tell when he was going into a chorus, I could tell when he was getting out of a chorus, just by watching."

Most of the time Fontana was too immersed in the constant blur of pure frenetic activity to fully comprehend the growing phenomenon surrounding his singer. "This is what you're thinking about," he explains. "'How are we going to get from here to there in the time limit we've got?' Somehow or another, we always made it. I don't know how. Sometimes we'd get there right on the wire, jump out of the car, set up, and play. We didn't have time to shave, change, or do anything. We'd do what we had to do, jump back in the car, and go somewhere else that same night."

To compound matters, the drummer recalls being "a day ahead of the press all the time. So we never knew—good or bad—what they were saying about us. That's why we didn't know what was going on." It wasn't until a couple of years later, at a show put on at the Dallas Cotton Bowl, that Fontana gave serious thought to Presley's impact and potential.

"I guess we had thirty-five to forty thousand people there. And Elvis come out of a tunnel—one of those chutes—on the back end of a limo or Cadillac. He looked like a young warrior out there—light bulbs flashing and the kids screaming. I said, 'My God, what was that?' Then I leaned over to Scotty and said, 'You know, I think Elvis is going to make it!'"

The RCA Days

"You gotta understand, I'm from England, where the BBC shuts down real early, and there was only one other station, Radio Luxembourg, with reception not so clear. I had this little transistor radio and one night I heard 'Heartbreak Hotel.' The signal would fade in and out and I was running all around my fuckin' room 'da dada da DA DA!' . . . and that's how I met Scotty Moore! Scotty is the guy who showed me what it was *that I wanted to do. Elvis was a great singer, but, since I was a guy—just in case you haven't noticed—it was the* band. *The band was what made it right for me. They call* us *the world's greatest rock and roll band. Mr. Fontana, Mr. Moore; the Hillbilly Cats!* That's *the world's greatest rock and roll band, for without 'em there wouldn't be any others. Give thanks, gives praises!"*

—Keith Richards

By mid-1955, Elvis Presley and the Blue Moon Boys were riding a genuine wave of career momentum. By virtue of "Baby, Let's Play House" hitting the country top ten, they played to bigger crowds and made slightly better money—and female hysteria over the good-looking singer grew more intense with each passing show. The man most responsible for booking the better venues and high-profile package tours was Colonel Tom Parker.

Parker, who had been Nashville promoter Oscar Davis's right-hand man and Eddy Arnold's manager during his initial rise to country music prominence, was a partner in Hank Snow Attractions, a concert-promotion venture. As has been documented by every music journalist from Albert Goldman to Alanna Nash, Parker was a crafty, if not downright devious, character. A cigar-chomping vulgarian with no particular sense of taste, he was also the hardest-working guy in his end of the business. Driven and tireless, he had a knack for making worthwhile connections, and he knew how to cultivate promising prospects.

Elvis Presley was one such prospect, although at the time Parker became aware of the future rock king, the promoter's attentions were focused on young Tommy Sands. A showbiz pro since the age of five, the Chicago-born Sands had sung on radio and television and had cut a few country records for the Freedom label before he even hit puberty. Of all the people who speak about Parker today, Sands is among the few whose comments aren't drenched in the bile of personal disappointment.

"He was very kind to me," Sands recalls. "I owe him my whole career, actually. He came into Cook's Hoedown Club in Houston when I was about twelve years old. He liked me and had [rhythm guitarist] Gabe Tucker bring me over to his table and he signed me to a contract. He was managing Eddy Arnold at the time and he was in town to do the Fat Stock Show in Houston.

"He signed me to his Jamboree Attractions and really, he managed me. As I got out of school that summer he brought me out to stay with him in Madison, Tennessee—which is where he and the first Mrs. Parker had their house."

Noting Sands's ambition to become an actor, Parker took the young singer on the road with him, charging him a 25-percent commission for whatever work they scared up. Sometimes he would encourage the boy to perpetrate little ruses, which he called acting lessons. "He knew every little diner and restaurant across every highway in this country," Sands reminisces. "One day he let me out on the road and said, 'Throw some dirt all over your face. Just around this bend there's going to be a diner. I'm going to get a table right up close to the big picture window. I'm going to be eating a big steak, and I want you to come up there and press your face up against that window and look so sad that you'll force the waitress to ask me to bring you in and buy you a meal.' I did that and it worked. That was what he called my 'acting lesson.'"

Sands never saw anything evil in Parker's actions. "I don't know what you would call his strategy, but he was brilliant. Self-taught, but a brilliant man.

The first post-Presley teen idol, Tommy Sands. COURTESY OF JOHNNY VALLIS

I'm sure he had a very high, genius-like I.Q. He thought of more things than any manager I've ever heard of before or since."

One oft-repeated tale is that Parker ran an animal act called Colonel Parker's Dancing Chickens. On the *Rockabilly Hall of Fame* Web site, Parker's widow, Loanne, claims there never was such a sideshow attraction. "This was a joke Colonel used to test the gullibility of people," she wrote. "It has been repeated and believed so many times that there is no doubt people are gullible!"

People may indeed be gullible, but Sands begs to differ with the widow's assertion. When the duo was low on cash, he actually helped set up just such a show in Albuquerque, New Mexico. "He had friends in all the circuses and tent shows around the country," explains Sands. "He went out and bought some things before saying hello to this friend who was running this tent show. He had me bring in this big box and some red velvet, and he stapled the red velvet around the box. Then he had me bring up a couple of barbecue grates, and he put coals in the barbecue and put tops on them. Then, when everybody came in that night, he had a big sign out in front: Colonel Parker's Dancing Chickens. Never Before Seen in This Country! The Favorite of Kings and Queens of Europe! And he put these chickens on the grate after he had lit the coals, and those damn chickens started dancing around and the audience went crazy."

The young singer's mother terminated the management contract after roughly eighteen months, but Sands never lost touch with Parker. While working as a disc jockey and a member of the *Louisiana Hayride* touring radio show in 1954, Sands saw Elvis Presley and the Blue Moon Boys. The experience changed his whole style. "Well, the first night I saw him was at the Eagle's Hall in Houston. Biff Collie booked him for a Saturday night show that was a lot like a small *Louisiana Hayride*. Then, Elvis walked out on-stage and all the girls in the Eagle's Hall started rushing the stage and screaming, and that didn't happen in country and western shows. That was the first night I realized that Elvis Presley was something special. And, the way he kept time with his left leg and moved it to the beat of the music—I thought that was so great. I thought he was sensational. I wasn't one of the guys standing around saying, 'What is it?' I was going 'Hooray! *Yeah*!'"

Parker had already heard of Presley through country music circles—and oddly, his Jamboree Attractions had previously rebuffed a booking inquiry from Scotty Moore—but Sands's appreciation supplied sufficient motivation for the cagey manager to take a serious interest in this new type of performer. Initially, his plan was to promote Sands as the next big thing. Less threatening in appearance than Presley, Sands made the girls scream too, but all they really wanted to do was cuddle the doll-like performer. Ultimately, Presley's ability to generate free publicity wherever he went tipped the scales in Parker's eyes. He never cared about the music one way or the other.

By way of compensation to Sands, Parker did help him. In 1957, when NBC was looking to book Presley on their *Kraft Television Theatre* production of *The Singing Idol*, the manager turned them down but recommended Sands for the starring role. He even picked up the singer's travel tab and asked for nothing in return. The show proved to be a star-making opportunity that resulted in a recording contract with Capitol Records, a million-selling single, "Teenage Crush,"and a movie career.

Of course, as of November 23, 1954, Presley already had a manager, Bob Neal. Neal had not been Elvis's first choice. "Elvis at the time wanted me to be his manager, but I was with Johnny Horton," recalls Tillman Franks who adds that he turned the position down because, "I didn't favor Elvis the way I did Johnny." Neal was a solid choice, both because he was close by and because he would work with Sam Phillips. Thanks to his WMPS radio show, Neal was well known and well connected throughout the mid-south, but he had a reputation among performers as only being able to book school gymnasiums and barn dances—nothing in the big money bracket. Parker clued Neal in to a lot of bigger offers, with the proviso that if his tips resulted in any future bookings, the disc jockey would pay him a percentage of the money earned from those gigs.

Bit by bit, Parker undermined Neal's position. First he impressed Presley by helping set up an audition for *Arthur Godfrey's Talent Scouts.* (Presley and the Blue Moon Boys failed to advance beyond the audition stage.) Next, he got the *Hayride* hepcat a brief, nonsinging appearance on country singer Jimmy Dean's popular *Town & Country Jubilee*, broadcast locally over WMAL-TV in Washington, D.C. He further showed up Neal, Presley's manager of record, by arranging a booking in Cleveland (on a bill that also featured Bill Haley and Pat Boone) that was filmed as part of popular DJ Bill Randle's short-subject movie about rock 'n' roll.

Pat Boone remembers the event well. "When 'Ain't That a Shame' was becoming a big hit, I went to Cleveland to be at a big sock hop with Bill Randle, the number-one DJ there. Randle met me at the airport and told me, 'I'm bringing a kid in from Shreveport tonight to be with you on the same show. A kid named Elvis Presley.' I said, 'Elvis Presley? He's a *hillbilly*. You've got him on your show tonight?' Not that I minded, but I was surprised. [There was] no chance that a hillbilly record could be played at a rock 'n' roll sock hop. I said, 'How did that happen?' Randle answered, 'Well, he was on Sun Records, but he signed with RCA, and I think he's going to be a big star.' So, sure enough, I met Elvis that night, and Elvis went on ahead of me. That's the only time we ever appeared on the same show. The audience didn't know him, and he had this slouchy and mumbly approach. His collar was turned up and his pant legs too long. He looked like a real greaser, which was not in at the time. It came in later, after the movies, but then he looked like that minority in most

Presley's chief rival in the teen sweepstakes, Pat Boone.
COURTESY OF RHINO RECORDS

high schools; kids from the wrong side of the tracks that most of the other kids sort of sneer at. Here comes Elvis and he lip-synchs a country sounding record, 'That's All Right (Mama)' or 'Blue Moon of Kentucky.' But he's wiggling and he's good looking—and I'm standing back and looking at the intrigue on the faces of these high-school kids. First they snickered and covered their mouths with their hands, probably saying little critical things, but then their eyes got bigger as they watched him move around the stage, and he was getting to them! Then the record was over and he said [mimics Elvis's voice], 'Thanks vurry musch.' And they looked at him like he was a hillbilly again. But he really did go over well when the music was playing, and it's a good thing I had a very big record, otherwise Elvis would've stolen the show."

Naturally, Presley and his bandmates were thrilled to share a stage with such major national stars and to show northern audiences what they could do. And, although the show had been booked by Neal, Parker made sure that Presley knew who'd really pulled the strings. (Due to some especially thorny contractual problems, Randle's film, titled *The Pied Piper of Cleveland: A Day in the Life of a Famous Disc Jockey*, was never released, sadly. Reportedly, the only print that still exists is missing its soundtrack.)

In a 1973 interview with *Rockville International,* Neal tried to put a positive spin on Parker's takeover of Presley's managerial contract. "Yes, I had a contract with Elvis," Neal stated, "and when, through part of my efforts, Parker got interested, we had a partnership agreement. You see, I was doing quite well with my radio program in Memphis. We had a record store, a large family, and I didn't really . . . well, I felt that Elvis was going to be very big, and I didn't want to get into the picture of being gone from town all the time. So, I preferred to stay there and more or less turn everything over to the Colonel with no . . . I mean, it was a friendly relationship all the way."

Despite Neal's positive take on events, it's clear that Parker had outclassed and out thought him on every level. He had befriended Neal and maneuvered him into testing deeper waters with Presley. Once the disc jockey had taken all the risks, Parker plucked control of Presley from his grasp before Neal could reap any meaningful rewards.

Then Parker began subtly defaming Neal to Presley's parents, which disgusted Scotty Moore. "[Parker] was working, brainwashing Gladys and Vernon and undermining Bob Neal and setting up deals for Neal. Lordy, some of the things are just unreal. Bob was just too nice a guy to really get in the trenches like that."

Neal claims it was his idea to change the Blue Moon Boys' deal with Presley, but the move has all the earmarks of a Colonel Parker hatchet job. Claiming that their agreed-upon split wasn't fair because it was Elvis, not the band, that was the attraction, they were offered two hundred dollars a week when they toured and half of that when they were idle. They squawked about it and threatened to quit, but at the time, it was more than they had been earning. However, the Parkeresque proviso that the band members pay all their own expenses was included. That punitive caveat would eventually create enough hardship and dissension to break up the band.

Parker seemed to declare war on the Blue Moon Boys the second he signed Presley (via his parents) to a promotional contract on November 23, 1955. Parker had been openly pulling the promotional strings for months prior to this date, and he became Presley's official manager of record on March 15, 1956. "Well, he didn't really show his stripes until he was actually in charge," says Moore of Parker. "The first thing he did when he started booking us was some tours with Hank Snow. And Hank's band, the Rainbow Ranch Boys, came to us and said Parker wanted them to start playing with Elvis and get rid of us. And we said, 'Well, if he gets rid of us, he gets rid of us.' They said, 'Don't worry, we ain't gonna play with him.' All these guys were great musicians in their own right, but they said, 'We don't play that kind of stuff, that's all.' That was just the first [incident]. It went on and on and on over the years."

Whereas Moore views the episode as the beginning of all the trouble, Fontana sees it as a good example of Presley's loyalty to the band. "The Colonel wanted me and Scotty and Bill to go, because in the first place, he couldn't control us. [He said] 'Be a little bit cheaper, Elvis. You'll make more money.' Elvis said, 'No, no, I'm not going to do that. They don't know what I'm doing, they've got a different style of music.' Hank had a good band, but they weren't doing what Elvis was doing."

Moore and Black—both veterans who had served during the Korean conflict—felt it was shameful that Parker demanded to be called by his honorary title, Colonel, and they instead referred to the porcine promoter as Parker or Tom. So did Sam Phillips. Fontana used (and still uses) the "Colonel" sobriquet, but he admits, "Oh, I didn't particularly like him. Nobody really did." He adds. "If you shook hands with him, you'd better count your fingers afterward. You had to watch him; he was always trying to do something to you. If you made a deal, you'd better have it etched in stone or you were lost. He was always ahead of you, you can count on that. We just stayed out of his way, did what we had to do, and if we needed anything done we'd see Elvis about it first."

Black, who first had the idea to start selling pictures of Elvis Presley to the fans, cleared a nickel for each photograph sold. It added up, and the money helped to support his wife and two children between bookings. Once Parker took over, the manager earned Black's eternal enmity by taking picture sales away from the bassist and keeping the profits for himself.

Smart, ambitious, and a master of long-term planning, Parker had earlier floated a rumor that Presley's Sun Records contract—which, at the time he first proposed a deal, had a little over a year left to run—was for sale. Phillips knew it was a setup, but he let the promoter fan the flames and he set a price. He had to. Despite some recent chart successes, his label was about to sink under the weight of several longstanding debts. After a flurry of bidding, Phillips sold Presley's recording contract, along with all of the singer's Sun masters, for forty thousand dollars and the right to fill all orders for his records through the end of the year. The money came out of different corporate pockets, but the result was clear. Elvis Presley was upgrading from the tiny recording company he'd called home to music powerhouse RCA Victor.

Of course, the most important deciding factor in Presley's move to RCA was Colonel Tom Parker. He had ties to the label dating back to his days of managing Eddy Arnold and promoting Hank Snow. RCA needed Presley. This new rock 'n' roll thing had thrown the recording company for a loop and it hadn't yet found a way to compete in that market. All of RCA's scouts and moneymen knew Presley would be big—a real cash cow. Subsequently, they let Parker have everything he wanted. More importantly, they put up with his constant "input"—first gratefully; later because they had no choice.

The brilliantly engineered deal ensured that Elvis Presley would get the full star treatment. It also allowed Phillips to pay his debts, invest in the Holiday Inn chain, and continue making pop music history by recording great hit records with the likes of Johnny Cash, Carl Perkins, Jerry Lee Lewis, and Charlie Rich. It was a rare instance where nearly everyone won.

However, Presley's band wasn't signed to any kind of a contract with the label. That's just the way it was back then; they were paid union scale, and they were given no compensation for any head arrangements or spontaneous creations of riffs or musical hooks they may have come up with. In a 2004 interview Alvin Lee told the author, "Scotty's solos were pieces of music on their own. He should receive royalties from them." The chances of that happening are slim to none. He was a contract-for-hire worker; no more, no less. When it came to safeguarding the creative input of sidemen and house bands, the musicians' union was useless. Eventually the lack of meaningful recognition of their talents ground at Moore's and Black's guts as much as the substandard pay and Presley's change in attitude toward his bandmates.

Part of that attitude change came from the need to hire bodyguards for Presley. The band had mixed feelings about it. On one hand, having the singer travel with them was good for band unity; on the other, they were musicians, not security officers, and it was hard enough to keep their young star on track from one gig to the next without having to worry about protecting him from screaming fans. Yet, from the get-go, Moore and Black had assured Presley's mother of her son's safety. "His mother was just like any other mother," Moore says kindly. "He'd never been out of the city limits, hardly. When we started going out and staying out two to three days, well, she'd come to me every trip and say, 'Watch him, make him eat good, make him get his rest, take care of him.' She'd tell Bill the same thing. Just a typical mom. He'd call her two to three times while we were gone, too."

(Incidentally, Barbara Pittman, whose own mother once worked alongside Gladys Presley, used to visit the singer's mother often. "Elvis's mother liked Bill better than Scotty," Pittman recounted. "He'd sit on the floor or back porch with her and have a beer and they'd talk and laugh." Unfortunately for Moore, Presley's mother mistook his shy, sometimes aloof nature as "sneakiness.")

As documented in several biographies, Gladys Presley spoiled young Elvis, in effect teaching the high-on-hormones-and-hubris teenager that he could do no wrong. Subsequently, the band suffered the unpleasant consequences of traveling in close quarters with a companion who had little regard for the olfactory senses of others. After traveling for hours on end in a hot car without air-conditioning, Presley, frankly, began to smell bad. "We had to ease him into more hygienic methods of living," Moore says in his book. "We had to coach him, without being insulting, you know, to take a bath." Pittman refuted this, saying, "I never smelled anything on him but good." But that was in Memphis. On tour, he was always, in Gordon Stoker's words, "semi-dirty."

Part of the dirtiness stemmed from the lack of readily available bathing facilities on the road during that era. Another factor was that the young star didn't want to deal with getting his smartly coiffed hair restyled after each shower. Still, many years later, various Presley confidants revealed that the King of Rock 'n' Roll's idea of bathing was to take a damp washcloth to his armpits and crotch before spraying on a little Brut cologne.

Black seemed to be the most offended by the youngster's odor. Once, when the singer refused to take his smelly stockinged feet off the dashboard and away from Black's face, the bass player abruptly stopped the car and, with murderous intent, chased Presley through a cornfield.

The most unusual result of all that traveling, heat, and sweat was a rather iconic fashion choice. Presley took to wearing his shirt collar folded up high over his sports jacket. Carl Perkins, who performed along with Elvis in many early shows, told Dan Griffin that the young singer wore his collar that way so

Elvis Presley (revealing an acne-marked neck) and Glen Glenn, San Diego, 1956.
COURTESY OF GLEN GLENN

he could hide the mass of painful acne that had marched up his back and onto his neck. Scotty Moore and rockabilly hero Glen Glenn have affirmed the truth of Perkins's claim.

Another difficulty the band experienced while traveling with the "Folk Music Fireball"—as *Country Song Round-Up* called Presley—was the singer's energy level, which manifested itself not only onstage, but also after the show. The guys were forced to help him wind down. "Yeah, we'd walk him down the road," remembers Fontana. "Whoever's turn it was. We'd stop and get a hamburger. He ate fast and got through his. So, I'd just walk down the road with him a little bit. Because once he got in the car, if he wasn't unwound, he'd stay up all night long—listening to the radio, talking. So, we'd walk down the road with him, maybe a mile or so, and then they'd come and pick us up. He'd get back in his seat and he'd go right to sleep."

Fontana also remembers that, while Presley was generally in good spirits, by the fourth week of a tour, he'd get irritable. "He'd get in an ill mood when he got tired. Because he did a lot of work, even when he was young. He worked hard onstage. We knew when he was in an ill mood, so we'd leave him alone. He'd go lay in a room for a couple of days, come out, and be fresh as a daisy."

Granted, every hard-touring band suffers from road weariness, and the road walks may have been necessitated by the adrenal rush of a great show, but many of Presley's symptoms suggest that he was using speed. Most biographies claim the rocker didn't even know about amphetamines until they were provided to him by an army sergeant who didn't want him to fall asleep on maneuvers. But Roy Carr and Mick Farren's book, *Elvis: The Illustrated Record,* maintains that Presley always had a pocketful of his mother's diet pills with him, even at his first Sun session. Barbara Pittman, who visited with Gladys Presley quite often, says that Presley's mother didn't take diet pills until the year before her death. Another view comes from childhood friend Lee Denson. Talking at length on the documentary *Why, Elvis?*, he claims that disc jockey Dewey Phillips got the nineteen-and-a-half-year-old sensation hooked on drugs, which, in turn, helped Presley overcome near crippling bouts of stage fright.

It's important to note that, in all the years that Dan Griffin was associated with Moore and Fontana (ten years with Fontana, six years with Moore and Fontana together), neither musician ever mentioned Presley's alleged early drug use. However, Moore's behavior during a chance meeting with a former policeman led Griffin to believe that Elvis Presley had been using drugs pretty early on.

"We were at the Jacksonville Theater around 1997," Griffin recalls. "It was after the *All the King's Men* album came out. They were taking us through the theater, and there was this older guy—older than Scotty and D.J.—and he said, 'Look at this poster. We've got this original poster from that show you did with Elvis in 1956.' He had been a policeman then; now he was a backstage security guard. He said, 'Do you remember that Elvis came offstage and we had to walk him around for an hour, and we ended up taking him to the hospital, where they had to pump his stomach?' Scotty said, 'Yeah, yeah. I remember that.' But he was trying to get away as quick as he could to end an embarrassing conversation. That gave me the impression that Scotty and the guard knew Elvis was on drugs."

On top of Presley's smell and "energy," the band had to constantly contend with sex-crazed girls wanting to get their hands on the singer. Louis Black remembers one show-time riot vividly. "I was big enough to be with Mama and Bobbie [Moore] backstage. [Suddenly] here came the crowd! Man, I remember Mama grabbing me by the collar and Bobbie getting up, and we were all running out the back. Scotty and Daddy were trying to get their musical instruments off the stage before [the crowd] ran 'em over and tore 'em up. We went out the back door and ran out to the car. They put me in the car. I guess Bobbie and Mama were in there too, and then Elvis got up on top of the car. I think that's where [reporters] caught him outside and took that picture of Elvis standing on top of the car with his shirt tore off."

Worse were the girls who always seemed to know where Presley was at all times. "I remember seeing Elvis's pink Cadillac," says Black's daughter Nancy. "When I'd get home from school it'd be sitting there. We'd go in and do our homework or whatever, and when we'd come out, names, addresses, and measurements would be all over that thing—in lipstick! I don't know if he had to paint it after that or what. I was like, 'What is this?' I just didn't get it until I was older."

The situation grew increasingly worse with each leap toward stardom. So, yes, a bodyguard was absolutely necessary for the handsome sex symbol. Initially that role was filled by Presley's friend from Humes High School, rugged Red West. Nearly everyone interviewed for this book has said virtually the same thing: If Elvis Presley ever had a true friend, it was West. "He just loved Elvis from the start, before he was big," affirms Tillman Franks. "When Elvis decided he needed someone to be with him, Red was the first one to do it, and Colonel Parker liked him all right." Moore, Black, and Fontana weren't particularly close to the red-headed Memphian, but they liked him, too. They viewed him as a regular guy who was doing a much-appreciated favor for a friend. West could also read a map and drive—an important consideration since, when Presley took the wheel, his mind tended to wander and he would often get lost.

West drove with Presley in a separate vehicle, which eased some of the tensions between the singer and his bandmates. Eventually, however, the idea of living off Presley's largesse didn't set well with West, and he joined the marines. (The two reunited after both men had left the armed forces.) Presley's attempts to replace him with various friends and relatives exacerbated troubles that had already been brewing within the band.

On the recording front, Presley's RCA debut, "Heartbreak Hotel," allowed the singer to break into pop music's mainstream. Second only to Bill Haley & the Comets' "Rock Around the Clock," "Heartbreak Hotel" was rock 'n' roll's greatest breakthrough recording. The perfect compromise between teen and adult tastes of the time in an era when recordings for each were played in the context of the same radio formats, it opened the door for Presley's much friskier, harder-driving recordings to follow. However, throughout the record's production, Presley and the Blue Moon Boys feared they were about to blow their one shot at the big time. Indeed, they had a tough time bringing together the sound for both sides of their first RCA single (which also featured "I Was the One").

Certainly the B-side song was an odd choice for the singer. The pedestrian Mae Boren Axton–Tom Durden composition parodies blues and rock more than it champions either form. So why did Presley choose to sing it? On one of the many Elvis-themed television shows produced after his death, Axton claims that she gave the singer a piece of the song so he could "buy his mama a house." The mother of singer/songwriter Hoyt Axton, the thoughtful lady also worked as Colonel Parker's PR representative in Florida.

Presley had known the song since he'd signed with RCA a couple of months earlier. According to Peter Guralnick and Ernst Jorgensen's book, *Elvis Day by Day*, he even tested the tune out live, telling the crowd at Bob King's nightclub in Swifton, Arkansas, "This is gonna be my first big hit record." Yet having learned the song so far in advance of recording it actually made it more difficult to capture in the studio. It happens sometimes that performing a song live creates a set idea in the mind of the singer about what the song should sound like. Then, when the artist finally takes the song into the studio, he or she is completely thrown by both the changed dimensions of the sound and the new environment.

Nevertheless, as a perk, RCA let Elvis run the sessions more or less his own way. The record label executives hoped that, in doing so, Elvis and his band would be able to recreate the strange, eerie sound of the Sun releases. Previously, RCA A & R chief Steve Sholes had hoped to achieve the Sun-sessions sound by hiring Sam Phillips away from his own label to produce Presley's sessions. Phillips turned him down cold, saying, "[T]here was no way I could contribute on a major label."

As Sholes saw it, the chief problem was that Presley insisted on having his road band play on his recordings as well. Such a thing wasn't exactly unheard of, but it was definitely not the norm. Most singers worked along with producer-picked session players in the studio. These seasoned pros could read charts, and they seldom made mistakes. A singer's road band was usually glutted with the cheapest musicians available, and these performers constantly made time-consuming errors.

RCA hired Nashville's most respected musician, Chet Atkins, to help supervise the session and to play guitar on the recordings. Instead of being honored, the Boppin' Hillbilly acted like he wanted to run his own recording date. It pissed off Sholes to no end. "Oh, Steve was all right," explains Fontana. "He was not a rock 'n' roll producer. Steve came out of the concert field of RCA. He would produce all the big orchestra things. He had to either produce Elvis or get fired. See, they paid like thirty-five or forty thousand dollars for [Elvis]. Back then that was unheard of, and Steve was the instigator of getting him on that label. So he had to knuckle down and make sure he got a hit or two."

As Gordon Stoker of the Jordanaires explains it, the real problem was that neither Sholes nor Atkins felt a connection with Presley. "Steve Sholes didn't understand what Elvis was doing and didn't really like what Elvis was doing," Stoker plainly states. "Then, Chet Atkins was just as bad. He didn't care for Elvis at all. I can assure you that Elvis didn't care for him, either."

Out of respect for Atkins, most musicians downplay the conflict between country's greatest guitarist and the King of Rock 'n' Roll. Not Stoker. The tenor background vocalist describes a scenario in which the two men were civil to each other, but were never in synch. "Of course Elvis didn't like Chet because of the first session," he explains. "Elvis had asked for the Jordanaires, and of course he didn't get the Jordanaires. Chet Atkins called me and said, "I just signed the Speer Family to the RCA label. Would you mind working with Ben and Brock Speer?" I said, 'Well Chet, I know them, but I've never worked with 'em.' He said, 'It don't make any difference. This kid's not going to be around long. He's just a passing fad. Just come in and do some oohs and ahhs.' So, on 'I Was the One' and 'I Want You, I Need You, I Love You,' you hear just me and Ben and Brock Spears.

"Well, as soon as he got to the session, Elvis said to me, 'Where are the other Jordanaires?' I said, 'Well, Chet didn't want me to use 'em.' You know, after that, he never liked Chet. He called him a sneaky son of a bitch. He never liked him as long as he lived because of that, because he knew Chet had pulled something over on him."

The Speer brothers–Stoker setup wasn't as cohesive as the full lineup of the Jordanaires would later prove to be. That said, the off-the-rack rock-a-ballad "I Was the One" allowed Presley to be a lead vocalist in a vocal-group setting for the first time, and he reveled in it. Swooping from despairing low tones to crying high notes, he fashioned a performance that made all the other white

Elvis Presley in the studio cutting a classic RCA hit in 1957. Courtesy of D. J. Fontana, RCA Records / Elvis Presley Enterprises

R & B singers seem cold and unemotional in comparison. "I Was the One" would go on to hit number eight on *Billboard*'s country chart and place in the top twenty on their pop chart, but it would be completely overshadowed by the song that Elvis would often mockingly refer to as "Heartburn Motel."

It took a couple of days to get the Nashville studio's cavernous echo under control, and Atkins had to come in and help steady the rhythmic tempo, but eventually—as had been the case with the torturous Sun sessions—it all paid off. Black's bass strutted in perfect unison with Fontana's understated, "strip-club style." He played behind Presley with a slow bump-and-grind beat that accentuated the erotic nature of the singer's performance. Pianist Floyd Cramer alternated tight rhythmic support with icy little blues fills that dredged up images of a thousand late-night barrooms. But if anyone made an impression equal to Elvis Presley's it was Scotty Moore.

No longer constrained by having to fill up every sonic inch of a recording, Moore slid into a pair of solos that aggressively aped big-band brass and ended in jazzy electric dissonance. Striking a perfect blend of Les Paul gimmickry and penetrating blues, his solos and fills heralded the ballsy new sound of 1950s rock. (During the early 1970s James Burton would appropriate a piece of Moore's famous riff for Presley's redrafting of James Taylor's "Steamroller Blues.")

A certified two-sided gold record, it spent eight weeks as the number-one pop record and a remarkable seventeen weeks as the number-one country disc. It even hit number three on the R & B charts. No other record had ever done that. Most importantly, its mammoth success convinced the RCA brass to just lay off and let Presley have a free hand at his sessions. Once they did, they reaped an incalculable fortune.

That said, not everyone dug "Heartbreak Hotel." None other than Sam Phillips was disappointed, calling the recording "a morbid mess." However, it was Stan Freberg, the self-proclaimed "last network radio comedian," who served up the most venomous attack on the song, Presley, and his fans. Freberg, a hip square who deemed rock 'n' roll "bad rhythm and blues," had just come off a series of successful Capitol recordings that spoofed the *Dragnet* television series, Mitch Miller's "The Yellow Rose of Texas," the Crew Cuts' version of "Sh-Boom," and the Platters' "The Great Pretender." To him, rock 'n' roll was a con job that catered to radio's lowest common denominator. ("OK, you guys," says his producer character on his parody of "The Great Pretender," "I distinctly understood the words that time. What have I been telling you guys? *Mumble! Mumble!*") Clearly, the comic wanted to ridicule the genre out of existence, or at least off radio playlists. But when it came to Elvis Presley, Freberg had met his match. His scathing comedic attack only served to validate the singer's startling newfound popularity.

Brilliantly recreating RCA's mechanical echo (as opposed to Sun's warmer slapback) Freberg caterwauls through "Heartbreak Hotel" like a demented Southern thug. In spoken asides, he takes a swipe at Presley's infamous gyrations ("Ripped mah jeans! Third pair today!") and demands larger doses of echo. Musically, he segues the signature piano and guitar licks into manic African tribal music and discordant instrument tuning. ("All right all right—that's close enough for jazz!") At song's end, Freberg's Elvis impersonation begins to drown in its own echo as he speaks for many parents of the era by commanding, "That's enough-ough-ough-ough! Turn me off-off-off-off!"

But nobody could turn the real Elvis Presley off now.

He was a star.

Presley's career was kicked into high gear through several sensational network television appearances, starting with his January 28, 1956, guest appearance on Tommy and Jimmy Dorsey's *Stage Show*. The perpetually quarreling icons of the 1930s and 1940s had put aside their long-standing rift and reunited in a last-ditch effort to revive the faltering fortunes of big-band music. *Stage Show* was something of a media event, one that Jackie Gleason—who owned the show—hoped would bring back "good music." It didn't exactly work out the way the comedy king had planned.

Within two years of Presley's first appearances on their show, both Dorseys would die of cancer, and Jimmy Dorsey's orchestra would score a posthumous hit, "So Rare," without him. Their short-lived television show is notable only because of the young rocker who lit up the screen there. Kinescoped performances collected on various DVDs show that Presley was seemingly born to perform on television. The black-and-white cathode-ray tubes made the already good-looking singer appear devastatingly handsome, and the harsh contrast of the lighting dramatized every little smile, sneer, wiggle, and lip curl.

Presley and his band (the name Blue Moon Boys had faded from their introductions with the move to RCA and was no longer their official public identity) made it all seem like effortless fun. However, performing live alongside such well-known music figures as Tommy and Jimmy Dorsey made for immense pressure. "Yeah, that was scary, playing along with [the Dorsey Brothers Orchestra]," confesses Fontana. "These guys were excellent musicians. We weren't such a big band, but when these guys played, boy, it sounded like thunder behind us."

A lot of the big-band cats resented rock 'n' rollers for pushing them out of the pop music limelight, but Fontana remembers the Dorsey Brothers and their orchestra—who supplied some messy fanfares and finales—quite fondly. "The Dorsey Brothers, they were really nice guys and they understood what we were doing. Louis Bellson was on drums, and I had met Louis a few years before that. So as soon as we had a little break, we'd go around the corner and start drinking coffee and whatever. He was OK, and all the rest of the guys were good. Usually string players are kind of funny, but everybody in the band was just as nice to us as they could be."

Despite dire predictions that Elvis "can't last," Gleason picked up Presley's options for two more shows beyond the original four he had been contracted for, which delighted RCA. With prime-time promotional appearances assured, the record label brought the singer and his group into its New York

City studios to cut songs for Elvis's first album, as well as some extended-play singles (EPs).

Studio technicians struggled to re-create the Sun sound. For the most part their efforts were futile, although their rendition of Arthur Crudup's "My Baby Left Me" comes very close. It was the first song to feature a Fontana drum intro. Although the drummer modestly says, "Aw, it's just four bars of nothin'," 1970s guitar god Alvin Lee states enthusiastically, "It's one of the greatest kick-offs to a song I ever heard." Indeed, it sets a jazzy tone for the R & B remake. Moore's EchoSonic amp adds a pleading halo to the bursting phrases in his fills and solos, while Black's descending bass notes raise a smile with their late-night-club jam flavor. Presley's finest early blues-with-a-beat vocal alternates crying confessional with betrayed anger and tension-relieving asides. So much texture in the course of one old blues tune; it was the type of achievement Sam Phillips would've killed to get out of them a year earlier.

"My Baby Left Me" was a solid R & B hit, but it was the Ink Spots–influenced, "I Want You, I Need You, I Love You" that hit the top spot on the pop charts. White radio still didn't know what to do with Presley's harder-edged songs. Self-parodying romance ballads played into his image, and they fit onto more playlists than did a guitar-oriented blues tune. Even though Presley was the embodiment of the new rockabilly movement, he wasn't able to break through with a fast song yet. That opportunity was opened up by a former Sun labelmate.

One of the first tunes RCA wanted cut was a version of Carl Perkins's "Blue Suede Shoes," which had scaled all three national charts at roughly the same time as "Heartbreak Hotel." Upon hearing the record, untrained ears at RCA thought that either Sam Phillips had pulled a fast one on them by releasing an old Presley master or they had somehow purchased the wrong singer. "No, Steve," Phillips replied to Sholes, "You didn't buy the wrong singer. Just be patient."

Recording cover versions of songs was a standard industry practice during the 1940s and 1950s. One hit song might be covered in many different versions—from pop and instrumental to polka, blues, hillbilly, and others—by a variety of artists. In the case of RCA and "Blue Suede Shoes," the label acted as if there was only room for one rock 'n' roll artist, and they wanted it to be Elvis Presley. With their superior distribution and radio contacts, RCA knew they could probably steal a hit record away from Phillips and Perkins. Scotty Moore remembers it this way: "The powers that be at RCA had been trying to get Elvis to cover [Perkins], and Elvis wouldn't do it out of respect for Carl. He'd tell 'em, 'He's a friend of mine and I'm not gonna do it.'" Presley of course relented, but he requested that RCA hold back his version, which features two biting Moore solos, from single release.

On March 22, 1956, Perkins and his brothers were involved in a car accident that killed their driver and put the band out of commission. (Jay Perkins, Carl's favorite brother and role model, recovered briefly but died two years later from lingering effects of the damage he'd sustained.) Among their first visitors after the accident were the Blue Moon Boys. "The whole bunch of 'em were banged up bad," remembers Fontana. "We were up in Virginia somewhere on our way to New York. Elvis was already there. They said 'Carl Perkins had just had a wreck.' So we said, 'Let's go see him.' We had another day so we weren't pressed for time. I don't think Carl ever forgot this. He said, 'Of all the people, I looked up and there you guys are. You looked like a bunch of angels coming to see me.'"

Perkins's accident was a classic case of bad timing. He and his band were on their way to *The Perry Como Show* in New York for their network television debut. Legend has it that Perkins lost public identification with his hit because Elvis Presley did the song on television while Perkins was hospitalized. It wasn't true. By the time of the Perkins wreck, Presley had already done the song on *Stage Show* simply because, like "Tutti Frutti" and "Shake, Rattle and Roll," it was a popular part of his repertoire. According to Moore, Elvis recorded "Blue Suede Shoes" to help out Perkins, an old friend, after his accident. "Elvis wasn't really thinking at that time that it was going to make money for Carl; he was doing it as more of a tribute-type thing. Of course Carl was glad that he did. It really helped as his record started going down."

In 1973, when he was opening for Johnny Cash, Perkins would introduce "Blue Suede Shoes" this way: "Here's a song that goes way back. A lot of people did it. Yeah, Elvis had a good one on it. And that boy Johnny Rivers has it out now, too. Now, don't boo. I hope it's a big hit for him, because I know that all them checks will go to a needy family in Jackson, Tennessee—that *I* happen to be the head of."

Moore admired Perkins's talent, but he didn't believe the guitar-wielding singer/songwriter had a legitimate shot at becoming the king of rock 'n' roll. "Carl was a nice-looking big hunk, like out-in-the-cornfield type," he explains. "Elvis was more like an Adonis. But as a rockabilly, Carl was the king of that." In the rockabilly revival of the late 1970s and beyond, Perkins's original "Blue

Suede Shoes" dwarfs Presley's in popularity. The funny part? Until Dave Edmunds brought it to Perkins attention in 1986, the composer and original performer of "Blue Suede Shoes" had played the song in Presley's style, not his own.

Some of Presley's television repertoire ended up on his first RCA album: a ridiculous version of "Tutti Frutti," the cover of "Blue Suede Shoes," and echoey bop renditions of "Money Honey" and "I Got a Woman." Pianist Shorty Long banged out some mighty impressive ragtime on "I'm Gonna Sit Right Down and Cry (Over You)" and the overly histrionic "One-Sided Love Affair." The most intriguing material, however, came from unreleased recordings made during Sun sessions, which Sam Phillips had relinquished.

The album, which mixed together Elvis's earliest recordings of "I Love You Because" and "Blue Moon" with middling rockers "Just Because" and "I'll Never Let You Go" showed just how far Presley and the Blue Moon Boys had progressed. The best of these Sun tracks, the hard-biting rock-a-blues tune "Trying to Get to You," showcased the band's tremendous confidence and distinctive guitar chops. Stylistically the most diverse album of the year, it quickly became RCA's biggest-selling LP to date. But it wasn't exactly a cohesive artistic statement. Greater performances were on the horizon.

As Presley's confidence grew, so did his studio chops, and while he was always polite, he never really paid Sholes any attention. "I hate to say it," observes Fontana, "but most of the producers we worked with were clock-watchers and note takers. 'Hey Elvis, that's two minutes and fifteen seconds; that's perfect time.' That's all they'd ever say." It was the singer himself who came up with production ideas, which he'd bounce off not only the Blue Moon Boys, but also his new collaborators, the Jordanaires.

Gordon Stoker, the lead tenor for the group, fondly recalls meeting Presley before he became a household name. "Well, we were working with Eddy Arnold, and we went to the Ellis Auditorium in Memphis to do a show. Elvis came back behind the stage to meet us, not to meet Eddy. He said that he'd been hearing us sing on the *Grand Ole Opry*, and he said, 'Man, let's sing some of those spirituals.' So, we got to singing with him in the room. That's when he said, 'If I ever get a major recording contract, I want you guys to work with me.' He was on the Sun label at that time. We didn't think anything about it; we had been told that by a lot of people. It didn't mean anything at all. But when RCA signed him . . . he asked for us. So, that started a relationship we had for almost fifteen years."

The Jordanaires' background vocals tended to smooth out Presley's and the Blue Moon Boys' rowdy edges enough for them to be played on pop radio. Equally important during those early sessions, their technical expertise (second tenor Neal Matthews had invented the Nashville Number System for arranging) helped the singer and his band communicate ideas to technical-minded people like Steve Sholes. Further, when Presley would mention that he wanted to do something in a particular black or Southern-gospel style, the quartet understood the reference immediately. Compared to that of the Jordanaires, Ben and Brock Speer's bag of tricks was virtually empty.

Stoker had started his career as the group's pianist and had already played on sessions for Carl Smith, Ray Price, George Morgan, Little Jimmy Dickens, and Johnny Horton. For Stoker, it wasn't that big of a stretch to go from country and gospel to R & B and rock 'n' roll, and Presley admired him for it. "You know, Elvis tried to play piano," chuckles Stoker. "He wasn't much of a piano player. Many times I heard him say, 'I can't play the piano. I can't dance. I can't play the guitar. What do they want me for?' We'd always say, 'Man, you've got what it takes. Give it to 'em.'"

Presley and the band had been giving it to 'em on television in between recording sessions and live dates. Their first appearance on Milton Berle's program showcased them on the battleship USS *Hancock* performing "Shake, Rattle and Roll," "Heartbreak Hotel," and "Blue Suede Shoes." During the final chorus of the latter, Bill Black—as he often did in their stage shows—turned the bass sideways, held it between his knees, and thumped it with both hands while he screamed with delight. Both the crowd and the singer loved it. The next day, however, Colonel Parker issued a stern edict: No more showing up my boy. Just play your instrument.

It wasn't the first time that directive had been issued to Black. According to Gordon Stoker, "When Bob Neal came on the scene he said, 'Hey, man, you've got to cut this out. You're not the star. Elvis is the star.' But Bill Black was getting almost as big a hand as Elvis. Of course Elvis thought it was funny, too. He would laugh at Bill. They finally made him quit doing it because he was almost outshining Elvis."

Asked if his father ever spoke of Parker's stifling of his stage antics, Louis Black responded, "Yeah. He hated that. There was even some talk of trying to do something with Daddy on a show of his own, and that type of stuff. The Colonel stopped that. He didn't want anything to distract from Elvis at all."

Another concern of Parker's was Presley's predilection for such comedy one-liners as "Get out of the stable, Grandma, you're too old to be horsing around" and "Well, folks, I'd like to shake, rattle, and roll for you all night long, but we've got a show tomorrow night at Alcatraz and we've got a long drive ahead of us." The manager wanted his boy to cut the comedy and just sing and wiggle. It should be a comfort to every comic who ever envied a romantic singer to know that the King of Rock 'n' Roll wanted to be appreciated as much for his wit as for his voice. He never stopped trying Parker's patience by yakking on stage, making silly faces, or, in later years, introducing himself as various celebrities. Each transgression would trigger a memo or a warning from the humorless Dutchman. Sometimes the singer fought back, but increasingly Presley just nodded his head and did as he was told. Early on, when he felt lousy about a Parker directive, he would talk to Scotty Moore.

"Elvis was very susceptible to things, and he was also loyal in a way. He'd come to me and say, "Colonel wants me to do this and I don't want to." I said, 'Well *tell* him! Sit down and tell him why you don't want to.' He'd sigh and say, 'Oh no, I made a deal with him. He's gonna take care of this and I'll take care of the singing.' I said, 'Well, don't come to me and tell me.' And it's a shame that he died not really knowing what it was all about. He was suspicious and stuff all along, but he just never would have guts enough to just really get in there and slug it out."

Parker got his way because he had done everything he said he would do. He got his boy a contract with RCA, made sure they promoted his records, put him on television, and was in the process of making him wealthy enough to buy a new home for his mother. Of course, Presley worked hard, but his band had been with him every step of the way, and they weren't getting anything out of it except sideman pay and union scale for recording sessions. Their efforts and creativity weren't appreciated in the least by RCA, who wanted to get rid of them.

"RCA and Steve Sholes, they've got letters back and forth [saying], 'Don't bring Scotty and Bill anymore,'" reveals Moore. "'They take time doing this and doing that.' But they never stopped and realized that none of us were session players. I mean, there's guys here in [Nashville] that don't even move their instrument out of a studio for weeks. I've kidded some of them that the producers will just run the tape down to where they want the eight-bar solo, and they don't even hear the vocal, and say 'fill it up.' And we didn't do that. And I couldn't do that. It wasn't my thing."

It wasn't Elvis Presley's thing, either. Sholes and RCA wanted to run his sessions like anyone else's: four songs per three-hour session, two three-hour sessions per night. They wanted to stockpile recordings for albums, EPs, B-sides, and fan-club releases. Yet, during most of the marathon recording sessions that were held, they ran up massive studio bills but got only two or three completed songs.

"Most of the time Freddie Bienstock, the publisher, would come in from New York and bring the material in," explains Fontana. "That's the first time anybody ever heard it. Of course, Elvis was a quick learner. By the second time through he had it the way he wanted it. So, it was all just head arrangements. We never knew what we were going to do from one song to another."

Moore adds, "When the publishing company started bringing him stacks of records and demos in to listen to, he could sit there and go through 'em, and when he give it like that [makes a thumbs-down gesture] you know he knew damn well he couldn't do it. Then he'd make another stack and he'd go back through them, and he could tell from that demo if he could do that song. There were a few things that we might not do because we couldn't adapt a key that would work."

Did Moore ever suggest a piece of material? "I never even gave it a thought that I should find something for him to sing, or anything; no. He had a good ear for the rhythm, not only on when he was playing rhythm guitar, but his voice. Some of the things, I couldn't see how he could sing 'em. But he could hear a song one time and just about know it."

Fontana remembers that Presley liked a lot of give and take in the studio. "Everybody contributed. He'd say, 'Well, what can we do here?' Scotty would say, 'Well, I'll play this, Elvis.' 'OK, try that.' Bill said, 'Well, I'll play this.' 'OK, let's put it together and see what happens.' We could play what we wanted to play, and if you go back and listen to those records, you'll find that, boy, they had the darndest feel in the world! They were tight. No horns or strings were in the way. We just played the heck what we wanted to play and it worked. Like I said, Elvis had a great conception of beat and tempo, and through his voice you could feel the beat and tempo. So all you had to do was follow his voice and it's going to be right."

As the lead guitarist, Moore was constantly going out on a limb for Presley and risking the ire of RCA by trying to learn a new approach to a song on the spot. Oftentimes, his timing would fail him, or a pick would strike a sour note. Yet, once he got locked in, he achieved what Presley wanted from him. The resultant quality—not to mention the commercial impact—of the recordings was astoundingly high. "Just like in New York we had 'Hound Dog' and 'Don't Be Cruel' on the same session," remembers Moore. "Don't that say something to you?"

"Hound Dog," which Presley changed from a stage piece that showed off his moves to a hard, guitar-driven rocker, is a prime example of how the singer's sound had progressed. In addition to alternating hard-raving electric rhythm with snarling fills, Moore lays down a tart, free-flowing lead that instigates dancing as much as it relieves the song's tense energy. Fontana's powerful drum fills between verses build more manic excitement, even though the tempo never changes much. Black's bass and Stoker's piano offer a simplistic but strong rhythmic underpinning. It's all tied together by the Jordanaires, whose gospel-tent-show hand claps and background vocals make the whole thing a distinctively smart pop record.

Presley and the band had done the song many times. A version quite close to the released rendition was heard during the Steve Allen tux-and-tails debacle. ("He hated that," says Moore.) Once again, familiarity didn't make it any easier for them to record the tune, which took over thirty takes to accomplish. "They weren't all complete songs," says Fontana. "We might do four bars up front and something might go wrong. So, you're not really playing a whole song. It's just thirty bits and pieces of 'Hound Dog,' but it wasn't a complete song—we would've been wore out. Elvis really didn't like to do a lot of takes. In fact, there were a lot of takes that shouldn't have been taken, and he said, 'Aw, no, that's good. I was singing it pretty good and you guys were playing it pretty good; let's just leave it alone.' He wouldn't do another. It had to be a train wreck before he would do another one."

It was on this session that Gordon Stoker's abilities on the piano came into significant play. Recalls Stoker, "Shorty Long went home on the first session that we did in New York. We had done 'Don't Be Cruel' and 'Any Way You Want Me (That's How I Will Be),' and Elvis said, 'I've got one more song I want to do, "You Ain't Nuthin' But a Hound Dog."' Shorty Long said, 'Well, I've already been here thirty minutes over and I've got another session and I have *got* to go.' So Steve Sholes said to me, 'Get over at the piano, Gordon, and play the piano on this.' So I did. In those days, they couldn't mic me to sing the 'ahhs' we did during the instrumental. So, the three guys had to fake their harmony, and it wasn't too good. . . . The bass had to jump up and sing baritone, and he wasn't too good of a baritone singer."

Thanks to the notoriety of the Berle and Allen television shows, "Hound Dog" had a waiting audience. The selection of Otis Blackwell's "Don't Be Cruel" had come through the demo selection process. Parker and Bienstock's minions persuaded the great songwriter to assign Presley a half share in the song in exchange for the hot singer doing it.

Much has been made of Presley's use of demos. The upshot of most of these discussions is that he lazily copied the songwriter's demonstration record (which usually had been sung by a singer who could imitate Presley's style) and that he didn't really offer anything creative. Some have even suggested that he copied Blackwell's demos note for note. Since Blackwell's demos haven't been released to the public (it would be a treat if they were) we have only his 1977 album for Inner City *All Shook Up* to guide us. Backed by a bar band called Grand Union, the writer of such hits as "All Shook Up," "Breathless," "Great Balls of Fire,"and "Handy Man" turns in raspy R & B performances that are occasionally enjoyable, but are almost completely dissimilar to the hit versions of the songs.

In many ways "Don't Be Cruel" was the group's greatest achievement. Not because of what they played, but because of what they didn't play. "I played the intro," Moore explains. "Tuned down the E string to a D, and played the little intro, and did not play another note in that whole song except a chord on the end. And a couple of guys said, 'Aren't you going to play on the whole song?' And I said, 'I don't need anything else.' You know, it sounded full, sounded great." Even the percussion is catchy and unique. "That's not my drum," laughs Fontana. "That's the back of Elvis's leather guitar case! There must be ten or fifteen of 'em like that, where Elvis is just playing the back of that guitar case—getting that 'pop' sound. He's playing it right on the mic while he's singing, and he was always right on top of it. We didn't have the electronics they do now, so we had to think of things to do to make it different. If we wanted a different sound, heck, we'd beat on walls, we'd kick things. He'd say, 'I don't like that.' So we'd try something else, and we'd just look around the studio to see if we could find something to make a little noise with."

At the heart of "Don't Be Cruel" are two other crucial elements—Presley's almost telepathic interplay with the Jordanaires and Bill Black's up-front bass lines. Plucking out an aggressive variation of Jesse Stone's rock 'n' roll rhythm, Black's work adds thickness and momentum to what is basically a mid-tempo doo-wop song. Recorded the same night, "Hound Dog" and "Don't Be Cruel" show the band and the singer off to their fullest advantage. Released on the same 45-rpm single, both sides hit number one on the pop, country, and R & B charts. No other record has done that before or since.

Presley and his original band were at the peak of their powers. With the recording field seemingly conquered, all that was left was for the handsome young singer to take the band with him to Hollywood.

The Movie and Army Years

"Elvis, his voice carried everything—the feeling in his voice and where he puts his words in the realm of it. I couldn't believe how he led everything. He was right on top of it. Elvis was one of those guys who sang a millisecond ahead of the beat, and that's where it* feels *great. I think that's what made him, outside of being one of the best-looking guys I ever saw."

—Glen Campbell

"Them ain't tactics, honey. That's just the beast in me."

—Elvis Presley as Vince Everett in *Jailhouse Rock*

1956 AND 1957 were peak years for Elvis Presley. His debut in the movie *Love Me Tender* was a box-office sensation (and truly, his then-undyed, pompadoured presence is the only interesting aspect of this otherwise dull film). The Blue Moon Boys, decried as "hillbillies" by studio brass, were not allowed to record the black-and-white Civil War drama's theme song or the three songs needed to flesh out the soundtrack.

"I'm not really interested in singing in the movies," Presley had told disc jockey Charlie Walker a year earlier. But his songs were the very reason that fans flocked to the movie. With the exception of the theme song, the tunes weren't great by any means, but the singer was assigned a writer's share of the royalties and he held the publishing rights to the songs, and that's all Colonel

Two classic rockers: Glen Glenn and Elvis Presley at the Knickerbocker Hotel, 1957. COURTESY OF GLEN GLENN

Parker cared about. Oddly, in the context of the movie, these folk-edged songs provide a welcome diversion from the turgid melodrama, and "Love Me Tender" became Presley's biggest ballad hit of the fifties. (Elvis liked to break the mood of the tune during live shows by changing the lyrics to, "You have made my life a *wreck*.")

RCA followed up on the romance angle of "Love Me Tender" with the release "Love Me." Although Jerry Leiber and Mike Stoller had written it as a piece of sadomasochistic comedy ("Tuh-reat me like a fool, treat me mean and cruel"), Presley delighted them by transforming the song into a ballsy love vow complete with a gospel finish. The songwriting team, who supplied material for the Coasters' greatest records, didn't particularly enjoy what the singer and his band had done with their "Hound Dog." "It had no groove," remarks Leiber, who nonetheless enjoys cashing the royalty checks. But "Love Me" turned out so well that the duo accepted offers to write songs for Elvis's future movie soundtracks.

On balance, the band was put to far better use on Presley's second LP, *Elvis*. Mixing tough-edged remakes of Little Richard's "Long Tall Sally," "Ready Teddy," and "Rip It Up" with the catchy Otis Blackwell original "Paralyzed" and the bluesy doo-wop of "Anyplace Is Paradise," the album showcases the band at their tightest. Playing with several styles, Presley not only offers a smart Jordanaires-led version of "When My Blue Moon Turns to Gold Again," but he also rhumbas, country style, through "How Do You Think I Feel" (which he and Moore had first attempted at Sun) and the tear-jerking Red Foley song that first got him noticed in school, "Old Shep." Oozing with authentic rhythmic feel, *Elvis* is one of only three truly fine start-to-finish secular albums the singer made in his lifetime.

Increasingly, the rocker was moving away from the bare-bones, guitar-oriented sound of the Sun days and into more piano- and chorus-dominated pop, with great commercial success. One notable exception was the song "Too Much." Built around a teen catchphrase ("Aw, man, that's *too much*!"), it wasn't much of a tune, but Presley attacked it with the same obsessive dedication he applied to everything in those days. For his part, Moore wanted to capture a carnival feel during his solo. On one particular take he got carried away, and the little guitar riff he was playing nearly ran away with him. The band did another take that was, in the guitarist's estimation, perfect. But the singer liked the one with the runaway guitar solo. Presley's instincts proved solid: "Too Much" spent three weeks as a number-one pop record. "My only jazz solo ever that was on a Presley record," Moore laughs. "There's one song I begged Elvis to let me do one more time, and he wouldn't let me."

Featuring a softer bop sound and a neatly executed hook, "All Shook Up" is the better-remembered record. Another "Presley beating on the guitar case" ditty, it sports minimal playing from Moore and Black; the song is, essentially, a duet between the rocker and the Jordanaires' tenor vocalist, Gordon Stoker. "I did several duets with him," informs Stoker. "'All Shook Up' was my biggest one. At the end I didn't do one of the 'yea-yeas' quite with him. I said, 'Hey, I didn't do that last yea-yea with you.' He said, 'What difference does it make?

If it ain't sold by then, it ain't gonna sell no way.' Of course, I wanted to do it over. But you see, you couldn't punch-in in those days like you can now."

During this time, semi-regular television guest shots kept feeding the frenzy over Presley and his music. "Yeah, all of them were good for him," Fontana says of Elvis's appearances on Steve Allen's and Ed Sullivan's shows. "Every time we'd work one of those shows, the tours would pick up. More people would show up. So yeah, we had a great time on those tours. That's all we did for a couple of years steady. But had it not been for all those television shows, we'd have still been in Arkansas, Louisiana, and Texas, doing the same thing."

For the most part, all of the shows' hosts and musicians were kind to both the band and its singer. There was, however, one exception. "The only guy who was kind of funny was Buddy Rich," remembers Fontana, who met his idol on *The Milton Berle Show*. "Buddy didn't want to talk to nobody. He didn't like rock 'n' roll; he didn't like country; he didn't like nothin' except what he played, but that was just him. So it wasn't no use gettin' mad. It was just his character and everybody knew it. The guy was a genius, so we figured we'd leave him alone."

Out on the road, the audiences' screams were getting louder and more constant (country singer Gary Bryant likened the sound to a "high, keening wail") but, according to Moore, the stage equipment never got any better. "Some of the big venues still only had a mic for Elvis and maybe Bill's bass. There wasn't any for the guitar amp or the drums or anything. You don't have all your monitors and the big sound system and everything [like now]." When an interviewer asked the guitarist how he was able to hear in all that noise, the normally quiet Moore responded with the most quoted line of his life: "Well, best I can tell you is that we're probably the only group in the world that's literally directed by an ass." After the laughter clears when Moore says that, he generally explains, "With D.J. watching Elvis and doing accents and things for him, we knew where we were at in the song. That's the thing. We couldn't necessarily hear his voice. And he'd come back in, and how he could do it was beyond me. He'd drop out and do all his dancing and stuff when I'm doing a solo, and he'd be right back there. He just had a great sense of timing."

With so many young women doing anything they could to meet Elvis Presley, one would assume that there was a lot of carousing going on by both the singer and his band. "No, not really," corrects Fontana. "People think we did a lot of things, but as soon as that show was over, we were packed up and we drove all night. We just didn't have time to do the things people said we did. The Colonel and them booking agents, man, they kept us hopping!" Fontana remembers the tours as pretty grueling. "We'd go out for two or three weeks at a time and by the time you got through with that tour, you were ready to go home and lay down!"

True enough, they were astoundingly busy, but there were memorable exceptions. Years later, Fontana told Dan Griffin about a few escapades. "On a trip through Richmond, Virginia, Scotty and Bill had their wives along on the tour," repeats Griffin. "D.J., still a bachelor, had met up with a rather talented young Elvis fan. After an enjoyable session, D.J. called Scotty's room, asking the guitarist to drive him to a music store to buy drumsticks. When Scotty arrived at his hotel room door he was ushered in, and D.J. promptly instructed the young lady to perform her tricks on his buddy. A satisfied and sly Scotty returned to his room and his waiting wife, telling her that D.J. had found an extra set in his suitcase and that he would not be needing a ride into town."

On another occasion, Elvis Presley himself baled his drummer out of potential hot water. Fontana related to Griffin that Presley tended to run wildly around the hotel to unwind after an invigorating performance. Then he'd retire to his room, generally alone. One night, after a show and in the wee hours, Fontana heard Presley's unmistakable voice whispering in the hallway loudly, "D! D?" Always polite, and unsure which room his drummer was actually in, Presley did not want to knock and wake sleeping parties in other rooms. He whispered at several doors until he found the still-awake Fontana and his date for the evening. Embarrassed, Presley asked if Fontana had a girl in his room; the drummer acknowledged he did. Presley informed Fontana that her mother was calling up his room, since his was the only name she knew. The angry mom informed Presley that her daughter was only fifteen and that she was heading into town with the sheriff. Shocked and totally oblivious, Elvis had denied it truthfully, but figured if there was a stowaway teenager in their midst, she would be in Fontana's room. A bus ticket was quickly purchased, and the overanxious fan was heading back to Mom in the opposite direction. Nothing came of the incident except for a few tense moments between Elvis and D.J.

In his book *That's Alright, Elvis,* Moore admits that adultery eventually broke up his second marriage. In contrast, the surviving Blue Moon Boys say that Bill Black—the oldest member of the group—never fooled around on the road. And so far, no female septuagenarian has come forward to dispute that claim.

As lucrative as the near-constant touring was, movies were the potential mother lode for Presley. In addition, the singer had aspirations of becoming a great actor. Not only did he want to be an artist of James Dean's quality (he never came close to achieving that), but he also wanted to be a true movie star. His early film contracts with Twentieth Century Fox and Hall Wallis at Paramount weren't gigantic, but they led to much bigger paydays later on. Equally important, they moved records for RCA and played to fans who would never get to see the dynamic singer in concert.

The best of these movies are *Loving You* and *Jailhouse Rock*. Both are filled with solid musical material, much of it written by Leiber and Stoller, with which the band acquits itself with furious panache. The theme to *Loving You* is one of those great drowsy-voiced ballads that only Elvis Presley could make sound so intimate and personal. Playing Deke Rivers—a minor-league variation of the lost young soul that James Dean had portrayed in *East of Eden* and *Rebel Without a Cause*—he hops onstage at a local political rally and rocks with utter abandon through "Got a Lot of Livin' to Do." (By some movie miracle, the band just happens to know not only what key he sings in, but also his style and everything else.) Creating a sensation, he saves a failing bandleader's career, anguishes over his parentage, and falls in love, first with the wrong girl, then with the right one. The movie offers nothing special in the way of a story, although the subplot surrounding Lizabeth Scott (the poor man's Lauren Bacall) provides some welcome misdirection.

The Blue Moon Boys all had roles as members of character Tex Warner's band. They wore western shirts, grinned a lot, and mimed playing their instruments. Initially, the boys—especially Bill Black—enjoyed Hollywood. Writer-director Hal Kanter told music journalist Albert Goldman that whenever a shapely woman would saunter by, the bass player would deadpan, "When I see something like that, it makes my asshole pucker like a yellow caution light."

Neither Presley nor the band liked recording at Paramount's sound studios. Union rules and requests for written arrangements, which usually only occurred to the group after they'd played a song several times, cramped everyone's style. Moore, however, enjoyed working with music director/choreographer Charlie O'Kern. "I did enjoy it because, there again, there was plenty of time, you could try different things, and Charlie or Elvis—if you don't like this or don't like that—nobody told you what to do. You just keep looking until you please yourself or whatever, you know, and that was fun doing that that way. Before he even went in and recorded it—forget the film."

The *Loving You* soundtrack, which took up only half of Presley's third album, remains fresh because the singer and band attack the material with so much enthusiasm. Even such throwaways as "Hot Dog" and "(Let's Have a) Party" (which resurfaced as a surprise hit for Wanda Jackson in 1960) were done with great flair. The success of both "(Let Me Be Your) Teddy Bear," which became a number-one hit, and the Leiber-and-Stoller-penned title track (which was a major radio hit even before it was released as a single) overshadowed two of the most dynamic musical performances of the period. Wailing through a speedy "Got a Lot o' Livin' to Do," Moore accents every open second with glittering guitar, while the piano pumps triplets like mad and the bass and drum add a driving, sexy nuance. Best of all, Presley sings with all the joyful release of a kid being let out of school for the summer.

Nearly as fine is "Mean Woman Blues," another S & M spoof masquerading as a blues tune. Better arranged than most three-chord rockers, it features Presley's impassioned vocal working off the Jordanaires' "doo-wahs" and hand claps as Fontana and Black lay down solid, inspired rhythm. Moore's guitar alternates little brass-substitute phrases with blues fills to set up one of the simplest, yet most intense, solos he ever laid down. The following year Jerry Lee Lewis would reinvent this tune for his first Sun EP; in turn, Roy Orbison would copy Lewis's version for his 1963 hit. Both were mighty renditions, but neither can compete with the searing chemistry exhibited on Presley's.

Another example of excellent band interplay is the title song for *Jailhouse Rock*. Another Leiber-Stoller composition, it's a dance-oriented remake of the R & B hit they wrote for the Robins, "Riot in Cell Block #9." While working up a variation of the reliable stop-time intro of songs like "Blue Suede Shoes," Fontana was reminded of a swing version of "Anvil Chorus" he once heard. Quickly, the band adapted this piece of an idea into the rife-with-danger mood setter we know today. Presley's raving is brilliantly underscored by Moore's tart electric rhythm (which creates the illusion that the song was being played at a faster tempo than it really was) and a wonderfully loud and twangy lead break that works nicely off session pianist Dudley Brooks's high-octave fills. These are the first sessions in which Bill Black played the Fender electric bass. Contrary to stories that proclaim he could not master the instrument, Black's work provides flawless timing and support. Together the group created a carefully contrived recording that conjures the feeling of utter personal abandon. If you don't like this record, you just don't like rock 'n' roll.

Fan club releases of the *Jailhouse Rock* alternate takes demonstrate how smart Presley was about honing a song's production. On "Don't Leave Me Now," he was content to continue working off Dudley Brooks's piano hook

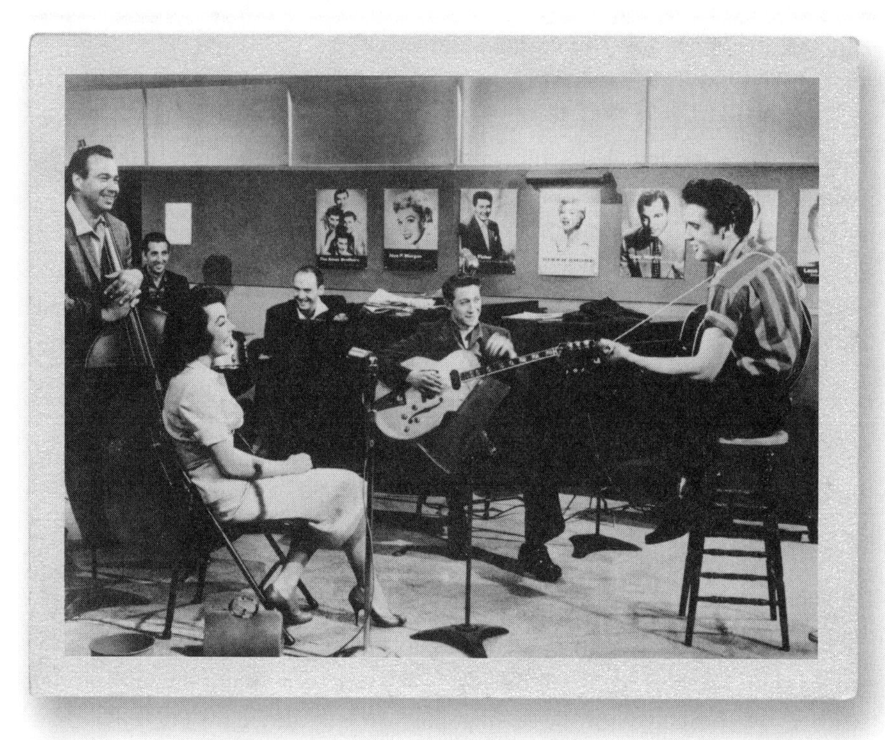

Bill Black, D. J. Fontana, Judy Tyler, Mike Stoller, Scotty Moore, and Elvis relax on the set during the filming of *Jailhouse Rock*, 1957. Courtesy of D. J. Fontana, RCA records / Elvis Presley Enterprises

until he fashioned a performance that sounded like last-call barroom pleading. For the Leiber and Stoller–penned "Treat Me Nice" (which had been written as a coy R & B ballad), the singer worked with Jerry Leiber to goose up the tempo, accentuate the guitar-case bongo-style slapping, and mix Moore's little jazz fills in and around the Jordanaires' vocal interjections.

The most infamous moment of these sessions involves "(You're So Square) Baby I Don't Care." Still struggling with his new electric bass (which was easier to hear during concerts) Bill Black reportedly couldn't master the song's intro. Frustrated, he threw the instrument down and walked out of the studio. Without saying a word, Presley picked up the bass and, with Leiber recording a guide vocal, recorded the part himself—and he did a pretty good job of it, too. (Years later, when the Beatles met Presley, Paul McCartney would comment, "Coming along quite promising on bass there, Elvis.") It's no surprise that Presley could play a little bass. He also fooled around with electric guitar,

Rocking out during a *Jailhouse Rock* promotional tour, 1957. Courtesy of D. J. Fontana, RCA records / Elvis Presley Enterprises

piano, and drums when he had time. But the fact that he would take up the bass man's instrument and complete Black's work, *Citizen Kane*–style, spoke volumes about the two men's often stormy relationship.

A self-made man, Black missed the freedom to responsibly do what he wanted, when he wanted. The previous year, he and Fontana had been forced to get Presley's permission to play in a recording session for another performer, which galled him. The session was for his old *Hayride* friend Johnny Horton. "[Bill Black] was really proud to play on 'Honky Tonk Man,' 'One Woman Man,' and 'I'm Ready If You're Willing' and one other song," states Tillman Franks. "We did four songs on that first session and Bill played on 'em, and Harold Bradley played the rhythm guitar." Franks, a pretty good bass slapper himself, explains why Black had been sought out. "It was my idea to get Bill. Johnny would have been tickled in a minute to have me play, but I told him that Bill Black could beat me. He could play a beat that I couldn't do. We called Bill up, and Johnny did most of the talking and asked Elvis if we could get Bill

Black. At that particular time, Elvis tried to cut 'em down on the money and all that, so Bill Black was kindly mad at Elvis anyhow. But we asked if we could come by and get Bill to play bass for us and he said, 'Well, tell everyone it's Tillman Franks playing the bass. Don't tell 'em it's Bill Black.'"

That teed Black off. In his view, it was bad enough that he wasn't sharing more fully in Presley's great success; now he was being prevented from taking credit for playing on three major country hits. Further, by this time the band members were no longer billed on posters or mentioned in announcements. The Jordanaires, on the other hand, not only received label credit for their work with Presley, but they were also allowed to do all the lucrative freelancing they wanted, provided they were there when Elvis needed them for his sessions.

The inequity of this situation makes the rock king seem like a grade-A jerk. Fontana says it's not so, that they all liked young Elvis. "Oh, *yeah*! He was the nicest guy in the world, absolutely. He never gave us a bit of trouble. He really couldn't give us a lot of hassle because we started together at the *Hayride* with Scotty and Bill. We were there before he was happening." Did Presley put on airs, as some books suggest, and call himself the King of Rock 'n' Roll? Fontana is adamant: "Never! He knew that the only king was the man upstairs."

Many of the problems were caused by Colonel Parker's directives, which usually arrived via telegram. Asked if the band had many one-on-one confrontations with Presley's manager, Fontana quickly asserts, "Not many, no. Me, Scotty, and Bill didn't deal with him much at all. If we needed anything we talked to Elvis about it, and he'd say, 'Don't worry about it, I'll take care of it.' And he would. The Colonel, he didn't like that idea. He wanted to be the main man, of course.

"Any time he'd give us a hard time about anything at all we'd say, 'Well, OK, that's right, Colonel.' Then we'd go to Elvis and say, 'Elvis, Colonel wants us to do so and so.' Then he'd say 'Aw, don't pay no attention to him. I'll take care of it. Don't worry about it; just forget it.' And, that's what we'd do."

Being inexperienced in band politics, it was tough for Presley to be in the middle of such disputes. The Blue Moon Boys could be a handful; Moore tended to brood and play the martyr, Fontana enjoyed the girls on the road far more than he lets on today, and Black was sometimes outspoken to the point of rudeness. Although by modern rock-musician standards the boys were very well behaved, they tended to stir things up and bring Presley down with their complaints. Since the singer was cushioned by his entourage from many day-to-day problems (especially during movie shoots), however, Scott, Bill, and

D.J. were actually more of a problem for Presley's handlers and bodyguards, and for Parker's organization, than they were for the artist himself.

Presley's deal with Parker was simple: Presley took care of the music, and Parker took care of business. Elvis could fight Parker on things like song choices, stage apparel, presentation, and travel arrangements, but when it came to the pay, promotion, merchandising, and billing conflicts, that was his manager's area. When the building tension forced Presley to take sides, he went with the side that had made him a millionaire. It's really that simple. But that didn't mean the singer actually liked his manager.

Generally, most people believe that Parker was around all the time, micromanaging every second of Presley's and the band's lives. If that had been true, the band's internal problems would have gotten worse faster. According to Gordon Stoker, the man who made Parker's rule bearable was Tom Diskin. "He was the go-between," explains Stoker. "Tom Diskin was a sweet man, a very educated, sweet, lovable man that Elvis highly respected. He couldn't stand the Colonel half the time. He couldn't stand the Colonel period, to tell you the truth. But he loved Tom Diskin. So everything was done through Tom Diskin to the Colonel. If the Colonel wanted anything done it was, 'Mr. Diskin go tell Elvis.' Then Elvis would say, 'Hey, Mr. Diskin. Tell the Colonel I'm not going to do so forth and so on.'

"He was very tactful in the way he told Elvis anything. The Colonel wasn't. Tom Diskin was a man who did so many things that were completely swept under the rug. He was responsible for a great deal of Elvis's huge success. The Colonel was behind the scene, but Tom Diskin was out on the front lines, and he would smooth everything over with everybody. He was the unsung hero, so to speak. But Tom Diskin wanted it that way."

Diskin, who was RCA's liaison man to Parker as well as a crucial part of Parker's Jamboree Attractions, didn't have the authority to finesse everything.

The pay issue had started earlier than most would like to admit. Barbara Pittman recalled witnessing a rather ugly confrontation about it between Moore, Black, and Presley at the Eagle's Nest in 1955. She claims that during a heated moment, Presley dismissed one of Black's arguments by saying, "You're just a two-bit bass player. I'm the star. You go out there and try it alone and see how far you get." Paul Burlison told Dan Griffin that Presley's lack of respect for the band was common knowledge in Memphis. Black and Moore—who were admired by the town's music community—did not want to ruffle feathers at the time, but their friends in Memphis loved to dig at Presley by saying, "You got a good voice, but without Scotty's picking and Bill's slapping, you would be nothing!" True or not, the singer hated hearing it.

It's important to remember that Presley had no say in putting together his first band. Sam Phillips did. If it hadn't worked out, Moore and Black would have gone on to the next project, leaving shy young Elvis to his own devices. We might never have heard of him. The best analogy regarding the breakdown of their relationship is that of the relationships among soldiers: although they wouldn't necessarily be friends in civilian life, they forge a strong personal bond in battle. Their camaraderie is based on mutual hardships in a specific set of circumstances over a finite period of time. However, when one becomes an officer it proves especially difficult to break the regular dogfaces from treating you like their old foxhole buddy whom they joked and got drunk with. Long after fame had hit Presley, Moore and Black tended to react to the singer as if he were the same shy, awestruck kid who needed to be told when to take a bath. Elvis wanted to be treated more like a star.

Sometimes Black tried to drive home his point about the band's lack of money through humor. "Well," chuckles Gordon Stoker, "Bill Black used to wear the filthiest T-shirts that you've ever seen. I don't mean that his body was dirty. He'd take showers and he'd put back on this filthy T-shirt. And I said to him, 'Why in the world do you wear those filthy T-shirts?' He said, 'Well, to tell you the truth, I think if Elvis sees me he'll feel sorry for me and buy me some new clothes.' It didn't happen. He didn't buy him nothin.'"

For his part, the practical Moore really wasn't counting on seeing the 50-25-25 split that the band enjoyed during the old days. He knew Presley was the star attraction and that neither he nor Black had a contract with either Sun or RCA. They received no royalties, just union scale for their session work. When they agreed to rescind their original partnership deal during Bob Neal's management reign, Presley rather generously offered Moore and Black 25 percent of his future royalties. Knowing that such a deal would also be unfair to the singer, Moore asked instead for a quarter of one percent of the royalties on future recordings by the band. Presley agreed, but the deal was never put into writing, and when Parker became involved in the day-to-day operations the notion was scotched. "I guess I just trusted him," Moore ruefully confessed to the *New York Times*.

"When the Colonel came onboard he said, 'Forget 'em, man. Don't give 'em nuthin',"' remembers Gordon Stoker. "'You don't owe them anything.' Scotty said to him, 'Should we get this in a contract?' He said, 'No man, my word is my bond.' Those are exactly the words that he said. Elvis told him, 'My word is my bond,' and his word was not his bond in that particular instance. But the Colonel was the cause of every bit of it."

Of course the royalty deal—which would have netted the trio millions over the years—wouldn't have worked. Moore, who has obsessively kept every document and official scrap of paper that has come into his hands, would likely have embarrassed both RCA and Parker by demanding continuing official audits, something that Elvis Presley never did.

Another sticking point with the band had been Presley's promise to allow them to record a solo project. Once again, the agreement was not put in writing. When Moore decided that he wanted to start setting up sessions, Parker pulled the plug. When asked to intercede on his bandmate's behalf and live up to his promise, Presley stood mute. Up to that point, most of the other problems the band had encountered could have been blamed on circumstance or on Parker. This time, the lack of character that Elvis Presley demonstrated became the true issue. It was at this critical juncture that Moore and Black lost faith in him.

The big loser in all of this was RCA. In light of the Bill Black Combo's subsequent success at Hi Records and Moore's work at Fernwood, it's apparent that Parker and RCA made a huge mistake by not having Moore, Black, and Fontana put out an album of instrumentals under the label's own auspices. Immensely popular jukebox items, good instrumentals were still hitting the charts with regularity into the late 1960s. An album titled something like *Elvis Presley's Band Plays the Hits* would have been a wonderful tie-in item for all involved: the band could've made some of their own money. Presley would have probably been accorded a share of the album's royalties for the use of his name. Parker would have gotten some free publicity for his "boy" while Presley was out of sight making movies, and he would have taken his cut of Elvis's royalties. In addition, he could have crowed that he was responsible for two great acts on RCA.

It's possible that Parker didn't want Presley's name associated with anyone else's for promotional reasons. In his mind, allowing Black to announce that he played on Johnny Horton's records would only serve to help Horton, who was one of his boy's competitors. But when Presley demanded that the Jordanaires be credited on his records, Parker made it happen. No one really knows why Parker seemed to hold a hatred for the Blue Moon Boys, but his actions sure seemed personal. Certainly the control issue holds water in this regard. After all, the manager rather notoriously ran off Leiber and Stoller—who were doing fantastic work with his boy—simply because they'd offered the singer some creative advice. However, the fact that Presley never insisted that his word be kept regarding the trio's solo project was the strongest sign that he felt no true loyalty to his original band. It's also a sure indication that he thought of himself as Parker's employee, not his boss.

Something had to give. On September 21, 1957, it did.

Scotty Moore and Bill Black, the original Blue Moon Boys, left Elvis Presley. Nearly everyone saw it coming.

"As a matter of fact, Elvis called me," remembers Gordon Stoker. "We were at the Knickerbocker Hotel, and he called me one day and said, 'Gordon, did Scotty say anything to you about leaving?' I said, 'Yeah, as a matter of fact, I think Scotty and Bill left this morning. They wanted more money and they didn't get it, so they took off.' "

It had been a long time coming.

As Presley's fame had grown, the Blue Moon Boys had felt more and more alienated—especially Moore, who was accustomed to guiding the troupe both musically and professionally. They had helped Presley achieve unparalleled chart success, and now his doe-eyed face was in movies. Scotty, Bill, and D.J. had thought that making films would be a glamorous respite from the road. But, while columnists and movie stars fawned over their singer, the band lived a largely miserable existence.

Suddenly, the music had become secondary to the silver screen. The material they were recording at inhospitable Hollywood studios was largely filler for soundtracks. Moore, Black, and Fontana appeared in five films. Just as they did on concert tours, during the filming of each movie they shared a bungalow, complete with kitchenette. To save money, they cooked their own food and pinched pennies. Even during a major motion-picture shoot, they were not paid on a scale that was on par with other actors.

Meanwhile, Presley's entourage (who would have to wait until the 1960s to be sarcastically dubbed the Memphis Mafia) shared a whole floor of the luxurious Beverly Wilshire with their boss. A plane mishap had made the singer nervous about flying, so members of the entourage drove him everywhere, while the band flew to gigs that were too far away for their own vehicle to drive to. Increasingly they felt disconnected from the kid they had nurtured back in Memphis. It didn't help matters that Presley's gofers—Marty Lacker, Lamar Fike, and Gene Smith—were often flat-out rude to the band.

Glen Glenn, a Los Angeles rockabilly frequently seen on local television's *Cal's Corral* and *Town Hall Party*, was introduced to Presley and the band in San Diego by his mentor, Fred Maddox. Later, Maddox introduced him to the whole crew. "He was real friendly," he said of the rock king. "Mostly, I talked to him about the country guys. He had been playing with Faron Young, and we talked about Tom Tall because he had just done this tour with Tom about a month or two before with the Browns. But I saw Elvis many times after that at the Knickerbocker Hotel, and that's how I got to knowin' Bill Black."

When the band wasn't required on set during the filming of *Loving You* and *Jailhouse Rock* Black would sometimes hang out with Maddox and Glenn. Occasionally he'd jam with them; other times they'd go fishing. Bit by bit, Black let some of the band's problems spill out. "Bill told me he was making more money before 'Heartbreak Hotel' hit. I think it was two hundred dollars a week when he was on the road and in Hollywood, and one hundred dollars

Bill Black, Scotty Moore, Glen Glenn, and guitarist Gary Lambert, in the band's room at the Knickerbocker Hotel, 1957. Courtesy of Glen Glenn

a week when they were just sitting around doing nothin'. Of course, he got paid a little for doing the movies, too. Here Elvis was making a million dollars and they were making two hundred dollars."

Even with session work and movie bit parts kicking in a few extra bucks, Black really didn't have enough money to do right by his family. Whenever he left town he gave his wife Evelyn fifty dollars for groceries and sundry bills and just prayed that the amount would be enough to feed his kids until he got home. Worse, the cost of long-distance phone calls in those days was prohibitive. Glenn recalls, "I was there many times when Bill would try to call the wife and check on the kids, and he would always gripe, 'Here I'm working for Elvis Presley, and I don't have enough money to even call my wife.'" Further, the tedious film work got them down. "I don't think Scotty cared too much for those movies," Glenn recalled. "D.J. didn't like 'em all that much, but Bill hated it."

Black also didn't like Presley's entourage (whom he would often refer to as "grubby little parasites"), especially Gene Smith, who has been described in some books as emotionally disturbed. "He wasn't emotionally disturbed," clarified Barbara Pittman, who was fond of Presley's cousin. "He was just a redneck." Probably fueled by both Presley's negative attitude and Colonel Parker's directive that contact with the band be minimal, Smith was often curt and abrupt with Black.

"The only reason I got in to see Elvis when I went up there was because of Bill," says Glenn today. "Even though Bill was not happy with Elvis Presley, he did this for me. He took me up there. Gene Smith, that was the one who was Elvis's cousin, if I had went up and knocked on the door, he would've said, 'Elvis ain't in. What are *you* doing here, anyway?' All the times I went up there, [Black] never hung out with the mob Elvis had with him."

Glenn clearly recalls the day that Black finally lost his cool.

"If Parker was around—he was an asshole sometimes—nobody could get in to see Elvis. One time Bill called up to see if Elvis was in, and they said, 'Yeah, he's in. But nobody can see him tonight, Bill. Parker's here.' Well, Bill got upset. He said, 'I'm going to go up there and I'm going to bang the door down. What do they mean I can't go up there?' I had to stop Bill from taking me up there. He was mad . . . and Bill was the kind of guy who could do something, you know. I think he could take care of himself pretty well."

Scotty Moore told Dan Griffin that this had been, indeed, the final straw for Black. Previously, the guitarist had learned that people were laughing at the trio's predicament behind their backs. To add further insult, "We found even the guys selling souvenir books were making more than we were," he told the *New York Times*. It galled the quiet but proud guitarist.

In Alanna Nash's *Elvis Aaron Presley: Revelations from the Memphis Mafia*, Lamar Fike gives the viewpoint of Elvis Presley's camp. He portrays Black as the ringleader, pacing around the hotel lobby and preaching revolt to his innocent bandmates. Gordon Stoker believes that Fike was merely "sticking up for Elvis" when he made those claims. He adds, "Bill was not stirring up anything. Bill had said that they deserved more money than what they were getting. It wasn't fair for him to have to work as a refrigerator repairman—which is what he was working as—and Scotty was just working at anything he could get when they weren't working with Elvis. They should have made enough money with Elvis to not have to do that."

"They wanted recognition, and they wanted a percentage of the profits, same as they got when they first started out," Fike explained to Nash. (According to Fike, Moore also wanted a cash payment of ten thousand dollars to "clear up some debts.") "And Colonel said, 'Fuck you. You're not going to get it. That's the way it is, boys, cut and dried.'"

Black and Moore promptly went home to Memphis, where they embarrassed Presley by informing the local press that the split was indeed a matter of money. "Scotty and I don't have fifty dollars between us," Black is famously quoted as saying. Despite Black's and Moore's coaching and need for solidarity, however, Fontana did not quit with them.

"Well, I tried to stay neutral," explains the drummer. "I knew they had a point. They had a *great* point. They should have gotten more money because that was the original deal, verbally. 50-25-25. They figured that they should have gotten more money and should have become quite wealthy. But the Colonel wouldn't let it happen. I never did understand why."

For his part, Colonel Parker lined up a new band for a benefit at the Mississippi-Alabama Fair and Dairy Show in Tupelo that consisted of guitarist Hank Garland, bassist Chuck Wiggington, and pianist Floyd Cramer. Fike told Nash, "They blew everybody away. Elvis turned around to me after the fair with a big grin on his face. He said, 'Shit, I didn't need Scotty and Bill anyway, did I?'"

Fontana remembers the show as going "all right," and that the screaming went on unabated. However, press reports of the time say that many longtime fans were calling out, "Where's Scotty? Where's Bill?" Presley himself claimed something intangible was missing from his superstar band, and he decided to hire Moore and Black back on a per-show basis until he left for the army.

"We went onstage and it was just like nobody said a word," says Scotty Moore. "Like we'd never been anywhere, said anything."

Yet, for all intents and purposes, that beautiful, creative partnership that had resulted in one of the greatest ascensions to fame in pop-music history was over.

How serious were the Blue Moon Boys about actually leaving Presley? Pretty serious. While shooting films in L.A., the discouraged backing band began talks with Ozzie Nelson. The entrepreneurial producer/writer/actor had recently started a record company as part of his empire, which he'd built on the success of his television series *The Adventures of Ozzie & Harriet*. Nelson had inquired about the Blue Moon Boys jumping ship to become the musicians behind his sixteen-year-old son, Ricky.

One of the band's favorite memories is their bass player's first encounter with the teen idol. "Scotty and D.J. told me that Daddy kind of halfway sleepwalked," chuckles Louis Black. "When he woke up, you ought to seen him: hair standing everywhere, and he'd come walking through there in his underwear and walked right on by Ricky Nelson and his girlfriends. He went over and got him a drink of water, walked right back by 'em and went to bed. Scotty and D.J. said, 'He didn't have no idea that anybody was even in there.' They said, 'You know who was here last night?' 'Naw, I was tired.'"

Presley's band liked the handsome, shy Ricky Nelson and took him under their wing—for better or worse. "We were friends with Rick," remembers Fontana. "He'd come to the hotel several different times and he said, 'Why don't you go talk with my dad?' We went up and talked with him. He was a hard-nosed businessman." While they considered the move to the Nelson camp, the much older and experienced trio spent time with teenaged Ricky—and arranged the youngster's first experience with oral sex in the process. An aging Presley fan, who stayed at the same hotel as the band whenever they were in town, wanted to meet the young television star. After an enlightening evening with her, the "irrepressible Ricky" wanted to hang with the Blue Moon Boys every night.

Due to the weekly television segment that featured his singing, Ricky Nelson quickly became as well known as Presley and Pat Boone. By playing behind him each week, Moore, Black, and Fontana would quickly become far better known than they currently were. According to Fontana, however, Ozzie Nelson bristled at some of Bill Black's ideas. "Bill kept saying he wanted to be an actor. And I think Ozzie wanted nobody to do anything except Rick and the family, which was understandable." This attitude cemented the Blue Moon Boys' impression that the elder Nelson was a tighter taskmaster than Colonel Tom Parker.

Fontana and Moore have different memories regarding what happened next. (Contacted through James Burton, Rick's surviving elder brother, David Nelson, does not recall the incident at all.) The drummer claims that Black's ambitious demands resulted in Ozzie Nelson turning them down. He believes they came up with a deal that Nelson would not accept. Moore told Dan Griffin that Nelson offered them barely more than scale pay and no guarantees of compensation during downtime. According to Moore, it was the musicians who, wary and still smarting from the fleecing that Parker had engineered, turned Nelson down.

Hindsight is twenty-twenty, and it can be argued that everything eventually worked out for the best; but it's also possible that the band's failure to join up with Ricky Nelson—with or without acting roles—may have been the biggest career blunder the Blue Moon Boys ever made with their eyes wide open. Although Ozzie Nelson was a strict, old-school disciplinarian during the big-band days (he liked his people neatly dressed, on time, and prepared), he enjoyed a very good reputation with his musicians. In addition, Ozzie, who had scored hits during the 1930s and 1940s with such comedic songs as "The Kid in the Three Corner Pants" and "I'm Looking for a Guy Who Plays Alto and Doubles on Clarinet and Wears a Size Thirty-Seven Suit," was generous—although not extravagant—with his players. After the big-band days were over, he found ways to keep several of his guys employed. He didn't particularly like rock 'n' roll, but he ended up treating James Burton and James Kirkland, who later appeared on the weekly sitcom, quite well indeed. Both used the show as a launching pad for prosperous studio careers in L.A., where they became part of the Wrecking Crew—the studio players who performed on literally hundreds of pop and country singles. Ironically, Burton would go on to fill Moore's post in Presley's TCB Band ten years later.

More importantly, son Ricky Nelson stuck up for his guys. Example? When producer Jimmie Haskell (one of the great underrated record men) tried to make the Jordanaires sing something that they didn't like, Nelson himself would politely command, "No. No. Let them do it their way." Indeed, Gordon Stoker claims, "I'd rather hear the Jordanaires with Ricky Nelson than with Elvis. He always had our sound right up front where Elvis actually wanted us." Yet, once the Blue Moon Boys rejected the Nelsons' offer, they were back to the same routine of hard work and relatively low pay.

Loyalty and need aside, the most obvious benefit Presley would have enjoyed by paying his band a better wage and picking up all their travel expenses was the reduction of his own tax load. A man who had quickly scaled the highest tax bracket in the nation needed all the legitimate business deductions he could get his hands on. Had he paid the Blue Moon Boys more, it's likely that the rock king would have been able to take home more pay after tax time. Parker had to know that, but instead of advising him to raise their salaries on that basis, he told Presley (according to Gordon Stoker), "If you don't pay 'em much, they'll continue working for you. If you pay 'em very much money, soon they'll have a bank account and they won't need you."

The Presley camp makes a big deal out of the year-end thousand-dollar bonuses the singer routinely handed out. These were not guaranteed, however, and usually depended upon the singer's goodwill at Christmastime. "He always gave us a Christmas bonus every year," reports Stoker, "and the bigger he got, the smaller the bonuses got." In the post-army years, Joe Esposito wrote the checks and did indeed pay out bonuses to Moore and Fontana. However, during Presley's early superstardom, when he was buying luxury cars like a drunken lottery winner, his band members had trouble paying their household bills. The only present Moore ever received from Presley was a watch that the singer was going to throw away after having been presented with a new Rolex. (The guitarist eventually made a present of the timepiece to country artist Ronnie McDowell.)

"You know, he didn't give D.J., Bill Black, and Scotty cars or anything like that. The Jordanaires, either," adds Stoker. "And, together, we made him what he was—on record, anyway. We encouraged him. He once told us, 'If it hadn't been for the Jordanaires, there might not have been a me.' We said, 'What?' He said, 'No, fellas, you guys have always taken an interest in me when I wasn't even interested in recording. You've always taken an interest in all this crap—this material'—he didn't call it crap, he called it the other word—'that they made me sing in these movies.' We'd help him with his arrangements and everything he did because we loved him. We didn't help him for the money. We did it because he was a friend and we loved him. At the same time, he just lost track of reality. What I would have done had I been him was help Bill Black and Scotty Moore, regardless of the Colonel."

"I think Bill had a good reason to be bitter," says Glen Glenn, "and he never brought Parker into it; he always mentioned Elvis." The way Black saw it, his deal was with Elvis Presley, not Colonel Parker. Black and Moore had left their wives and children behind to basically fend for themselves while the musicians helped the singer become something. They were told they would benefit, and not just by having jobs. While Moore never placed full blame on the singer, he often expressed disappointment over Presley not demanding more control of the situation.

Fontana, who had no family commitments at the time, felt he had no right to strike because Presley had done everything he'd promised, salary wise. His unwillingness to walk out with Moore and Black probably cost the Blue Moon Boys their bargaining leverage. When Presley hired the two men back on a show-by-show basis, which resulted in a small raise plus paid travel expenses, the singer made sure Fontana received a pay increase as well. If there were ever any hard feelings between the drummer and the other band members, however, they never showed. Fontana and Moore continued being close friends and work associates long after Presley stopped being their primary employer.

A remark, made by Lamar Fike during his recap of the salary dispute, deserves some attention. "I don't blame Scotty and Bill and D.J. for trying, but they could be replaced," he told Alanna Nash. "You could have put them in the Seattle Fair and they wouldn't have drawn twenty people. Musicians have a tendency to forget that."

If Presley's founding musicians were replaceable, then by the same token the boys in the Memphis Mafia were absolutely disposable. It should be noted that, in all the time they were with the rock king, no member of Presley's entourage ever made as meaningful a contribution to the singer's career as did Scotty Moore or Bill Black. None of them ever created a lucrative opportunity or a new form of music. A few Presley associates (Joe Esposito and Jerry Schilling in particular) developed some show-business skills over the course of time. Most, however, were flunkies, gofers, spies for Parker, and enablers. "All the guys were capable of doing things that needed to be done," explains Fontana. "Except a couple of them—they weren't capable of doing anything. I just don't want to mention their names. They know who they are. They were really gofers and hangers-on." By their own admission, some of the guys spied on Presley so that Colonel Parker could keep the singer under his thumb.

Over the long haul, Presley's reliance on the Memphis Mafia actually hindered his career. During the mid-1960s, Glen Campbell (who at that time was an ace session man) was hired to help Red West and Charlie Hodge work up some demo material for the fading rock king. The idea was to create better material than he was getting for the movie soundtracks. Campbell remembers West's compositions as "nothing special." When asked if he thought the men surrounding Presley had had the singer's best interests at heart, he replied, "Yeah, I guess. But really, he should've gotten better people to handle things for him than just those guys."

The presence of Presley's entourage didn't just keep his bandmates at bay; it also revolted longtime friends like Tommy Sands. "Elvis was used to all his friends running after him, and of course he had that Memphis Mafia around him—those nine or ten guys that lived off of him and got paid every week. They ate his food, drank his drinks, and shared his women, and I was never like that."

It is ironic that, in later years, members of the Memphis Mafia would complain about the same issues that they'd sniggered at Moore and Black over. Presley balked at paying anyone in his entourage more than a couple of hundred bucks a week. His father, Vernon, was always blamed as being the tightwad, but Elvis was the earner; he could have demanded raises for anyone at anytime, and he chose not to do so. As a result, by 1976—a year before his death—most of Presley's pals would be out of his life.

They were easily replaced.

In 1958, however, the most curious fallout from Black's and Moore's failed pay strike was the fact that Moore stopped playing lead guitar on Presley's studio recordings. You can hear a final taste of his lead in the intros and fills of 1958's "Wear My Ring Around Your Neck." After that, Moore retreated to the rhythm slot. Legend has it that he turned to Chet Atkins one day and said, "Chet, I have run out of things to play." Atkins, who *never* ran out of things to play, was taken aback: "This is your style; come up with something." When Moore couldn't—or, more precisely, wouldn't—he asked that session ace Hank "Sugarfoot" Garland be brought in. Was he better than Moore? In terms of both versatility and quickness in grasping what was needed, yes. Garland may have been the best guitarist ever. But Scotty Moore invented the guitar style he used with Presley. Garland's genius—at least as far as Elvis Presley's music is concerned—came into play when he expanded upon Moore's style.

Gordon Stoker feels Moore's withdrawal from playing lead was simply the result of awe and hero worship. "Well, I saw it happening, and I know why he wasn't playing lead. You just don't play lead in front of Hank Garland. You don't play lead in front of Grady Martin, or even Harold Bradley. See, Scotty was always very limited, and Scotty knew, more than anybody, that he was very limited. He had a certain thing that was just needed at the time. But these guys who came along were much better, and they beat him at his own game, so to speak. I'm not putting him down, because I love Scotty, but that's what the truth was."

"Hank was just so good that he could play anybody's style," Moore states enthusiastically. "He'd listen to you for five minutes and play rings around you. He was just that good, and in your style. He'd always try to play something that he thought I would play. That was how good he was. And simple. [Presley's 1961 hit] 'Little Sister' is a good example."

Like Moore, Garland was a jazz fanatic who had a great feel for blues, country, and rock. His guitar work brilliantly echoes Moore's on such hits as "A Fool Such as I," "I Need Your Love Tonight," "A Big Hunk O' Love," and "I Got Stung." During their few stage appearances together, Presley introduced him as "one of the finest guitarists anywhere in the country."

In 1961, at the peak of his renown as a session guitarist and recording artist, a car accident would end Garland's career. Some say that the event was the result of deliberate foul play and that there was a murderous conspiracy in place, but no evidence confirming those claims has ever materialized. As a consequence of the brain damage he sustained in the wreck and the hundred shock treatments he endured afterward, Garland would never play guitar again. Mentally impaired, he lived with his brother Billy until his death in 2005. In 2004 an Associated Press reporter asked him about Elvis Presley. After much deliberation, he smiled and answered, "He was real nice."

After Garland's accident, when Presley needed a lead guitar on his Nashville sessions, he employed Grady Martin or Harold Bradley. If Moore was petulantly holding back his skills, it wasn't apparent to Gordon Stoker. "He always seemed to enjoy Elvis's company, and they always had a nice talk. Everything was very pleasant, but he just didn't want to do the lead when you had a much better lead man sitting in the chair beside you. Scotty was a man who was a little bit in awe. Of course, on a lot of the sessions there was Chet Atkins, who was a very good lead guitar man too."

Presley viewed Moore as the session leader: the guy who would count into the songs and explain his wants to the other musicians. In truth, few musicians remember Moore or Fontana ever providing suggestions on how to work with the singer. Some studio veterans even grumbled to Ernst Jorgensen (*Elvis*

Presley: A Life in Music—The Complete Recording Sessions) that if Presley hadn't wanted them there, Moore and Fontana would not have been hired for the sessions. Was jealousy a contributing factor in such statements? Surely. But the remarks are not completely inaccurate. Nashville studio pros had high standards, and they did not accept others into their ranks gladly. By 1967, Fontana would gradually work his way into the Nashville studio call sheets. Moore would have to prove himself back in Memphis.

During the autumn of 1957, though, with an army induction looming and a movie contract forcing his hand, Presley rehired Moore and Black for two very good reasons: First, none of the Nashville pickers would have given up their lucrative session gigs to work for the comparatively meager salary the Blue Moon Boys earned for very long. Second, Moore and Black were dedicated to the singer. "He knew that he could depend on us for whatever," observes Fontana. "He never worried about us being late or not showing up, drunk, or whatever."

Ultimately, it reassured Presley to see familiar faces in the studio. He knew in his heart of hearts that he owed Scotty Moore some kind of allegiance. Of the two founding Blue Moon Boys, Presley was closer to the quiet guitarist. The singer probably would have kept Black around just to make Moore happy. But Black exhibited admirable resolve. He played a few more session dates and a final tour with Presley, and that was it.

According to Glen Glenn, during his final tour with Presley Black extracted a satisfying measure of revenge for the way he'd been treated by the singer in years past. "During that last tour that Elvis did where he went up the Pacific Coast, Bill told me, 'Now we're making big money. We're getting it now.' I don't know what they were getting, but it was better than two hundred dollars. When they drove out, Bill had Elvis's credit card so he could buy gas, food, or anything he needed for the trip. Bill kept showing me that credit card. I remember him saying, 'Glen, look what I got. I've got his credit card. I'm going to buy any damned thing I want.' Then he laughed and said, 'He owes me.'"

Elvis Presley's 1958 army induction came after the filming of *King Creole*, the soundtrack of which eschewed guitar-based rock in favor of horn-based New Orleans jazz. The futures of both band and singer were clearly up in the air. "Really didn't know what was going to happen there," admits Moore. "Of course, I'd already done the service route, and I think I told him 'Good luck.' I thought they might get him into special services or something, try to do something like that. I really had no idea what was going to happen."

Fontana's first reaction to Presley's draft notice was lighthearted. "Better him than me! I had already been to Korea and back, so I wasn't about to go again." The drummer is alone among his peers when he says that he knew the Elvis phenomena wasn't over. "The Colonel wouldn't let it be over. That's why I say to give him credit for being what he was. He was a good promoter. So he wasn't going to let it be over. I didn't even think about that."

Returning to Shreveport after Presley's induction, the drummer resumed playing in all the little clubs he'd performed in before hooking up with the Blue Moon Boys. Soon he latched onto a six-month gig playing behind Lefty Frizzell. Fontana remembers having a good time playing music with the country legend, but, "He was a hard man to work with. He was drinking a little, so you never knew what mood he was going to be in when he came onstage. So, we just learned to follow Lefty and do the best we could." (According to Northwest rockabilly Bobby Wayne, who toured with him, Frizzell's favorite cocktail was vodka and buttermilk.)

One of the Frizzell road trips to Los Angeles resulted in a story that Fontana retells with his usual dry sense of humor. Road weary, the musicians wanted to look up an old flame who had been a regular fan of Frizzell's band and several other touring country acts. When Fontana inquired of her whereabouts from the club owner, he got an unexpected reply. "Yeah, he told us the old girl had left hangin' out with country hillbillies and 'gone pop.' She was blowing the Lawrence Welk band!"

Rockabilly legend Gene Vincent also hired Fontana to become a touring member of his band, the Blue Caps. "Yeah, I was with the Blue Caps for about forty days," recalls the drummer with a laugh. "Things got a little bit out of hand with that bunch. They were a little bit younger, and I never knew what them boys were going to do, y'know. Some of them guys were always getting into hot water for one thing or another. I was afraid that I was going to be thrown into the same pot. So, I got back to Dallas and I said, 'Gene, I think I just won't go back out with you anymore, if you don't mind. I've got other things to do.'"

Even though Vincent's band was populated with traffic-light drag racers and malevolent hotel-room wreckers, Fontana remembers the singer of such hits as "Be-Bop-a-Lula," "Lotta Lotta Lovin'," and "Dance to the Bop" as a great artist and showman. "He was the *nicest* guy in the world. He was drinkin' quite a bit back then, and he had that bad leg. [Mangled in a motorcycle accident, it would torture him the rest of his short life.] I think that had a lot to do with it. He just stayed in pain all the time. Sometimes you could see through his pants—that old nub was soaking wet with pus and one thing or another. He was sittin' on it, layin' on it, and he was a helluva showman. He'd throw that leg around like there was nothin' wrong with it. He had that metal brace on all the time. How he got around that good, I don't know. I don't understand it, but he was very good at it. I mean, he was *good*."

The drummer's respect for Vincent's talent didn't stop him from playing jokes on Capitol's answer to Elvis Presley. At every diner that he and the Blue-caps would stop at, Fontana made a beeline for the jukebox, where he'd punch

Mr. "Suzy Q" himself, Dale Hawkins. COURTESY OF DALE HAWKINS

up all the Presley songs. Fontana would then sit across from Vincent, and as the songs played, he would innocently remark, "Man, listen to those *drums.*"

That same year, 1958, Dale Hawkins (of "Suzy Q" fame) hired both Moore and Fontana to play on a particularly tasty version of Jimmy Reed's "Ain't That Lovin' You Baby." Hawkins's label's chief, Leonard Chess, seemed less tolerant of the guitarist's need to warm up than Presley had been. "That was a good time," Hawkins chuckles. "That was [when] Scotty and D.J., Dean and Mark [Mathis], myself, and Margaret Lewis came up. There was an LP put out in 1984, *The Chess Rockin' Rhythm Series.* If you listen to it, you'll hear Leonard cussing everybody out saying, 'Scotty, get them fuckin' butterfingers out of you, man.' He called D.J. a 'banana-nosed hooker.' And all we did was—man, we just stopped playing and gave him the finger [laughs]. And we wouldn't play no more until he left. That's how we did 'Ain't That Lovin' You Baby.' What Scotty did [to get that guitar sound] was, he tuned the third string from the top down to a D, which gave it that hollow-body, open sound."

Moore himself tried to stay busy during Presley's tour of duty. He did a three-week tour with Roy Orbison before the singer achieved national fame, then decided to try producing records for Slim Wallace's Fernwood label. Jack Clement reports that the idea to produce had probably been on Moore's mind since 1955. "Well, I'm the one who got 'em hooked up. I had been offered this job at Sun Records, and I had built this little studio in Slim's garage in my spare time while I was [belatedly] going to college. Scotty came along, and he was interested in learning that stuff—engineering and so on—so I hooked him up with Slim. In fact, I gave Scotty a book about recording techniques and stuff. So, he just sort of stepped into what I was doing really. They went on and built a new studio down on Main Street in Memphis."

Fernwood, named for the street the garage studio was on, was started by Wallace, a local truck driver/nightclub owner and part-time musician, with Clement in 1955. Fernwood's first artist was supposed to have been Billy Lee Riley, but when Clement took their initial disc to Sun for remastering, Sam Phillips heard it and offered both Clement and Riley a contract with his label. Scotty Moore casually knew Wallace through music distributor Bill Fitzgerald.

By the time Moore arrived in late 1958, Fernwood still hadn't progressed much beyond an idea. Local rockabilly Ramon Maupin's "No Chance" had sold a few copies locally, but the label wasn't really run as a serious business. Organized and determined, Moore changed that immediately. Made a partner and vice president, he began seeking out acts, booking studio time, assembling a regular studio band, and trying to make sense of the makeshift studio. "Slim had a few friends and neighbors of his that were coming over from Arkansas that he was trying to cut records on," chuckles Moore. "I think I went out and bought another microphone or two, or some other kind of equipment, and it was still kind of 'Raggedy Ann' put together." One has to wonder, if during this process, Wallace wasn't hoping that the guitarist could seek out and develop another Elvis Presley. "Slim didn't say," answers Jack Clement. "But if *I* wanted to find another Elvis Presley, Scotty would be the guy I would put in charge."

"I think Slim brought Scotty in there for his name and to keep the studio busy," says Joe Lee, who played piano and sax on many Fernwood sessions. "He did. As far as custom recordings go, we got a lot of those. People would come in and want a band to back 'em up, and we did a lot of that."

The first call Moore made was to Bill Black. With little money coming in, Moore, Black, and saxophonist Joe Lee formed a new group called The Scotty Moore Trio. The first and best thing they cut together was an instrumental titled "Have Guitar Will Travel," which was inspired by the popular Richard Boone western television series *Have Gun—Will Travel*. From the song's jump, Moore showed he had kept up with current musical trends by imitating and improving the sound of guitar-slinging teen sensation Duane Eddy. Opening and closing with a deep, comic voice announcing, "Have guitar, travel *any*time," he trades tasty riffs with Black on electric bass, while Fontana's cymbal-heavy shuffle drumming creates a distinctive, catchy dance beat. Hampered by poor distribution, "Have Guitar Will Travel" never really made it out of Memphis. Years later, when the whole Fernwood catalog was released on CD by Dave Travis's Stomper Time Records, the instrumental was hailed as one of the great lost hits.

The Scotty Moore Trio was a relatively short-lived proposition. Through Moore's contacts, they broke in the new act in some of the same Memphis clubs that they'd played together four years earlier. "We played some pretty raunchy places in those days," recalls the trio's sax player, Joe Lee. "They needed the money." When he was otherwise unoccupied, D. J. Fontana would play drums, and for dances or shows they would hire vocalist Gene Simmons (a former Sun artist who, in 1964, would enjoy a hit with "Haunted House"). Their stage act consisted of hits of the day (with Simmons occasionally singing one of Elvis Presley's tunes) and danceable instrumentals with a jazzier edge.

Regardless of the venue, Black continued cutting up whenever possible. "We did a show in New Orleans where the stage was built over Lake Pontchartrain," says Lee of the Scotty Moore Trio's best gig. "It was a big rock 'n' roll

Bill Black, Scotty Moore, and Joe Lee working at the Fernwood studio, 1959.
COURTESY OF JOE LEE

thing. We backed up the Big Bopper. He was a hoot. Nearly everyone on the show had a million seller. That was a good memory, because we stayed in a nice hotel in downtown New Orleans and had a lot of fun. Bill was always carrying on with the crowd. I don't care if it was a fancy restaurant we were eating in, he'd just stand up and say, 'I'm Bill Black and I used to play with Elvis Presley.' I'd just laugh myself sick and say, 'Sit down Bill, you're embarrassing me.'"

According to Lee, when people made the inevitable inquiries about Presley, Moore and Black were unfailingly polite, although Black enjoyed joking, "When we first started working with Elvis, we had no idea that we were making a monster." The line always got a laugh.

Billed as "Scotty & Bill (formerly Elvis Presley's band)," the trio even headlined a show at the *Louisiana Hayride*. "They had some good memories of that place," remembers Lee, who was referred to on the show's posters as "and others." The *Hayride*'s popularity had slipped considerably since Presley had performed his final show there in 1957. It was no longer a star-making vehicle, but Moore and Black put their best efforts forth for a surprisingly big crowd. "We pulled one of those vaudeville deals in Shreveport one time," laughs Lee. "Thomas [Wayne] was up onstage singing, and Bill started to hassle him. He slipped out into the audience—we'd do that every so often—he slipped out in the audience and started yelling up at the stage, 'Hey, I can do better than that!' So, we'd stop playing while they argued back and forth. It was all part of the show. On that gig, they had some security officers and they started coming over there to get him! He had to say, 'Hey, hey, this is part of our act.'"

The aforementioned Thomas Wayne would ultimately provide Moore with his biggest success on Fernwood. "I lived on Belle Avenue in Memphis," he explains. "Luther Perkins, who was Johnny Cash's guitar player, his brother Thomas Wayne Perkins lived only a couple of blocks over. Thomas was my paper boy. And he'd bring the paper by, and, in fact, if we were doing any rehearsing there or anything, at my house, he'd come in. In fact, he broke a glass on my coffee table one day. He sat down on it and he cracked it. But he was always there, wanted to sing. So finally, we took Thomas and cut a couple of sides on him. He had a good voice."

Immediately, Moore, Black, and Sun drummer J. M. Van Eaton helped Thomas Wayne forge a mini-rockabilly classic, "You're the One That Done It," backed with the teen rock-a-ballad "This Time." Initially issued on Fernwood, the company leased both sides to Mercury Records in March 1958. The pockets of airplay the disc received was encouraging, and the response to Wayne—who was no Elvis Presley onstage—was strong enough to raise hopes.

Moore picks up the story from there. "And then I met these two writers, Gerald Nelson and Fred Burch. They had this song, 'Tragedy.' They wanted to know if I had anybody that could cut it. I said, 'Well, you can try. Maybe you can cut a demo on it, or whatever, to see what we can do with it. It won't cost you anything,' 'cause it was just Bill and I that played on it. Thomas brought these three little girls from high school to sing on it."

Although more of a ballad than Sanford Clark's "The Fool" or Jody Reynolds's "Endless Sleep," Wayne's version of "Tragedy" achieves a true state of rockabilly noir. The poetic teen lament had previously been cut by the songwriters with their band the Escorts, and Moore used that version as a demo. But it was his production expertise that made the final disc unique. "We took it to the Hi Records studio. They had just bought a new mono-tech machine. We cut the song there and took it up to WMPS, because they had two machines, and we put the delays, the slap on the thing, 'cause that was the big thing back then."

The B-side, "Saturday Date" was beyond insipid. On that song, Nancy Reed, Sandra Brown, and Carol Moss (the De-Lons) carry much of the lyric between Joe Lee's sax turnarounds. It was the type of teen dreck that was fast edging rock 'n' roll off the national playlists. Yet, in one of those twists of fate that only happened in early rock 'n' roll, it was "Tragedy" that got noticed.

"It laid around for two or three months," remembers Moore. "All of a sudden there was a disc jockey up in Kentucky—Lexington, I think. He was doing an all-night record show, and he started playing 'Tragedy.' A promoter in Buffalo, New York, heard it and called after a couple of weeks to get some information on it. He said, 'You want to hire me as a promotion manager, I can make this thing a nationwide hit.'"

"Slim called us down there at the auditorium," says Lee. "He said, 'We've got an order out of Buffalo, New York, for thirty thousand records on that thing.' In those days, everybody was broke, and Slim asked, 'The main thing is: how are we going to pay for the pressing? I don't have that kind of money to pay for thirty thousand records.' Well, Scotty had met this distributor in Buffalo when he was with Elvis. We got back to the office the next day and I said, 'Why don't you just call him up and say, "We don't know you, and we don't have any kind of record of your credit. If you'll send us half of the bill, we'll go ahead and send you the records next week."' So, Slim did that. The man said, 'I'll do better than that. I'll send you the money for all thirty thousand if you'll send me sixty thousand.' So, he wired the money and we started pressing records."

"This was back in the days when, if you had a distributor," clarifies Moore, "if you could get him to order a thousand records you were going to have to give him a hundred free. In those days, it was payola, but it wasn't payola. Just free goods rather than marking the price down."

To get the money they needed to press sixty thousand copies, Fernwood made promises to pressing plants (eventually Moore would write out checks totaling $250,000), brought in a local attorney as a partner, and set up a tour on the eastern seaboard, where the record first caught on. After appearing on Dick Clark's *American Bandstand,* "Tragedy" became a top-five pop hit, and it reached the R & B top twenty. Less than one year after his former singer had entered the army, Moore had proved he could fashion a dual-market hit with yet another artist.

Interestingly, Wayne, like Presley, was born in Mississippi and went to Humes High in Memphis. He was one of the many aspiring vocalists in the area who flat out knew that Moore and Black had shaped Elvis Presley's career.

Moore and Black skillfully guided the youngster through show dates, disc jockey interviews, and television appearances. The kid was loyal and eager, but their success was short lived. A classic one-hit wonder, Wayne would see his next two Fernwood singles flop. With no new hit records, the label was dying on the vine. "Never could get another [hit] on him at all," laments Moore. "Back in those days, there were so many different artists with one song. Thomas wasn't the most handsome guy in the world; I thought maybe that was part of it. We should not have let him do any TV. You know, who knows?"

Wayne's final shot at Fernwood came with "The Girl Next Door Went A'Walking," which he cowrote with singer/songwriter Bill Rice. Featuring Moore's trio as well as guitar hero-in-training Reggie Young, sax man Joe Lee, pianist Carl McVoy, and a vocal group that sounds suspiciously like the Jordanaires, the song was an obvious Elvis Presley knockoff. Unfortunately for Wayne, by the time the tune was released, in 1960, Presley had been honorably discharged from the army, and all the Elvis wannabes that had sprung up during his absence were out of business.

After he rejoined Presley, Moore managed to persuade the returning rocker to record "The Girl Next Door Went A'Walking." Heard on the excellent *Elvis Is Back* LP, it is a note-for-note remake of Wayne's original, but it sports a far more exciting vocal. Wayne, meanwhile, hung in there for a while, cutting sides for Capehart, Phillips International (the Sun subsidiary), and Santo record labels without success. In 1961 "Tragedy" was remade into a top-ten hit by the boy-girl group the Fleetwoods, and Wayne's original version was soon forgotten. Wayne's final days in the music business would be spent working as a technician for Moore on projects with soul singer Joe Simon and former Beatle Ringo Starr. Wayne died in a car accident in 1971.

From 1958 to 1960, in the course of just two years, Fernwood went from being a nothing company to a budding major independent label and back to nothing. This wasn't Moore's fault. He had actually accomplished quite a lot with the studio end of the business. Not only had he christened the new Fernwood studio on Main Street, but the guitarist/producer had also recorded some promising talent that would make waves in the future, most notably sax star Ace Cannon, teenage guitar whiz Travis Wammick, and the nucleus of what would become the Bill Black Combo. Ultimately it was Slim Wallace's lack of cash, connections, and vision that doomed the little label. Fernwood ended its days leasing masters to other labels and making vanity recordings for people who walked in off the street.

However, Sam Phillips was impressed enough with Moore's work at Fernwood to offer him steady work as a producer at his new studio at 639 Madison Avenue. Prior to that offer, Presley had returned and needed a band to play on both his new album and the upcoming *Frank Sinatra Timex Show: Welcome Home, Elvis.* In Moore's autobiography, *That's Alright, Elvis*, James Dickerson reports that the guitarist still believed in Presley and felt everything could work out between them. Presley also raised the guitarist's hopes by asking if Moore would consider going back on tour and, during slack times, run a studio inside Graceland. Neither venture would materialize.

During the 1950s, Frank Sinatra was notorious in his disparagement of rock 'n' roll, calling its singers "cretinous goons." Yet, when he wanted a boost for his low-rated series of Timex-sponsored specials, he sought out the king of the so-called cretinous goons, Elvis Presley, to make his first highly anticipated post-army guest appearance. Colonel Parker made Ol' Blue Eyes pay through the nose for his hypocrisy, too—$125,000 to be exact. Regardless of the record-high fee and Sinatra's concession to rock music's greatest icon, the booking was a mistake.

Originally broadcast on ABC in May 1960 (it is now available on DVD), the program was a flop in many ways, but mainly because it didn't make good use of Sinatra, his "Rat Pack," or Presley. After a lukewarm musical number, "It's Very Nice," which introduced the uniform-clad rocker with seriously undermiked vocals, the show quickly devolved into the usual variety crap. Two dance numbers (one depicting an Asian wedding; the other, a tribute to the Chipmunks) were flat-out time wasters. Further, as was evidenced by the lifeless sketches, the Rat Pack's fabled chemistry didn't translate well to the small screen (perhaps because Dean Martin wasn't there). Even Nancy Sinatra, not yet the tough-talking, go-go-boot-wearing hip chick she would become a few years later, presented boring, safe, middle-class entertainment.

Some moments do shine, though. One is Sinatra's solo rendition of "Witchcraft" (a number-six pop hit in 1958). Others feature Sammy Davis, Jr. (who basically stole the show) doing his celebrity impressions and offering a number from *Porgy and Bess*. And then there was Elvis Presley, the man around whom the television show supposedly centered. Looking awkward in his Vegas-style tux and singing his hastily recorded current hits "Fame and Fortune" and "Stuck on You," the Hillbilly Cat demonstrated professional chops and admirable self-mocking humor, but none of the cathartic abandon of his pre-army performances. In 1957 Ed Sullivan's cameramen had been instructed to film Presley only above the waist to keep from offending the Catholic League of Decency with the singer's trademark moves. In contrast, Sinatra's crew panned out to a wide shot during "Stuck on You," hoping (probably praying) that Presley would bust a wild move or two. But, except for a bit of a choreographed flourish during the song's bridge (to the sound of forced female screams), he did little more than snap his fingers and bounce on his heels in time to the music.

Worse, in a duet spot that featured Sinatra crooning "Love Me Tender" and Presley offering his rendition of "Witchcraft," the older vocalist effortlessly outsang the rocker, who couldn't hit his low notes. *Welcome Home, Elvis* wasn't a complete embarrassment for the singer but it is a textbook example of how poor showcasing can hamper even the most talented of performers.

Sinatra was, of course, thrilled over the substantial boost in his Nielsen ratings, but he didn't make time to hang with Presley and the band. "Frank was . . . you can't get too close to those guys," Fontana explains. "See, he had to do the whole show. He produced it; he did just about all of it. So he was busy. He'd wave at you, or something like that. That would be about it."

The lame showing, the fabled Sinatra coolness, the pressure from RCA to get things back into high gear; in the great scheme of things none of it mattered. Elvis Presley was back home, and for the time being, Fontana and Moore—along with bassist Bob Moore, pianist Floyd Cramer, and the Jordanaires—were back with him. The only person missing from the reunion was Bill Black, who had gone on to better things.

The Bill Black Combo

"I've done what I wanted to do because I love it. I love playing music. And I'll tell you one thing. You want to know why these people are drunks? You want to know why they're on dope? It's because they're talented, but they don't have the love for it. You've got to love it, because it will take you away from your family. It will take away from the things that you care about."

—Bill Black to his son, Louis

IT WAS THE biggest news story in the entertainment world: Elvis Presley had returned home from the army. "Well, the first thing I have to do is cut some records," he told reporters. "Then, after that, I have the television show with Frank Sinatra. Then, after that, I have the picture for Mr. Wallis, and then I have two for Twentieth Century Fox."

By March of 1960, plans for Presley's career were going full-steam ahead, but first he had to hold court at a get-together thrown in his honor. Gordon Stoker remembers a particular guest from the singer's past in attendance.

"I never will forget when Elvis got out of the service. There was a big party up at Graceland for all of us. Bill Black was there. I don't know if he was invited or just came, but he was there anyway."

After Presley's official induction, things hadn't looked too bright for the former Blue Moon Boys. "Scotty lost his car because he didn't have the money to make the payments," recalls Stoker with disgust. "Are you kidding me? Was that fair?" Fontana had returned to playing small clubs when not freelancing with big-name acts such as Gene Vincent and Lefty Frizzell. Bill Black worked at an appliance store and did session work at Fernwood to keep his family fed, and he somehow managed to hang onto an old Studebaker, which he kept running by making repairs with his own two hands. He'd also formed his own band.

Now, here it was: 1960. Black's new group, the Bill Black Combo, had recorded two instrumentals, "Smokie, Part 2" and "White Silver Sands," that had scaled both the pop and R & B charts. At their peak, the band had guested on Dick Clark's *Saturday Night Beechnut Show*, and they had signed to appear in a movie that would beat Presley's first post-army film *G. I. Blues* into theaters. In order to keep him at the label, Hi Records founder Joe Cuoghi gave him a share of the profits and creative carte blanche. The previous week, Bill Black had become a star, and he hadn't needed a controlling, blowhard manager, or found it necessary to break his word to a friend, to become one.

Everyone at the party knew about the conflicts between Presley and Black. Doubtless, some were holding their breath, believing that something ugly was about to occur. Stoker picks up the story. "Well, the Bill Black Combo had two records in the top ten at that time. Then, somebody said in front of Elvis, 'Hey Bill! Good grief. I see that the Bill Black Combo has two big hits in the top ten.'

"And Elvis said, 'Yeah man, mumble mumble mumble.' Or something like that.

"So, Bill stuck his thumbs under his armpits, grinned, and said to Elvis, 'Yeah Elvis, I always *wanted* to help you, but you wouldn't let me.'

"Under his breath Elvis said, 'Yes, yes, son of a mumble mumble.'"

Most onlookers laughed. Stoker knows he did. It was a perfectly played piece of situational comedy. "Of course," continues Stoker, "Elvis was extremely jealous that Bill Black had that success, when he should have been happy for him."

Black didn't come to the party to rub his triumphs in Presley's face. (That was just a happy by-product of showing up.) The bass player actually intended to offer belated condolences over the death of the singer's mother. The madhouse that was Graceland in the days leading up to Gladys Presley's funeral had kept him from calling or visiting in person. The former partners leaned their heads in and spoke quietly for a moment, then Black left without further incident. It was probably the last time Bill Black and Elvis Presley saw each other face-to-face.

There was some talk that Black would return to Presley's backing band, but it was only talk. "All of a sudden, he came out with that Bill Black Combo, and that's all he needed," admires D. J. Fontana. "He didn't need to work for anybody else."

By now a savvy music veteran, Black knew he would never pose a serious commercial threat to Elvis Presley. That wasn't the point at all. Often described as the "boisterous clown" of the group, Black proved to be the smartest of the Blue Moon Boys. Once it had been determined that he and Moore would never be anything more to Elvis, professionally speaking, than no-profit-sharing servants who were given little or no credit, he left Presley's organization and started his own. Further, his antiauthoritarian streak prevented naysayers and fat cats from snuffing out his dreams of becoming a performer in his own right. His son, Louis Black, said it best: "You could never get anywhere telling Daddy that he couldn't do something."

Black's first hits had provided the perfect "I told you so" to both the egocentric manager and "snotty-nosed kid" who had undervalued him. Soon, records by the Bill Black Combo would be on nearly as many jukeboxes as records by Presley, and the bass-playing bandleader had no reason to think that would change anytime soon.

But then, the headaches started.

Unbeknownst to most Presley insiders, Black had foreseen going out on his own as early as 1957, when the disgruntled bassist had considered starting a band with Glen Glenn. "When Bill quit Elvis," explains Glenn, "his first idea was to start a group, with me as the singer, called the Continentals."

Glenn, a favorite of the modern-day rockabilly crowd, had cut a few truly fine sides with guitarist Gary Lambert, including "One Cup of Coffee" and "Everybody's Movin'." But, by the time Black proposed the Continentals idea, those records had already come and gone without a trace. (Today they are considered genre classics.) It would have been a fine opportunity for the Missouri-born cousin of Porter Wagoner to join forces with Black and begin the next stage in his career.

"If I hadn't gone in the army, I would have probably been playing with Bill," agrees Glenn, who remembers his last contact with the bass player. "I was already in the army, in basic training, and my dad called and said, 'Bill Black called me last night. He said he wanted to talk to you, but I told him you were drafted into the army.' Bill told him, 'I've got a record contract for him.' I was already with Era, but Bill was determined to get me on records.

Bill Black and rockabilly cult hero Glen Glenn, 1957.
COURTESY OF GLEN GLENN

But he told my dad, 'I'm leaving to go back to Memphis. Tell Glen I'll see him later.' But I never saw him again."

Had it not been for his love of music, Black actually might have lived out his life running Able Appliance. Asked why her father got into the appliance business, Nancy Black-Shockley replies comically, "He was hungry." Most accounts say that the bass player was a pretty good salesman who enjoyed talking to customers. When the Fernwood money started coming in, even old pal Scotty Moore shopped there. "We were always close," says the quiet guitarist.

"When me and my wife moved, we bought all new kitchen stuff. We had one of his contractors come in and remodel it for us."

Indirectly, Moore was responsible for the Bill Black Combo sound. For Fernwood's sessions, he had hired some of the area's best up-and-coming musicians, including teenage guitarist Reggie Young, pianist Carl McVoy, sax master John "Ace" Cannon, and drummer Jerry "Satch" Arnold. Some, like saxophonist Martin Willis ("The finest musician I ever knew," says Roland Janes), had seasoned their recording chops over at Sun Records. The first session to bear Black's name as producer was for Bill Rice ("All Alone," "Let's Give Love a Chance"), and Black found it very easy to achieve a snappy groove in such accomplished company.

Joe Lee, who recorded at Fernwood as Joe Lee and His Sextet, dabbled as the label's A&R man and arranger when he wasn't playing gigs or running his own Alley Records label. He knew that Black had a definite vision for a simple, danceable instrumental sound. "Yeah. As a matter of fact, he had played some

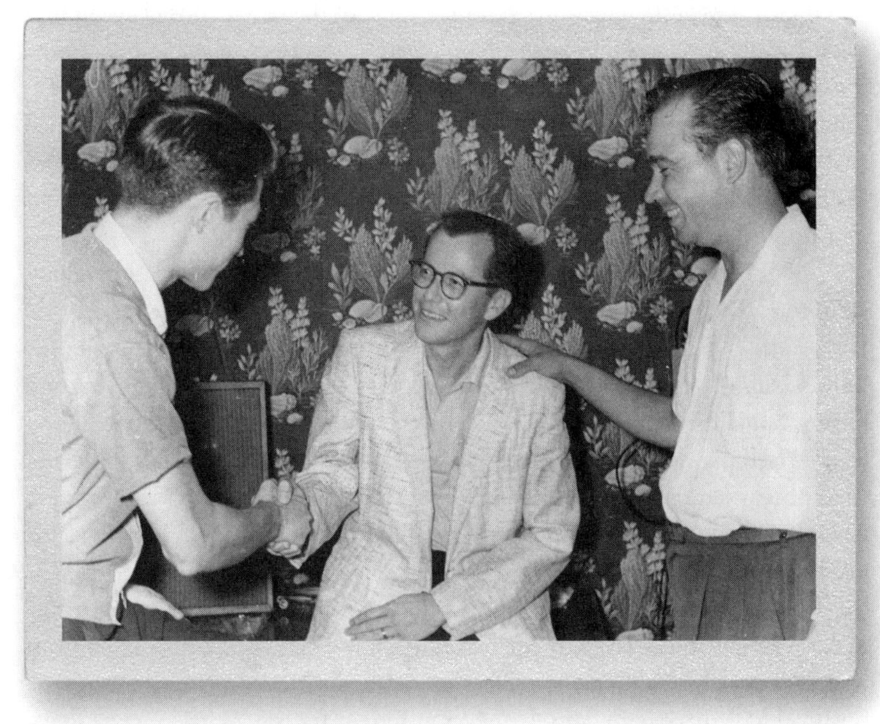

Scotty Moore, Joe Lee, and Bill Black, 1959. COURTESY OF JOE LEE

test recordings of some things for me," recalls Lee. "He said, 'You know those honky-tonk days, man?' I said, 'Yeah.' He said, 'Well, that's the sound I want. I want some honky-tonk music, man. Let's try our best to get *that* sound.'"

Lee's "Jo's Mix," which features Moore, Black, Fontana, Young, and McVoy, clearly anticipates the Combo style. Another Fernwood group, the Tarantulas, led by Bob Tucker, also contained some elements, particularly the single-note organ playing of Bobby Emmons, that would be adopted by Black after his move to Hi Records.

A trained musician with a degree from Memphis State, Tucker believed that Black was a master of the stand-up bass, but merely professional on the electric. "But he had a talent for recognizing the commercial viability of what he was doing," says Tucker, who also helped book the Combo. "In other words, he knew he had something, and he rode it all the way to the wall."

Although Black had been working up the sound at Fernwood, it was the owner of Hi Records who made the Combo a reality. Gene Simmons recalls: "Joe Cuoghi said to Bill, 'You know, they know you all over the country, and everybody likes you. Why don't you pick some of the better musicians around town and try and cut some instrumental stuff?'" As the owner of Poplar Tunes, the best-connected record-distribution outfit in the mid-south, when Cuoghi spoke, people listened. (It was on Cuoghi's advice that Sam Phillips stopped splitting his resources between Billy Lee Riley's "Red Hot" and Jerry Lee Lewis's "Great Balls of Fire" and put everything behind the latter. The gamble paid off beyond Phillips's greatest expectations.)

Despite his promotional savvy and his power as a distributor, Cuoghi hadn't been able to get many results with Hi (a friendly allusion to the term *hi-fi*). Formed in 1957, the label started with eight different partners: Cuoghi, his lawyer Nick Pesce, three friends who each invested five hundred dollars, and former Sun Records associates Bill Cantrell, Quinton Claunch, and Homer "Ray" Harris. (A former Sun artist, Harris's "Come on Little Mama" is the best "psychobilly" record of the 1950s.) Cuoghi displaced Cantrell as president when he bought up the outside investors' shares. Almost immediately, the label had a hit.

Ace Cannon chuckles as he remembers the circumstances. "Me and Ray Harris, Joe Cuoghi, and Carl McVoy and Johnny Bernero, a drummer, went to RCA in Nashville, picked up Chet Atkins, Ernie Newton, and we were cutting Carl McVoy's record 'You Are My Sunshine,' 'Tootsie,' 'Little John's Gone,' and 'Daydreaming.'"

McVoy, a cousin of Jerry Lee Lewis and Mickey Gilley, had transformed Jimmie Davis's "You Are My Sunshine" into a bright, mid-tempo rocker. It garnered plenty of airplay in the region, but a booking on Dick Clark's prime-time Saturday night show caused orders for the record to come flooding in, and Cuoghi didn't have the cash for more pressings. Caught in a typical independent label bind, he sold the master of "You Are My Sunshine," as well as McVoy's contract, to Sun Records for twenty-six hundred dollars. It was one of the few hit records that Sam Phillips actually purchased. McVoy went on to cut several more singles for Sun that stiffed.

By the time Bill Black came onto Cuoghi's personal radar, Hi Records had released sixteen flop singles in a row and was close to going out of business. One of the discs, Jay B. Lloyd's "I'm So Lonely" backed by "I'll Be Alright," featured backing by the then-unnamed Bill Black Combo. Presumably, Cuoghi made Black an offer during this session. It turned out to be a smart move.

Ray Harris, who engineered all the Combo's sessions, told *Rockville International* that "Smokie, Part 2" required "about two straight weeks of cutting on that song, which means three hours every evening." Black and company were trying to gel as a musical unit, but they were also looking for a something catchy to make part of their sound. It came when guitarist Reggie Young decided to break up the monotony with a little trick he'd developed.

"So Reggie Young came in one day," Harris explained to Dan Griffin, "and said, 'Ray, we're not getting anywhere this way. Let me play you something that I did today.' And he got a pencil and tuned his guitar down and started beating a rhythm. Bill picked up the bass, and they started. That's the way we got 'Smokie.'" Young's "pencil lick" (which nearly resulted in the band being called the Reggie Young Combo), combined with Black's bass and Hank Hankins's supplemental guitar rhythm, gave the tune a low, funky bottom that highlighted McVoy's piano trills and Willis's scorching alto-sax riffs. The tune was brilliantly simple and easy to dance to.

Other sessions, including the ones that produced "White Silver Sands," were executed more quickly, but in truth, all of them were hard. "I can remember when Bill Justis [whose instrumental hit "Raunchy," on the Sun label, predated the Combo's work] would come down and direct some of the sessions with us," explains Martin Willis. "I can remember doing take sixty-three. We would play these takes so many times that my jaws would give out and I couldn't play. Doing thirty or forty cuts on one tune was nothing. Imagine playing the same solo thirty times. Nowadays, they do one, maybe two or three, and then you are done."

Memphis sax legend Martin Willis, 1959. Courtesy of Martin Willis

Recording in a relatively technology-free era, the band had to improvise certain techniques as they went along. "I don't think a lot of people know this," informs Willis, "but the reason that our records sounded so great on the radio is because [the band] would plug the playback into a little, tiny, portable transistor radio and see what it sounded like. If it sounded good on that, that was the take they would use."

"We were just trying all kinds of different gimmicks," laughs Ace Cannon. "I've seen us cut records where Satch [Arnold] wasn't even using a set of drums. He'd play on an upside-down cardboard box. For an echo chamber they had a basement. You'd open the door and there would be no steps down to the basement or nuthin'. They'd have to lower you into the basement. I remember cutting a song called 'Sunday Blues.' I had to put taps on my shoes and walk down there on that concrete and act like I was somebody walking down the street and whistling. So, here I was pretending to be walking down the street while I was playing saxophone."

According to disc jockey George Klein, there was little doubt that Black's previous association with Elvis helped the Combo secure their initial radio play. "I think they got a lot of attention because he was Elvis's former bass player," states Klein. "Because there wasn't but three guys who could touch Elvis, and

Billboard's **"most-played instrumental group of 1962."** Courtesy of Martin Willis

that was Scotty, D.J., and Bill. So, here comes Bill with a real nice instrumental group. So yeah, the Elvis connection helped him out a whole lot." Of course, Joe Cuoghi put "formerly with Elvis Presley" on nearly every piece of promotional literature he issued. That said, if listeners hadn't enjoyed the Combo's offerings, the novelty of a Presley-related instrumental recording would have worn thin fast.

Released in 1959, "Smokie, Part 2" became a number-seventeen pop hit, but it hit number one on the black music charts. It was just as big with jukebox operators throughout the country. Their follow-up, "White Silver Sands" (which featured Bobby Emmons on organ), did even better, hitting number nine on the pop charts and number one on the black charts. Quickly, Hi had the group record an album and go out on to the road to promote it.

Unfortunately, Reggie Young, whose pencil thwacking on the guitar helped make the records so catchy, couldn't tour because he had been drafted. "I went into the service from 1960 to 1962," Young remembers. "I spent two years in Ethiopia while the band was touring all these great places."

As singer Gene Simmons remembers it, the Combo leader's connection to Presley didn't mean a thing to certain club owners. "Those first couple of years we were booked by the Show Artists Corporation of Chicago, and they didn't handle nothing but black groups. We played that year with the Ike and Tina Turner Revue in Regal theaters and South Chicago. Two or three shows a day, and we're the only white boys on the show."

At one gig, recalls Simmons, "Well, we went up there about three to four in the afternoon and started setting up on the bandstand. The owner of the club, who was a black guy, he came out and said, 'Shoot, now look-a here. I thought I told the man that I put in an order for the Bill Black Combo.' Just like he had ordered ham and eggs. Bill said, 'Well, I'm Bill Black and this is my Combo.' The club owner just shook his head. He would not believe it. Bill looked around and said, 'Man we'd better hit a medley of our songs, because this guy doesn't think we're the real deal.' They did a medley of 'Smokie' and 'White Silver Sands' and maybe one off the album, like 'Cherry Pink.' Then the owner came up, and these were his very words, he said, 'Go ahead on, motherfucker, you the Bill Black Combo, all right.'"

Part of this cultural confusion stemmed from the fact that pictures of the Combo's musicians were not featured on their early albums. According to Simmons, when the band requested that their pictures be put on future albums, Joe Cuoghi had a ready answer. "He said, 'You've got to think of it this way:

about 90 percent of your sales are coming from black people, and a lot of those stations still think you're a black group because the sound feels funky and black. What do you think would happen if they saw your picture on those records?' Bill laughed and said, 'Well, let's wait a while.' It was going too good." When pictures were finally featured, they were usually only of Black, which prevented Hi Records from having to explain the group's changing lineup. Some band members, like Carl McVoy, had day jobs that interfered with recording and touring. Others, like Martin Willis, were involved in several projects at once. Some were replaced because they couldn't take the grind of continual touring.

Sears department store had also given the Combo a boost when it decided to use their LPs to demonstrate the store's new stereo consoles. Another showcase for the group's recordings was a little more left-field. "That sound also came around at a time when striptease clubs were big all over the country," remembers Bob Tucker, who joined the band in 1963. "You could not go into a strip joint in America without a chick taking her clothes off to a Bill Black record. More women undressed to that shuffle than anything else. I mean, we're ahead of Johnny Mathis in getting chicks' clothes off of them. And I remember one time, we had cut a version of 'Harlem Nocturne' and some trade paper reviewed it. It mentioned the fact that strippers liked Bill Black music, and that this one was perfect for their act. 'So, all you strippers out there, put this one on and take 'em off.'"

Despite two big hit records and plenty of weekend bookings, Black continued to work at the appliance store for a while. Naturally, his band razzed him about it. Willis remembers saying, "Now, this is not a refrigerator, Bill; this is a bass. You can carry this one." On stage, the sax man recalls Black using the comedic bits he'd first employed during his days with Elvis Presley. "One of the favorite ones that he would do in front of a big audience, he would go to wipe his brow after we got through the tune, and he'd pull a huge pair of women's panties out of his pocket. He'd wipe his face with those and the audience would break up."

Black's willingness to give—and take—a joke was instrumental in keeping his crew happy. "He had a low-pressure approach to guiding a band," Willis points out. "He almost let the band do whatever they thought was necessary, but when it came time to make a decision he did that without any equivocation. I was his roommate on the road, and I guess I probably knew him as well as anybody. As far as a person is concerned, you couldn't ask for a better human being. He was just like a typical down-to-earth guy from Tennessee. He had to deal with a lot of high-pressure guys in New York, but he had a way of doing it. He had that experience and was always ready to jump in there and play."

The ability to keep his guys loose was much appreciated by the band's various members. If you watch closely, Black can be seen doing just that in the 1961 teen flick *The Teenage Millionaire*. Not much better than the Alan Freed movies of the 1950s, the film stars Jimmy Clanton as a bored millionaire orphan who wants to break free of his trustees, date a little, and sing a lot. Whenever he hears a song he likes by Jackie Wilson, Dion, Chubby Checker, Marv Johnson, Jack Larson, or Vicki Spencer, he imagines the respective artists performing it in "Fabulous Musicolor"—a process that tinted the film's normally black-and-white footage with various pastel shades of blue and red.

In the movie, the Combo can be seen miming (Black's electric bass isn't even plugged in) their hits "Smokie, Part 2" and "White Silver Sands." Except for Black, this was the band's first time in front of a movie camera, and they were scared stiff. By now an old pro at moviemaking, Black began talking to his band, trying to get them to relax. What exactly was he saying? "I can't repeat some of what he said," laughs Willis. "He would purposely try to break us up, and especially try to get me to laugh. You can't laugh and play a saxophone at the same time. He always picked on me, especially onstage. He'd come up and say something in my ear while I was playing and tried to get me to break up. Anyway, if you look at that film closely, you'll see that he's talking to all of us. He'd always pick on Emmons; he'd say something ugly about Emmons, and you can't tell unless you're a lip reader. So, he made the whole thing fun."

Later, on a live local television show, Willis would extract a measure of playful revenge. "We were pantomiming, and there is this part on 'Smokie' where the guitar plays and then I come in at the middle of the phrase. As a joke, I didn't do it. I didn't stick the saxophone in my mouth, and the saxophone was playing away [in the background]. Black wasn't paying attention, and when he finally noticed, he went nuts. Then I went to miming the sax again and said, 'Oh, are we supposed to play here now?'"

The Teenage Millionaire was a cheap-enough production to have probably turned a profit in the drive-in theaters where it played, but no one could truthfully say it was a good movie. At the same time, it helped to blow the band's cover with black record buyers—as did the group's appearance on *The Ed Sullivan Show* (where they performed a medley of "Don't Be Cruel," "Cherry Pink," and "Hearts of Stone"). But that exposure didn't seem to hinder overall sales of the band's records. In fact, the Combo was voted *Billboard*'s number-one instrumental group of 1961.

Another noteworthy trick in the Combo's bag was eighteen-year-old Bobby Emmons's use of a Chord-a-Vox piano attachment that provided a "roller-rink organ" sound. The sound is especially prominent on their version of "Don't Be Cruel." Black does his trademark aggressive bass line while Emmons plays the part Elvis Presley would have sung. The result was a number-eleven pop and a number-nine R & B hit.

The Chord-a-Vox was also the basis of some of the cheesiest-sounding records ever made. "I've heard it described as rock 'n' roll Muzak," confesses Bob Tucker. "That's not far from the truth, but it has a feel to it. I cannot tell you the number of accomplished musicians that I've hired throughout the years to fill a slot here and there who couldn't play it. It was just too damn simple for them."

As Ace Cannon recalls, the device was sometimes more trouble that it was worth. "One day we had trouble with it on a job that didn't amount to nuthin' the night before. We got in the motel room and Bill and Bobby worked on that Chord-a-Vox all day long to get it to work. Bill was mechanically minded. So, him and Bobby had that thing on the motel floor and they worked on it all day long. 'White Silver Sands' starts out with the keyboard. So it was important. Well, they got that keyboard working and we got on that show that night and when it came time to do that song, Bobby flipped on that Chord-a-Vox and tried to get those same notes and not a damned sound came out of it!

"Bill unstrapped that bass, threw it on the floor. It bounced three or four times and must have skidded about twenty-five feet across the stage! I don't know whether they thought it was in our act or what! Bill gave that little ol' smile that he always had and got over there and started working on that damned Chord-a-Vox right in the middle of that song. When it finally got to working, he strapped that bass back on, and it was out of tune from being thrown, and started playing again like nothin' had happened."

Although Black is revered by modern rockabillies for his efforts with Presley, those same aficionados blanch at his work with the Combo because it was often calculated and corny. Regardless, eight of their singles hit the pop top forty, and all of their albums charted respectably well. Just as important as fans were jukebox operators. It seemed they couldn't live without these danceable shuffles, and the bassist delivered them with assembly-line regularity. According to his son, Louis, whenever Black was working on a new song he kept in close touch with his old partner, Scotty Moore. "Scotty said that Daddy would record a song with this little group he had and he'd ask, 'What do you think about it? Do you think it's going to sell?' They'd kind of share ideas on it."

From the start, Cuoghi knew he couldn't pay Black as cheaply as he did other recording artists (approximately three cents a record) and expect to keep him on the label. So he struck a deal that gave the bass man a percentage of each record's profits and allowed him to set up his own publishing and subsidiary labels. In exchange, Hi Records got the first option on anything Black recorded. Willis guesses that Black's yearly take was around one hundred thousand dollars or more—good dough for that era.

However, according to his sax-playing roommate, this newfound affluence didn't change Black's basic tastes. "We were coming in from a tour one day and we stopped in West Memphis, Arkansas, to gas up at one of these little truck stops," chuckles Willis. "This is the guy who had five million-selling records in a row, and we stopped at a truck stop's dry goods section, he goes over to a shirt rack and starts taking shirts off of it. I think it was Hank Hankins who turned around and said, 'Here's a guy who's making a hundred thousand dollars a year, and he buys his shirts in a truck stop.' That broke us up for the rest of the tour."

Once the new deal with Hi was finalized, Black set up his own studio, along with a publishing imprint, which was named Lyn-Lou after his first daughter, Nancy (who Black nicknamed "Linda Lou"), and a record label, which was named Louis Records for his son, Louis. One of the hit-making entrepreneur's more successful outside ventures concerned a teenage songwriter named Billy Swan. A band he sometimes played with, Mirt Mirley & the Rhythm Steppers, drove from St. Louis to Memphis to record for Black. Swan was just along for the ride. "My friend Jimmy Boyer was the lead singer for them," recounts Swan. "So, we went into Satellite [Studios], and Chips Moman was the engineer, and they did one song called 'Little Miss Heartbreak.' That's the only one they had with 'em. Then Jimmy Boyer, who was standing against a wall drinking a Coke, said, 'Well, Swan writes songs.' So Bill said, 'Well, play me something.' So, I played him three, and 'Lover Please' was one of 'em. So, they did 'Lover Please.' The record came out on Louis Records."

Mirt Mirley & the Rhythm Steppers' version of the song didn't click, but Black liked the song well enough to rerecord it with another of Swan's friends, Dennis Turner. "That record started getting some action in St. Louis," explains Swan. "Shelby Singleton—he was head of Mercury at that time—wanted to lease the master from Bill and put it out on Smash. Bill didn't want to lease the master." Undeterred, Singleton had Clyde McPhatter record "Lover Please," and the song became the R & B pioneer's final top-ten pop single.

Many hardened music-industry pros would've sought to take advantage of a teenager with a hit song, but Swan calls Black "the fairest publisher I ever worked with." Martin Willis echoes that statement, adding that he was a fine employer as well. Did that mean he paid better than other bandleaders in the area? "We were so poorly paid by everybody," laughs Willis. "That's like saying, 'my leprosy is better than my cancer.' I would say yes, Bill would make sure that we were really taken care of, especially on the road. He paid us regularly, on time; you never had to worry about money when it came to Bill. He always made sure the session money was in. I was probably paid a better scale, and more promptly, by Bill than anybody else I worked with."

Black was also good about maneuvering around the schedules of his various players. Carl McVoy, who worked full time in construction, needed to stay close to his business. So Bobby Emmons was hired to fill in when McVoy could travel or make a session date. Willis, in particular, posed a problem. Besides his work with the Combo, the married-with-children sax man fronted two other bands—The Marty Willis Band and the Dixieland All-Stars—when he wasn't attending college classes. (Willis would eventually receive his PhD in hotel and restaurant management.) Once the Combo was going strong, Willis asked that he be excused from most out-of-state tours and shows. His road replacement, Ace Cannon, was a particularly apt choice; it was he who had inspired Willis to take up saxophone in the first place. Willis would continue on and off with the Combo until early 1965, but today most people remember Cannon as the band's saxophonist.

Willis says that perception doesn't cause any friction between the two. "We used to laugh about it. In fact, I still kid him about it. I say, 'I'll spot you three years and still blow you off the stage.' We actually went to the same junior high school in Memphis. I was a lot younger, but he and I are actually very great friends. There never was any jealousy or hurt feelings, because I play a totally different type of music. He played the, I guess you'd call it, barroom-type saxophone, and I played rock only when I had to. I was more of a schooled musician. I played a lot of jazz flute, and I played jazz clarinet in the Pete Fountain style."

Cannon, who, like Black, had been playing in bars since he was ten years old, enjoyed the mix of pop, country, blues, and rock that the band demanded of him. Cannon's sax can be heard on the Combo's hit renditions of "Don't Be Cruel" and "Josephine." His sax work is distinguishable from that of Willis's in two ways: Cannon honks with more passion on the rockers, and he exhibits the sensual tone of Syl Johnson on ballads. It is the latter quality that has kept him a perennial favorite with fans of mood music and romantic jazz for more than four decades.

At the time that Black hired him, Cannon had never been more than a couple of hundred miles outside of Memphis. "When I first started with him, he also rented my car from me," laughs Cannon. "He was giving me ten cents a mile and a salary. And I was making more with the car than I was the salary." The colorful sax player was quite close to Black. They had been friends and neighbors for years, and his association with the Combo would have lasted much longer if it hadn't been for his chronic drinking. "I just started too early with it," he admits. "Getting out there in the music business and playing places where I wasn't even supposed to be. I just got too early a start on it. Joe Cuoghi and Sam Phillips and all of them have said that there ain't no telling what I would have been if I hadn't drank."

When he did imbibe, the sax player did things he would be ashamed of later. "I used to do all those performances where I'd slide around on the dance floor with my knees," Cannon says of his drinking days. "People would gather around me in a jam session and yell, 'Go, Ace, Go.' Jumping off the bandstand used to be a part of my act. They used to put sawdust and things like that on the dance floor so you could slide. One time I was playing this place that put some sort of wax on the floor, and when I hit the floor, I fell over forward, and I thought the damned horn was fixing to come out the back of my head. And people didn't know if that was part of the act or if I was drunk. To the public, it was like, 'Hell, he plays better drunk than he does sober.'

"Then it got to where I'd make fans mad. One time, they thought I hadn't done a show because I was asleep in my van, and they set a fire underneath my truck. I was really inside the office sleeping on the couch—I wasn't able to play. But they were mad enough that I wasn't there that they would light a bunch of newspapers under the truck. They came to hear me, and by God, they were going to hear me.

"I remember a show out in El Monte, California. They had some group out there called The Masked Marvels, and I wanted to play with 'em onstage. I done got snockered before the job, and I went out on the bandstand while they were playing. It got to the point where security had to lead me off. They locked me up in a car or something in the parking lot. They might have locked me up for my own protection. Anyhow, I couldn't get out.

"Then me and Bill almost fought in Rapid City, South Dakota, and I wound up in the jail there." When asked if Black ever drank on the road, Cannon responds, "Yeah, but he didn't let it go to his head like I did. Me and Bill had lots of clashes over the booze. If both of us got drunk together, you did not want to be around us.

"It finally got where the people who were running the show at London Records [Hi's corporate partner] up in New York told 'em that they had to get rid of the horn player. I was messing up out on the road and everything else, drinking too much. I think they replaced me with Charles Chalmers." (Cannon didn't completely quit drinking until after a 1995 car accident nearly resulted in his foot being sheered off.)

Firing Cannon was tough for Black. Yet he still liked the hard-drinking sax player enough to provide him with a golden opportunity—a chance to make his first hit single. "What we did was take the old song 'Columbus Stockade Blues,' an old country thing that Jimmie Davis wrote a long time ago," explains Cannon. "Me and Johnny Bernero went in there and changed the format, slowed it down, and made a blues out of it called 'Cattywampus' at first."

Cannon and Bernero took the tune to Bill Justis at Sun, who was looking for a follow-up to his hit, "Raunchy." Justis's rendition of "Cattywampus" has more horns and is faster, but it doesn't compare to the version Cannon later cut, which he rechristened "Tuff" (as in "Man, that hot rod sure is *tuff stuff!*"). "They put it on Bill Black's label [Louis Records] first," says Cannon. "It was what they called a sleeper. It slept for about six months before it ever really done anything. Then one day somebody called me and said, 'Cannon, we've got a hit on our hands.' I said, "What do you mean?' 'Somebody in Mobile just opened up "Tuff." They're changing the call letters on their radio station to WTUF, and there's a big celebration down in Mobile and they want you there. The record is starting to make waves in a whole lot of other places.'" Distributed by Hi, "Tuff" hit number seventeen on the national pop charts and number three on the R & B chart. A smart, more aggressive adjunct to the Bill Black Combo sound, it put Cannon's career into high gear as jukebox operators all across the country clamored for the record.

Cannon would score a few more hit singles with Hi, but like Black, he would discover that his market was increasingly becoming album oriented. Black himself would move into theme albums such as *Bill Black's Combo Plays Tunes by Chuck Berry*, *Bill Black's Combo Goes Big Band*, *Bill Black's Combo Goes West*, and *Bill Black's Combo Plays the Blues.*

A Southerner In New York—

Black's Swinging For Twist

By RHEA TALLEY STEWART

NEW YORK, Dec. 9. — Bill Black and his combo, all from Memphis, were playing away for twist dancers on the bandstand of the New York night club, the Roundtable, in an incongruous setting of murals of King Arthur's Knights, when one of the boys exclaimed:

Mrs. Stewart

"Look, there is a girl doing the UT!"

The UT, Bill explained later for the benefit of those whose knowledge of Twist is not so esoteric, is a super-form of the twist, in which that frenetic dance is done in double-time. Whatever anyone has to say about Twist goes double for the UT. And those initials stand for University of Tennessee, where it originated.

Bill Black, Playing For Twisters

"We went around later asking various people where they were from, and sure enough, this girl called out, "I'm from Chattanooga!" Man, she was dancing like a maniac!"

Bill, who first achieved fame playing bass for a fellow-Memphian, Elvis Presley, is well-known in rock and roll circles. "Don't Be Cruel," "White Silver Sands" and "Josephine" are records of his that are by-words in the teenage set. The engagement at the Roundtable, which begain three weeks ago, is a landmark in his career, for this is a smart East Side place, with a sophisticated clientele. And Bill was hired for his knack with twist music.

"Oh, I've been playing twist for five or six years," says Bill, whose combo has traveled all over the country. "But those were always young people. It's one thing to see 17- and 18-year-old kids doing that, an another thing to see the people at the Roundtable, rich people in big fur hats, with chauffeurs waiting outside, people that have so much money you can't even think about it, older dignified people, to see them twisting."

Bill says, "Funny, all the requests we get for a slow number come from young people. The older ones are crazy about the twist. It has got so now that the only dance numbers you can play are the twist, the old-fashioned cha-cha, jitterbug and the

preciate a revealing dress on a shapely form, but they can observe in all their oddity the gyrations of the overly plump, the awkward, the past-middle-age. "It sure is a way of getting rid of your inhibitions."

The boys in the combo, all from the Memphis area, are Hank Hankins on guitar, Jerry Arnold on drums, Martin Willis on saxaphone, and Bobby Emmons on piano. The vocalist is Gene Simmons, who comes from Tupelo, Miss. Bill himself plays the electric bass. "That's because other boys in the band do the other instruments better than I do. I started out on guitar."

These boys have made records on the Hi label (that's a subsidiary of London Records) which have sold about four-hundred-thousand copies in the past two years. The newest is an album called "Twist Her" . . . well, what else would it be called? . . . a rearrangement by Bill of various twist tunes with vocal settings. This will be the fifth album of the Bill Black Combo, which has made nine singles also. Theirs is the only instrumental group ever to have a record in the top 100 for a solid year; the record that scored this hit is called "Saxy Jazz."

"You know, those records sell in England, Africa, Australia . . . man, we're big in South

scraped your feet like you were mashing potatoes. We went to the British West Indies with a fellow who was billed as the Mashed Potato King of the World, and man, did they go crazy about him! Then there was a dance that I think would have caught on if it didn't have such an odd name. It was called the Slop."

"Oh, I've been playing the twist for five or six years," said Bill Black in a December 9, 1962, article in the Memphis *Commercial Appeal.* COURTESY OF MARTIN WILLIS

The Combo's final top-forty hit was 1962's "Twist Her," a fairly lively, sax-led rocker that was released at the height of the twist craze. "Oh, I've been playing twist for five or six years," Black told columnist Rhea Talley Stewart in a Memphis *Commercial Appeal* article that focused on a show in New York. "But those were always young people. It's one thing to see seventeen- and eighteen-year-old kids doing that, another thing to see people at the Roundtable, rich people in big fur hats, with chauffeurs waiting outside, people that have so much money you can't even think about it, older dignified people, to see them twisting." In the article, Black notes that all the requests for slower numbers came from young people, proudly states that his records sold well in England, Africa, Australia, and even South America.

It took a lot of hard work to make that happen.

According to Louis Black, his father, who would often run up phone bills in excess of fifteen hundred dollars, worked around the clock, but was still a good parent. "We didn't see a whole lot of Daddy, but when we did it was quality time." His sister Nancy concurs: "That's why I don't think we were aware that he was gone all the time, because when he was home, he spent time with us. He was not, 'Y'all leave me alone. I'm tired.' I remember sitting on his shoulders and combing his hair."

Black often took his son to the studio with him, where the bass player shared what he had learned about the personal art of record promotion. Says Louis, "Daddy told me, 'When I'm in a town, if I've got a little extra time, I make a point to see these DJs. I sit there and talk to 'em, and I would remember something about them from last time. Because when I left there last time, I would write something down from the conversation, like that their mother was sick or whatever happened in their family personally. So, when I come back and I've got a few minutes, I'll call one of 'em and just shoot the breeze with 'em. I'll say something like, "Hey, how about your daughter Mary? Is she doing OK now?"' He said, 'That makes people feel close to you.' 'Now,' he said, 'these records that you're mailing out? I'm going to ship these out to these people, and when they get it they'll say, "Oh man, there's ol' Bill Black. Yeah, I'll give him a spin here."'"

Shortly after the *Commercial Appeal* article had been published, Black decided to pull himself off the road and—in a move that would have made Col. Tom Parker envious—send out different versions of his Combo to different regions of the country simultaneously. (No one can authoritatively say how many version of the touring band existed at the same time. Ace Cannon says two, Martin Willis says two or three, and Bob Tucker believes as many as five separate units hit the road under the Combo name.) Black told Scotty Moore, "Nobody knows I'm the bass player. Nobody knows the difference." When fans who did know the difference would ask, "Where's Bill?" Bob Tucker or whoever was fronting the group that night would answer, "Bill couldn't make it tonight. He said to say hello and play this one for you."

"We would cut the records and they would go on the road," states Martin Willis. "The personnel in these groups changed from time to time. Bobby Tucker was put in an as a leader of one group. Anyway, we would cut these tunes, and these other groups would go out on the road and promote them."

Black didn't exactly retire from live performances. Martin Willis remembers playing local gigs with his old friend, and Billy Swan saw Black at a *Shower of Stars* live television show in 1964. Mainly, however, he wanted to stay home and concentrate on his business, his family, and his health.

As long as Martin Willis could remember, Bill Black had been taking headache powders—the kind that's poured into a glass of water and drunk. "He had this headache all the time and it would be really severe," Willis recalls. "I remember saying to myself, 'I wish somebody would *do* something.'" Despite the sometimes blinding pain, says Willis, Black never missed a show.

Initially, doctors thought Black was suffering from a sinus problem. Louis Black remembers the treatment. "They'd stick these things up his nose—they looked like long chopsticks with stuff on the end—and they'd run that thing halfway up in his head. I was in there and I couldn't hardly watch it. Then they'd take it out, and of course all that mess would drain out. He would feel better and then go home."

After sinus treatments and headache powders no longer did the trick, doctors determined that Black was suffering from a malignant brain tumor. "I know it wasn't until sometime in '64 that they began treating him seriously," reports Black's son. "Before then, they thought it was the sinuses. He had a bump behind his ear that never would heal right, and he asked his doctor about it one time, and his doctor told him that it was just some type of cyst, but it was OK." Later, they surmised that cyst was the start of the cancer.

Black was operated on twice. Each time his memory and motor skills were affected a little more drastically. He would repeat questions to the family they'd already answered and lose his temper unexpectedly with old friends. His daughter Nancy noticed a sadness in his eyes when he spoke. "He knew he was going to die," recalls his son. "Mama told me one day just as I got home from school, she said, 'You know what your daddy said today?' This was when he was sick at home. 'A funeral went by and he said, "That reminds me. I have to get all my stuff in order."'"

During this ordeal, Evelyn Black, in daughter Nancy's words, "still had to be mama." She tried to keep the younger kids' minds off their father's illness by playing games, cooking meals, and doing all the things mothers do, but it wasn't easy.

During the lengthy hospital stays, Black was visited regularly by Scotty Moore, D. J. Fontana, Ace Cannon, various other friends and family members, and writer James Cannon. Eventually his condition worsened, and there was talk of a third operation and even more brain-tissue removal. However, the doctor in charge—a friend of the family—advised against further surgical procedures. "I'm telling you that the best thing to do is let him go home now," the doctor told the Blacks, "because if you keep him here, they'll have to take out some more brain again, and each time it's going to be worse. Right now, the medicine is working on him. He's better off if you leave him alone and he'll just go into a deep sleep."

"And that's the way it was," adds Louis Black. "I sat up with him about four months off and on."

Bill Black died on October 21, 1965.

His funeral at the Bellevue Baptist Church—the biggest church in Memphis at that time—attracted, by Ace Cannon's estimate, "two or three thousand people at least." Even people who'd seen it coming were devastated by the loss. Bill Black was not even forty years old.

There is a popular misconception that Elvis Presley basically ignored his former bass player's illness and eventual death. It's not true. Bobbie Moore, who had reconciled with her husband at the time, remembers visiting Graceland with Scotty and D. J. Fontana, where they gave the concerned singer updates on Black's condition. Further, Louis Black clearly recalls Presley riding from Graceland alone on his motorcycle to comfort the family. "He didn't come to the funeral, but he came out to the house and saw us. He said, 'I'm not going to be there because your daddy's funeral and your husband's funeral will turn into a circus.' He said, 'I wouldn't do that to him.' He told us then before he left, 'If there's ever anything that y'all need, you just let me know and it's yours.' That's what he said."

Presley was always kind to the Black kids, especially Louis, who afterward would occasionally drop in at Graceland. "Every time I was out that way, I'd stop and his uncle Vester Presley would call him down. He only told me one time not to come up. He said, 'You don't want to come up here today. I've got some of these Hollywood cats up here and you don't want to be up amongst this stuff.'"

The Black children didn't know that their dad was special because he'd been in show business, had helped Elvis Presley, and had made hit records. "Being as young as we were—and I don't want to say that we were in diapers or anything—but now it seems like it affects me more," says Nancy Black-Schockley. "He was always 'Daddy.' He never was 'Bill Black' to me. I wish I had been more in awe of who he was out in the world."

"I really wish that I could have had him a lot longer," agrees Louis. "I would like to have had time to really spend with him, and time enough to brag on him a little bit so he'd know I was proud of him."

With Black's death, his musical legacy began to slip through the cracks of history. Evelyn Black would remarry approximately a year and a half later. To keep peace in the new family setting, Evelyn discouraged her kids from asking too many questions about their late father. It wasn't until after her death in 2003 that Louis and Nancy—the children who are old enough to remember life with "Daddy"—felt right about speaking publicly about him.

They still receive royalties from the reissues of the Bill Black Combo material, but more than monetary gain, they'd like to see their father's contributions honored. "I want Daddy in the Hall of Fame," says Louis Black. "Because [Scotty and Bill] did have a lot of influence on the way Elvis did, whether anybody wants to believe it or not. Because I've heard that from more than one person that was there. I'm not taking anything from Elvis at all—that was a happening—but a lot of behind-the-scenes things went into it."

From the author's viewpoint, there is no question that Bill Black belongs in the Rock 'n' Roll Hall of Fame. If Paul McCartney can be inducted three times—as a Beatle, a member of Wings, and a solo artist—then his most prominent predecessor should be inducted twice: once as Presley's sideman, and second for his hits with the Bill Black Combo.

After Black's death, Bob Tucker and Larry Rogers revived the Combo concept. Called the Bill Black Combo during Black's life, Tucker's group paid homage to their fallen leader by calling their version Bill Black's Combo. Around the time of her remarriage, Black's widow sold Tucker and Rogers both the right to use the name "Bill Black's Combo" and the Lyn-Lou Studios for seven thousand dollars.(Louis Black still owns the band's original name, the Bill Black

Combo.) At the time, it was probably a fair deal. Unfortunately, with the studio went their dad's original stand-up bass, the one he'd played with Elvis Presley. (As a side note, when Black started the Combo he phoned Tillman Franks and said, "Tillman, I'm leaving the entire stand-up bass field to you.") Afterward, the instrument fell into disuse.

It's important to note that when Black passed away in 1965, his family had no inventory of his belongings at Lyn-Lou studios. Black kept few records of any transactions, and it was difficult for the family to know about any deals Black had made with people before he fell ill. As a result, friends and associates parted with precious items, including the upright bass that was his pride and joy. Through Bob Tucker, that acoustic bass ended up in the hands of Nashville entrepreneur and publishing magnate Buddy Killen, who sold it to Paul McCartney's wife Linda in 1974. Black's family got nothing. It is the dearest wish of Black's children to see that bass again. It is a touchstone of their early lives.

Employing different personnel, Rogers and Tucker kept their various line-ups of Bill Black's Combo on the road, working primarily weekends, and they took the group to Columbia Records. There, the band changed its style to country, and it went on to win *Billboard*'s Country Instrumental Group of the Year in 1976. They recorded briefly for Mega Records before returning to Hi in the hopes that they'd catch lightning in a bottle a second time. It didn't work. "The times were changing," comments Ace Cannon, who also returned to Hi late in his career. "[Producer and late-sixties label partner] Willie Mitchell took over Al Green and he just did so well with it." Green's massive success placed Hi's commercial focus strictly on soul and urban R & B. In this new musical milieu, the Combo's easy listening variations of jazz and rock seemed embarrassingly campy.

The ironic part of Black's saga is that most of his Combo musicians went to work for producer Chips Moman, who would use them on Elvis Presley's best latter-day studio album, *From Elvis in Memphis*.

Many lament the fact that Black didn't live long enough to give his viewpoints on Presley's rise and the breakup of the Blue Moon Boys. If they expected fireworks or juicy gossip from the bass player, they would have been disappointed. "Bill was no rumor monger," points out Martin Willis, who adds that most of his late boss's Elvis stories were not only humorous in nature, but featured himself as the butt of the joke. Ace Cannon agrees, adding, "Bill had too much going on himself to worry about what Elvis was doing."

Further, Black's success had wiped away any residual anger from the old days. "I'm sure there was a certain amount of creative friction, because our daddy had his own mind, and his own music in his own head," speculates Nancy Black-Shockley. "There may have been some of that, but once he got on his own and his own combo was going, I don't think he would have said anything bad about any of them."

Louis Black agrees. "I don't think he would have said anything to hurt the image of Elvis in any way. I just don't think that he would, no matter what. I can still remember when Elvis would come out to the house, on Christmas or whatever, and bring Daddy a present of some type. They were always like two buddies that hadn't seen each other for a while."

Bill Black did say something that perfectly summed up how he felt about his days with Elvis Presley. It comes via Billy Swan. "I went to his house once when we were in Memphis," Swan recalls fondly, "I vividly remember walking into this room, and there was a 78 rpm Sun Record on the wall in a frame. It was 'Mystery Train.' I just remember him pointing and saying, 'Now *there* was a record.'"

Fading into the Shadows

Elvis Presley's army discharge should have signaled a return to a busy touring schedule for Moore and Fontana. Yet, despite a few live shows for charitable events in Hawaii and at Ellis Auditorium, most of their work was in the studio. The first order of business was fresh recordings. "Stuck on You," which was backed by the excellent honky-boogie of "A Mess of Blues," shipped two million singles, but only 1.4 million sold. That was great for anyone besides Elvis Presley, who was enjoying one of the biggest storms of positive publicity in his life.

RCA reasoned that Presley's post-army sales were down 25 percent because his audience had begun to change. Many of the teenagers who dug him the utmost in 1958 were now in college digging folk music or working a day job in 1960. Perhaps that's why the faux–Mario Lanza approach to "It's Now or Never," which appealed as much to adults as to teens, scored so heavily on the *Billboard* pop charts (it held the number-one spot for five weeks). The rocker's voice had not only stayed in good shape during his army stint (home recordings from that period show him practicing diligently), but it had also developed an adult tone, emotional depth, and nuance. This newfound vocal maturity was vibrantly on display during the singer's first marathon sessions in Nashville.

Moore, who no longer tackled lead guitar or song arrangements, was among the first musicians called, mainly because he and Presley thought alike in the studio. "Yeah, we always seemed to have the knack of knowing what each other was pretty much thinking," explains Moore. "Even after he got into the movie things, and a lot of things I didn't even play on, I would still be there, be the leader of the session. I guess it was just him knowing I was there, if we wanted to go back and do something simple, maybe that was it. It's hard to say. He wasn't doing it out of charity, I know that, 'cause I had a gig going in Nashville, with the studio and everything. But I still felt loyal—I guess hoping that more songs would come out like we'd done earlier."

Working with a studio group that included Moore, Fontana, bassist Bob Moore, pianist Floyd Cramer, drummer Buddy Harman, guitarist Hank Garland, sax master Boots Randolph, the Jordanaires, and Charlie Hodge, Presley made the best album of his early career. Covering all the stylistic bases, he transformed Peggy Lee's jazzy "Fever" into a panting R & B showpiece. Clyde McPhatter and the Drifters' "Such a Night" exhibits Johnnie Ray's girl-teasing salaciousness. 1950s doo-wop got a nod with such rock-a-ballads as "Soldier Boy," and "Thrill of Your Love." The album even features a German folk tone (courtesy of Hodge's harmony) on the soldier ballad "I Will Be Home Again."

Better still are the blues rockers. "Dirty, Dirty Feeling" and "It Feels So Right" feature Garland's hard-twanging, quasi–Scotty Moore guitar leads, and the mixture of begging and arrogance imbued in "Like a Baby," make for some wonderfully salacious moments. Yet the clear highlight is Presley's remake of Lowell Fulson's "Reconsider Baby." Basically a late-night blues jam, the song is remarkable in that every instrumental element works, from Cramer's high note runs and Harman's swing to Moore's acoustic strumming and Garland's tasteful electric riffs. The true standout element, though, is the wailing, jazz-fed sax solos of Boots Randolph, who quickly became a regular at the rocker's Nashville sessions.

"He did that 'Reconsider Baby,' and I don't believe anyone played a saxophone solo on one of Elvis's records but me," Randolph told the authors. "Elvis liked what I did and I think he would have liked to have put me on more of his stuff, but somehow it didn't always fit, and that's a feature spot."

In the twist era of teen pop, slick musicianship and packaging were more important than raw, elemental playing. As a result, the saxophone made the jump from an R & B staple to a pop music solo instrument with ease. When he wasn't cutting his own enormously popular albums, Randolph was playing an integral role in the creation of Presley's early-to-mid-1960s sound, providing both supporting rhythm and driving leads. He had already done similar work on such Brenda Lee hits as "Sweet Nothin's," "That's All You Gotta Do," and the perennial seasonal favorite "Rockin' Around the Christmas Tree."

Randolph, whose "Yakety Sax" was a 1963 smash, found Moore and Fontana friendly but wary. "I met Scotty and D.J. on the first Elvis session in Nashville, at RCA Studio A, I believe. From that point on, I liked 'em. They were friendly guys. They made me welcome there. They were a little bit shy of the sax, I think. But they had all been friends of Bill Black, and Ace Cannon was part of his group down in Memphis, and I think they accepted the sax as being a part of rock 'n' roll. So, I think that maybe Elvis tended to go that way because of the major sound of what was happening.

"They knew I was versatile with the different sounds, and I got to be the guy they would hire to put on the sessions, but sometimes I'd record only one song all night. They knew that sooner or later he'd run into something that he'd like to put the sax on. That was true in that one particular case ['Reconsider Baby']. I played background and baritone sax on a lot of his stuff. It wasn't always real dominant. 'Return to Sender' was one of the biggest things I played baritone sax on. I did it on some other things, like the soundtracks that we did for the movies. I think I was on about eight or ten different movie soundtracks."

Randolph doesn't remember Moore or Fontana giving him any particular advice about playing with Presley. "I think they felt I should just contribute whatever I could to those particular recordings, and if I felt like playing something, then I should go ahead and play it. Then, if they didn't like, they'd tell you. That's how the Nashville sound was developed. They left everybody alone and each guy had his own position."

Studio work led to Randolph being given a guest spot on the last live show Presley would do for eight years, the March 25, 1961, benefit for the USS *Arizona* Memorial Fund. "That was really exciting," grins Randolph. "That was one of the highlights of my career. We went over to Hawaii and raised money for the *Arizona* Memorial. Of course, I had never been in anything like that before. You had fifteen thousand screaming kids, and he had a charisma about him that was just spooky. You couldn't explain it; it was just there. I wasn't a part of that very long. I only did a couple of those things. But Elvis then started doing a lot of movies, so he wasn't doing a lot of personal appearances. Then, when he got into the Las Vegas thing, well, after that I never got involved with him very much."

The live show—which was released in 1980 on RCA as the limited-edition boxed set *Elvis Aron Presley: 25th Anniversary*—was a solid screamfest for fans and demonstrated Presley's sparkling chemistry with his new band line-up featuring Randolph. It also featured rousing live renditions of "Such a Night" and "Reconsider Baby," and it ended with a six-minute version of "Hound Dog."

Despite the confidence Presley displayed in performing the newer material in concert, the much-hyped studio LP these songs were drawn from, *Elvis Is Back*, was a relative failure. One of Presley's finest blues-drenched achievements, its initial run sold around two hundred thousand copies. In contrast, the mediocre soundtrack to *Blue Hawaii* (which features the romantic ballad "Can't Help Falling in Love") became his biggest-selling album of all time.

Part of the failure of *Elvis Is Back!* stemmed from the fact that Tom Parker wanted Elvis's single recordings and regular LP releases to be distinctly different. Figuring that fans might not buy a single if the song was also on an album, Parker issued the edict that no singles be immediately released from *Elvis Is Back!* The strategy had worked with Presley's first two non-movie-related albums, but it didn't this time.

Another problem was Presley's fan base. History has not been kind to the string of soundtracks the singer recorded after his stint in the army. Most of these soundtracks contain only one or two good songs; the rest is throwaway material. However, the early 1960s soundtracks were monumental sellers in a way that the far superior *Elvis Is Back!* was not. Conclusion? Elvis Presley's recorded output was only as good as his most rabid fans would allow. Early on, Presley's loyal fans would buy anything he released. Had they been choosier about the purchases of the soundtrack albums, it's likely that Parker and RCA would have insisted on better material recorded in a less rushed fashion.

Initially, Presley and his crew cut some great singles between movie soundtrack sessions, most notably "(Marie's the Name) His Latest Flame" (for which bassist Bob Moore created the rhythm hook), "Little Sister," and "(You're the) Devil in Disguise." After a while, RCA was begging Parker to get his boy back in the studio to cut some fresh material for the singles market, but the canny manager wouldn't do it. Subsequently, the label began to fill the void with material from their vaults, such as an incendiary version of Chuck Willis's "I Feel So Bad," "Such a Night," and the spliced-together 1958 remake of Jimmy Reed's "Ain't That Loving You Baby."

Fontana says that Presley knew from the start that the movie contracts were going to compromise his music. "It just got from bad to worse," the drummer recalls. "The songs got so bad, and Elvis knew that. But the contracts were signed, and the Colonel said, 'Don't make any waves. Just do the best you can.' And Elvis would tell us, 'You know, guys, the songs are not the greatest, but we're going in and we're going to do the best we can with what we've got to work with.' He never would fluff the songs off or just try and get through 'em; he did his best."

Scotty Moore concurs, adding, "The only time that Elvis really wasted time was when he got into the movies and he would [need to] deliberately just get psyched up to do the material. And I will say once he got psyched up, he would do the stuff and do it the best he could, really. But he didn't want to."

The remaining Blue Moon Boys no longer enjoyed anything about the moviemaking process "It's really no fun, not no fun at all," remembers Fontana. "You sit around all day and then shoot thirty seconds and stuff. Get up at five in the morning and all that. We said [to Elvis], 'We'll go home and we'll do the soundtracks.' He said, 'OK, I'll call you for the next one.'"

Years later, Fontana told Dan Griffin that the filming of *G. I. Blues* was the final straw for the two musicians. For the German beer garden scene in which Presley sings "Blue Suede Shoes," Moore and Fontana were presented with their costumes—green lederhosen with Alpine caps. The duo took one look at the corny garb and promptly demurred.

Neither man fit in with the scheme of the movie soundtracks, either. They were both play-by-ear men who used head arrangements and worked with Presley's suggestions and whims until they all found something they liked. In Hollywood, the expense of motion pictures demanded that every moment be charted, arranged, played with precision, and executed as quickly as possible.

Many of Presley's 1960s soundtracks feature the talents of guitarist/arranger Billy Strange. Boasting one of the most impressive resumes of his era, Strange scored films, arranged hits for Nancy Sinatra, recorded (uncredited) as part of the Ventures when founding members Nokie Edwards and Bob Bagle went in the army, and wrote hit songs with Mac Davis. He began playing guitar on Presley's movie sessions with 1962's *It Happened at the World's Fair.*

As a guitarist of the first rank himself, Strange felt that Moore had "always done wonderful stuff for Elvis." That said, he was never asked by anyone connected with the films to replicate Moore's original rock 'n' roll sound. Further, the movies did not allow Presley to work in his accustomed manner. "It was just the same as any other movie. You score according to what the producer and director wish. They pick the spots that they want music in. You discuss then what kind of music they want—whether they want brass, or a rock 'n' roll rhythm section feel, or whatever it is. Then, most of the time, you never see them again. They sometimes come to the recording sessions, but very seldom. And they very seldom ever made changes once the decisions were made to put music in a given area of the film. The one place where Elvis did have say-so was the songs that were cut. You scored around him, naturally. You did whatever Elvis or the movie called for to display his wares in the best fashion possible. You arranged around that."

Although Moore and Fontana played on several soundtrack sessions, Strange never personally worked with them. "Well generally, we worked with what is now known as the Wrecking Crew: Hal Blaine, Carol Kaye, Larry Knechtal, Glen Campbell, Don Randi, or another piano player, depending on what the project was." When asked if Presley's men might have played on demos from which the movie-studio groups worked, Strange answers, "Yes, we worked from that, but we did not work from prerecorded tracks that anybody did. In other words, we did everything live in our recordings."

According to Strange, it was likely that Elvis Presley was looking for a different sound. "Well, you must remember Elvis had always recorded in Nashville or Memphis, Tennessee, with the same crew of people since the beginning. When he came to California, those people weren't here, and I think it was a conscious decision on his part to use and facilitate something in the California style of moviemaking and record making that did not exist in Tennessee."

Further, Strange, who now lives in Nashville, opines that the recording cultures of the two areas were distinctly different. "Because of the kind of work that the California musicians were called upon to do, you had to read music," he explains. "Tennessee was a different animal entirely. Here they finally got around to what they call reading the number charts. Now, you'll find that there are a great number of California musicians living here because the record industry is very good here."

Of course, James Burton, Glen Campbell, and "a lot of other young guitar players at that time" didn't read music, either, but they were experienced enough with charts and the Los Angeles studio setup to deliver whatever a session needed. Did Campbell, who played on the *Viva Las Vegas* sessions, know that Presley wasn't happy with his soundtrack material? "Oh, yeah," Campbell says, adding a whistle to his response. "Well, he liked the song ["Viva Las Vegas"] OK, but the other songs in the movies he thought were very mediocre. Parker was probably getting a kickback from the guys who wrote it and everything. It wouldn't surprise me. I had the same thing happen to me. To get Glen, you'd have to slip a couple of hundred on the side to my manager. Agents—they did that a lot back then."

Strange concurs. "I think that became the Colonel's forte. In other words, he made deals. He also made deals with songwriters and publishers on an awful lot of material that Elvis recorded and did in films. He wanted them all assigned to Elvis Presley Music or Gladys Music."

For his part, Parker never interfered with the execution of Strange's job, made suggestions about the music, or personally approached him about signing away the rights to his songs, which include "Clean Up Your Own Backyard," "Memories," and "A Little Less Conversation" (the latter would be remixed into a surprise international hit in 2004). The manager left the high-pressure tactics up to music publisher Freddie Bienstock.

"Well, that was the case for years," recalls Strange. "When we used to cut things for Elvis, Freddie used to send my songwriting contract back so the credits read it was by me, Mac Davis, and Elvis Presley, and all I would do was take a black marking pencil and scratch through everything he wrote in it except the title and my name. I wasn't about to give everything away to Freddie Bienstock."

Asked if anyone at the movie studios confronted Parker about his method of doing business or handling of Presley's career, Strange chuckles in disbelief. "You've got to be kidding. No, nobody talked about *anything* the Colonel did. At the time, he was a second God. He was the big dog."

While Presley was spending eight to nine months a year making movies, the former Blue Moon Boys were raising families. Fontana and his girlfriend Barbara married and had two sons, David and Jeff. Moore's second wife, Bobbie, gave birth to their daughter, Andrea. Both men were looking to make a living any way they could. In Moore's case, he had a steady (albeit unspectacular) wage coming from Sam Phillips, who had expanded operations from his new Memphis studio at 639 Madison Avenue, to a second studio on 7th Street in Nashville. "I went by one day just to see his new studio and say hello," Moore remembers, "and lo and behold, he made me an offer I couldn't refuse. I left Fernwood, went to work with Sam at the new studio as production manager, and it was just shortly after that he came to Nashville and bought out a studio that Bill Sherrill was involved in. And then he remodeled this whole, huge Masonic building. It was a huge studio."

Most of Moore's production efforts at Sun were steady, well-recorded works that—like most of the label's recordings once they left their original Memphis studio at 706 Union Avenue in late 1959—lacked a distinctive edge. By the time Presley's guitarist was on Phillips's payroll, the label had undergone some startling reverses. Johnny Cash, Carl Perkins, Roy Orbison, and others had left. The scandal over Jerry Lee Lewis's marriage to his thirteen-year-old second cousin, Myra, had effectively killed his mainstream recording career. Phillips, whose radio interests and investment in the Holiday Inn chain made him wealthier than the record business ever would, seldom showed up at his studios anymore. When he did, he was sometimes drunk and difficult to handle. During one inebriated tour of the studio during a recording session, Jack Clement asked him to shut up or leave. Phillips fired him for "insubordination."

It turned out to be a stupid decision. After a brief fling with his own Summer Records label (the company's slogan was "Some 'er hits, some 'er not. Hope you like the ones we've got."), Clement took his hit-making prowess to RCA, where he eventually interested Chet Atkins in a young black country singer named Charley Pride. "Well, actually, it started back at Sun Records," Clement recalls. "Sam had discovered a white guy that sounded black, sort of. I was saying, 'Why don't we get a black guy and teach him to sing country?' Well, it must've been five or six years later when I got to Nashville, I heard a tape that Jack Johnson had made with [Pride]. I listened to it, and it wasn't near as good as he sounded in the studio, but it was good enough for me to tell, 'This guy sounds like Hank Williams or somebody. He's a real country singer—nothing fake about it.' So, I agreed to pay for a session. Anyway, I took the demo to Chet [Atkins], and he turned it down at first. But one day, I ran into Chet and he said, 'What'd you ever do with that colored boy?' I said, 'Well, I haven't done anything yet. I'm thinking about pressing it up myself.' He said, 'Well, I've been thinking about that. We might be passing up another Elvis Presley.' Those were his exact words." Pride would eventually recorded fifty top-ten country hits for RCA.

Compared with such colorful in-studio personalities as Phillips and Clement, the shy, often withdrawn Moore didn't make much of an impression at Sun. Most, like drummer J. M. Van Eaton, remember him more in the role of engineer. One of his first charges was the easily combustible Jerry Lee Lewis, who laid much of his Old Testament wrath upon Presley's guitarist. "He'd back Scotty into a corner and start preaching at him," reports ex-wife Bobbie Moore, "and oh, how Scotty hated that."

"But I've always admired Jerry's talent," insists Moore. "I was just never fortunate enough to be around him when he had his head straight. I think we respected each other musically. Get him to sit down and be Jerry Lee and he'd play some piano. I mean he really could."

Moore's sessions with Lewis were cut at the Madison Avenue studio (706 Union Street having been abandoned late in 1959). At first, Moore didn't have the luxury of recording those famed keyboard runs because the pumpin' piano master had been kicked out of the musicians' union for nonpayment of dues. Moore got around the issue by having Lewis overdub vocals on "When I Get Paid" and "Love's Made a Fool of Me," the worst-selling disc of his early career. The most successful cuts Moore oversaw were the eerily slow remake of Chuck Berry's "Sweet Little Sixteen," which hit the bottom of the national Hot 100 chart, and a version of Jimmie Rodgers's "Waiting for a Train," which was cut during the same session as "Sweet Little Sixteen" and which would be released in 1970 and become a number-eleven hit on the country charts.

Moore and Lewis never really formed a friendship, and the guitarist didn't take any crap off the Killer, either. Fontana clearly recalls an early 1970s disc jockey convention where, after Lewis told Moore that he wasn't good enough to play in his band the Memphis Beats, the two men started throwing punches. "We were at one of the conventions for the disc jockeys here or something and, of course, Scotty knew Jerry from the Sun days," Fontana laughs. "I don't know what happened; I think it was just a personality clash. They happened to be at the same party in the same hall, and they probably had been drinking a little bit, you know. But the next thing I knew, Scotty came over the top of the table, and they started rasslin' around, just fightin'! I was there with my wife, and I told her, 'We better get out of here. I know both of these guys and I don't want to have to get in there and take up for one and not take up for the other.' So her and I left. I don't know how long they fought. I walked out the door when I saw 'em rasslin' in the middle of the floor. Last time I looked, Scotty was beatin' the fire out of Jerry. When I saw him later, Scotty said, 'How come you didn't help me?' I said, 'Well, I think you were doing all right. You didn't need me in there.'"

Fontana had some trying experiences with Lewis himself when he joined the wild pianist on some road dates during the early 1960s. He quit after Lewis had a temper tantrum because a pilot would not turn the plane around so he could retrieve some misplaced pills. "He's probably one of the finest talents that I've ever seen," comments the drummer. "He does it all, and he's just a great talent! Sometimes you don't know what Jerry might do; that's just the way Jerry is, I guess. He's not going to change, that I know of."

One of the people Moore came in regular contact with in Nashville was Billy Sherrill. It was Sherrill, working out of the Nashville studio with the group of sessions players who were regarded as the A team, who actually produced Lewis's best-known recording from that era, a smart remake of Ray Charles's "What'd I Say," a top-thirty hit on the country, pop, and R & B charts. After Phillips sold the Nashville studio to Fred Foster at Monument Records, Sherrill parlayed a job with song publisher Al Gallico into a staff position at Epic Records. The move would make the youngster a force to be reckoned with in the years to come. His remarkably successful work with Tammy Wynette, David Houston, George Jones, Charlie Rich, Johnny Paycheck, and many others would signal the rise of the pop music–friendly countrypolitan sound.

One of Sherrill's first ideas when he got to Epic was to record Scotty Moore. "He was in with the boys in New York," says Moore, "and he had decided—and it was a good idea, really—he wanted me to do all the Elvis tunes in instrumentals. He had already gotten the go-ahead." Moore had been after Sam Phillips to let him record instrumentals as Bill Black was doing, but Phillips kept putting the guitarist off. This project seemed the perfect solution: a risky idea on somebody else's nickel. The plan was to do the initial hits, the movie hits, and current Presley hits in succeeding volumes. Moore was especially intrigued that the albums would be sold through the Columbia House Record Club. "And that's what sold me on it," says Moore. "I said, if it's in the record club, it's going to sell records. OK, soon as all the paperwork's done, then they come back and say, 'Well, tell you what: just do the main hits this first one out, and let's see how that's gonna do.'"

Barred from using Presley's name on the cover, Sherrill called the LP *The Guitar That Changed the World.* It was an apt, dramatic title that didn't quite fit the guitarist's modest personality. Once again, Moore wanted some recognition from Presley to help him sell his wares, but he had to go through Colonel Parker to get it. "I did ask him something about Elvis writing the liner notes," he remembers with disgust. "No way. I don't think it would have cost him too much to have done that. After it was out, I sent Parker up a copy of it. I've got a letter back from him saying, 'Well, good luck with your project' or something."

Moore's work on *The Guitar That Changed the World* is actually pretty strong. On it he updates his guitar sounds with some pleasing fuzz tone, plays tasteful bits of melody, occasionally imitates Bill Black's bass riffs, and lays out some fine straight leads. Also, Fontana delivers some spot-on drumming against

Bob Moore's smartly struck bass lines. However, the production, which featured the Jordanaires singing many of Presley's parts, often plays out like nostalgia-theme Muzak. It's a nice novelty item for completists, but it's not "the great lost album."

The sad part for Moore was not the album's poor sales (he claims to still owe production costs on it), but the fact that Sam Phillips was so enraged over what he viewed as the guitarist's defection to a major label that he fired him. It happened just as the Memphis soul movement of the 1960s was about to explode. Today Moore laughs at the bad timing. "You know, I hadn't been up here six months and Memphis just busted wide open. I mean, Stax, American, everything was just going. And so I said, 'Well, I guess everyone just wanted me to leave before things would start happening,' you know?"

For his part, Moore had already been in the process of taking over Roy Studios in Nashville and renaming it Music City Recorders. Bobby Bare and Jerry Reed, who both cut demos there, thought it was a top-notch facility, but neither spent much time with Presley's guitarist because Moore was always attending to business. He had discovered his niche as an engineer, and he worked sessions by musicians ranging from Joe Simon and Arthur Alexander to Ringo Starr.

Perhaps his best freelance production was the 1966 Frank Frost album *Harpin' on It*, for the Shreveport-based Jewel label. The Arkansas bluesman was a former Sun artist who had previously worked for Robert Nighthawk's band. At the time of the Jewel sessions, Slim Harpo was enjoying a big hit on Excello Records with his "Scratch My Back." It was hoped that Frost could nick a part of that sound and rack up similar sales figures.

Augmenting the trio of Frost, Sam Carr, and Lee Bass with Nashville session ace Chip Young on bass and harmonica man Arthur "Oscar Lee" Williams, Moore kept the sound simple yet rhythmic. In the process, he made an album that boasted the intimacy of Harpo's singles for Excello and the catchy drive of Jimmy Reed's work for the Chicago-based Vee-Jay label. The lead single, "My Back Scratcher," was a solid seller in the south, and the album (which was re-released in 2001 by the English Westside label) proved to be one of only two genuinely enjoyable LPs Frost would cut in his lifetime. Further, Moore had shown that he could fashion a first-rate album without picking up the guitar—something he was doing less and less frequently at his studio.

"I'd go by there every day," recalls D. J. Fontana. "That was my watering hole. That was my drinking spot, over there." Although the drummer didn't notice that Moore had stopped playing guitar full time, he observed that, "He was over there at that studio from ten in the morning until two, three, four the next morning sometimes. So he really didn't have a lot of time to play at all. He was busy trying to keep his business going at the studio."

Fontana, on the other hand, was playing quite steadily. "Oh yeah, I moved to Nashville in 1966. At first I was only coming in town to do Elvis's sessions, and I met a lot of the local guys. So when I moved here, it was a little bit easier for me. I knew Floyd Cramer, and he hired me for a lot of his *Class* albums. There were two drummers; we were playing percussion and things like that.

"Floyd was real good to me. He'd say, 'Come on over, you'll get paid whether you do anything or not.' They'd have me play tambourine, maracas; they always wanted you to do something. Anyway, once I knew all the guys, they started calling me. That's what it takes—you just have to know who's calling musicians. I just got in early. There weren't that many drummers in town;

D. J. Fontana and Elvis Presley relax during a recording session at RCA's Studio B, Nashville, Tennessee, September 12, 1967. COURTESY OF D. J. FONTANA

I think there were five or six guys that played all the sessions. So I just happened to fall right in there. Buddy Harman, he's a well-known drummer in town, and he'd be doing three or four sessions a day, and if he was busy he'd say, 'Call D.J., he'll do it.' So everybody that I knew helped a little bit. I cut with everybody in town at that time. Mostly country acts."

Fontana did so many sessions (three or four a day, for more than twenty years) that most are long forgotten by the drummer, although he does remember a few highlights. "We did several little things with Johnny Cash," he states proudly. "We started one night to do something with Mother Maybelle, and then Mother Maybelle got sick, and so Johnny said, 'Well, let's go to the house and eat.' June [Carter] took us to the house, very beautiful home up there on the lake. Afterward we all went home. We still got paid.

"But I had worked with them, and I have worked with Dolly Parton and Porter Wagoner—I did some early stuff with them, some albums. A guy named Tommy Overstreet, I did all his—"Gwen" [a top-five country hit in 1971] and a bunch of others. There's so darned many of them. I did Lynn Anderson's "Cry" [a number-three hit in 1972], then I did a Christmas album for her. It was just a mixture of things that I learned how to do, but I don't remember who all the artists are now. I did one session with Orbison—he was still on Monument at that time, I think. They had about thirty or forty pieces in there; he used to cut with everybody together. He didn't like to overdub much, either."

While Moore and Fontana were working in Nashville, Elvis Presley was looking for a new sound for his recordings, or at least a way to get back to what he did best. Difficulties that arose while Presley was recording a version of Jerry Reed's 1967 country hit "Guitar Man" necessitated sending for Reed and his gut-string acoustic guitar. According to Reed, his session with Presley wasn't out of the ordinary. "It wasn't any different. Except he was pretty and I wasn't," jokes the singer/songwriter. "Best-looking man I ever laid my eyes on. Made me wonder if I wasn't born wrong."

Reed, who was a year away from recording the country-crossover smashes "Amos Moses" and "When You're Hot, You're Hot," recalls that his recording dates with Presley featured neither Moore nor Fontana. "They weren't on those sessions," recalls the guitarist. "[The musicians] were all Nashville studio pickers—Bob Moore on bass, Buddy Harman on drums, Chip Young on rhythm guitar, Charlie McCoy on harmonica. You know, he used the A players when he was recording in Nashville. D.J. and Scotty weren't involved."

Any other artist might have worried that the bigger-name performer was trying to steal a hit away from him. Not Reed, who responded with comic incredulity, "Are you kiddin' me? Lord no. I was, 'Elvis is going to cut *my* song. Come on, Elvis. Get *on* it, Elvis!' You think I cared about my record? Have you lost your mind?"

Years later, the complete version of Presley's "Guitar Man," which features an impromptu segue into "What'd I Say," showed what Presley had intended to achieve with the song all along: free-form rock with an acoustic country feel. At the same session, the rocker sang another of Reed's compositions, "U.S. Male." "After we cut 'Guitar Man,'" remembers Reed, "this steel player said, 'Sing him another one, Reed.' I said, 'No, I've got one, that's enough.' Elvis said, 'No, have you got anything else?' I said, 'You might like the "U.S. Male," I don't know.' 'Play it!' So I played it, and he said, 'Let's cut it.'"

By modern standards, "U.S. Male" is as politically incorrect as a song can get, but the sneering, spoken intro, bongo-style guitar riffs, and full-out rockabilly release on the chorus signaled that Presley was back to making records his way. Unfortunately, both the malaise caused by the continual release of mediocre movie soundtracks (especially the later ones) and the rapidly changing musical climate of the late 1960s adversely affected the success of both "Guitar Man" (which topped out at number 43 on the pop charts in 1967) and "U.S. Male" (which hit number 28 on the charts in 1968). It was the relative failure of these well-crafted records that threw enough of a scare into both the singer and his manager to attempt something as unique as the televised Singer-sponsored comeback special, *Elvis*.

After several cinematic turkeys, which culminated in *Frankie and Johnny*, *Easy Come, Easy Go*, and *Stay Away, Joe*, the singer's profile as a performer couldn't have been lower, nor could critics' perception of his music have been worse. Even Presley's most devoted fans had tired of his formulaic films, which Presley himself dismissed as "travelogues," and their kitschy soundtracks. Presley had already been working with newly appointed musical director Billy Strange and his cowriter, Mac Davis, to update his sound for *Live a Little, Love a Little* and *The Trouble with Girls*. Strange immediately provided a more contemporary pop sound. For the latter film, he even anticipated the rocker's move into Memphis soul with the antihypocrisy gospel-blues of "Clean Up Your Own Backyard."

Since Strange was already in tune with Presley's tastes and knew all the Los Angeles musicians, the rocker wanted Strange to be part of his upcoming NBC television show. "I was part and parcel of the planning stages of it—picking the songs and so forth," reveals Strange. "Then Steve Binder and I got into a big hassle. He says he fired me, but he didn't. I quit. I was doing a picture for Elvis at the same time that I was doing the *'68 Special* [as the television special is often called] and it came down to that it was such a damned hassle. I could work the picture on my own and not have to worry about Binder or anybody else. So, I just quit and did the film instead."

Before he left, Strange had pitched a song to the singer that would provide a romantic counterpoint to Reed's "Guitar Man," which was scheduled to be performed during the show. "Mac [Davis] was at my house, and he sang me the first eight bars of the song, and it stuck with me," he says of "Memories." "The day I went to rehearsal for the *'68 Special*, Elvis said he wanted a big, big ballad, and he named some ballad that he had recorded years ago. I said, 'How about this? Memories, pressed between the pages of my mind.' He said, 'That's great! I love it.' I said, 'Great, I'll bring it to you tomorrow.' I went home, hashed it out, did a quickie tape of it and brought it in the next day. Elvis bought it and set up a recording session and did it." In contrast to the show's staged (and ultimately forgettable) production numbers, "Memories" played out like a poignant anthem. However, it was the sit-down portion of the show that still resonates with viewers today.

Naturally, when the idea was proposed, Presley's first instinct was to call D. J. Fontana and Scotty Moore, although the guitarist and the singer were no longer close. "I was in the studio here in Nashville, working," Moore recalls. "And when I got home my wife said that Elvis had called. And I said, 'Oh, really?' I was kind of surprised. And she said 'No, really.' And I asked 'Was it him on the phone?' And she said, 'Oh yeah,' 'cause she had met him. I asked, 'Well, what did he want?' And she said, 'Well, I don't know. I told him to call back in a couple of hours.' And he did. He called back. He said he was fixing to do this TV special and wanted to know if we'd come out there and work on it with him. And I said, 'Sure.'"

Today, Scotty Moore hates it when people refer to his last television appearance with Presley as the *'68 Comeback Special* as if that was actually the name of the show, and he politely reminds them that it was actually called *Singer Presents: Elvis*. The guitarist's objection notwithstanding, the fact is Americans love drama, and Presley had given them plenty of it: first with his rags-to-riches leap to fame, next with his induction into the U.S. Army, then with his triumphant return to civilian life and movie stardom. At this juncture, like many rapidly fading stars had done before him, Presley was using network television to remind people how good he truly was when he was allowed to do his thing.

Ostensibly, the one-hour program was talked up as a Christmas special, but producer Steve Binder knew what the stakes were and came up with some daringly different ideas. "We had a good time on that show," recalls Fontana, who played a guitar case instead of drums. "We just did that little thing in the round. That's the segment they really wanted. They wanted it to look like we were sitting around the living room, doing nuthin', just talking and playing. 'Whatever comes in your mind, you do it.' There was nothing to read, no dialogue. They said, 'We don't have anything for you guys to do. Just do what you do best. Just play and see what happens, and we'll turn the cameras on. When we get tired, we'll turn 'em off.' It's about what they did."

Binder's idea was to feature an informal segment that doubled as a return to Presley's simpler, more honest form of music. The problem? The core band hadn't jammed with their singer since the early days. Indeed, Moore remembers the Blue Moon Boys getting stale on the road. "We got in a rut," he admits, "playing the same thing night in and night out. And I would try to get D.J. and Bill and say, 'go get the snare drum and bring it up, and the bass.' [They'd reply] 'Ah, no, it's too much trouble.'"

Then there was Presley himself. While singing at home with the Memphis Mafia, he usually sat at the piano and played gospel tunes. So, in essence, the television special's producer was asking him to fake a casual atmosphere during the segment. Moore remembers how Binder probably got the idea. "Steve Binder wanted us to get into the dressing room and have a jam session," the guitarist explains. "I don't remember seeing a tape recorder. I didn't know that he was taping the stuff. But we got in there, and were horsing around and doing all the old stuff. And that's where Steve got it. In fact, he said, 'This is what I want you to do. I want to get you out there. I don't want you to rehearse anything; I don't want to rehearse camera shots. The only thing we're going to do is lights. Just do whatever you feel like doing. The only thing I'll ask you to do is if you'll just do it twice, before two different audiences.' And that's how that all came about. He had nothing planned, as far as I know, unless it was going to be just a stand-up concert type, do two to three songs."

Of course, there were some difficulties in getting the act out of the dressing room. While Moore's stage fright was acute enough to necessitate the hiding of a whiskey bottle in his guitar case, Presley's was a full-blown panic. For reassurance, the rocker brought three of his crew up onstage with him: Alan

Fortas; Lance Legault (a future regular on the 1980s TV show *The A-Team)*, who banged on a tambourine; and Charlie Hodge, who played inaudible acoustic guitar and sang a little harmony. Hodge and Presley had known each other since the rocker's army stint in Germany. Once the singer learned that Hodge had gone to the Stamps Gospel School and been a member of Red Foley's Smokey Mountain Boys, they became fast friends. How any of that qualified him, or any of the Memphis Mafia, to share television time with three pioneers of rock 'n' roll is anyone's guess. Yet Hodge did contribute. He cued Presley into stories and songs, and he laughed sycophantically at all his boss's jokes while cutting off Fontana's few spontaneous comments. (During Presley's Vegas years, Hodge would continue to play a part in the singer's shows by handing the jumpsuited singer both his drinking water and the cheap rayon scarves he tossed into the audience.)

In his introduction of his two surviving band members, Presley couldn't resist the impulse to shave two years off of his association with them (perhaps in an effort to make himself seem two years younger?). "The guy on my left is the guy who played guitar for me when I first got started in 1912, uh, 1956," Presley says. "This my guitar player, Scotty Moore. This is my drummer; he's from Shreveport, Louisiana. I met him about ten years ago—D. J. Fontana."

Presley looked especially handsome in his black leather outfit, a fashion statement that had first been dreamed up by English television producer Jack Good for Gene Vincent. The returning King looked every inch the roadhouse rockabilly, even when he allowed a look of cringing disdain to cross his face while referring to his first record as "That's All Right Little Mama."

Presley continues with his introduction, "When we first started, we had just a guitar, a bass player, and, uh, another guitar." Watching the footage and observing the way in which Presley looks over at Scotty and D. J., stumbling meaningfully, it seems that Presley was trying hard not to mention Bill Black by name. Then he launches into "That's All Right (Mama)." Musically, the performance is fine, raw stuff, the likes of which hadn't been heard since Presley had been billed as the Hillbilly Cat. The desperate, almost hysterical, pleading rasp in his blues belting put the world of contemporary music on notice: Elvis Presley could still rock.

However (as DVD compilations of the live segments show), it's clear that the trio was rusty and out of synch. During "Heartbreak Hotel," Presley kept forgetting the words, and Moore had to be cued into his solo. Better was their solid, soulful version of "Love Me," which is less dependent on Moore's guitar work. After performing "Love Me," Presley commanded affably, "Hey man, let me trade axes with you."

Moore's first thought as he exchanged his electric guitar for the singer's acoustic model was, "Uh oh, there goes a string or two." Moore swears the guitar switch was a spontaneous act. If so, it is a case of Presley's instincts triumphing once again, and he proceeds to lay down a thrilling, hard, electric version of bluesman Jimmy Reed's "Baby What You Want Me to Do."

In short order, the singer begins bashing open chords through splendid, desperate versions of "Lawdy Miss Clawdy" and "Trying to Get to You," proving himself to be a first-rate garage rock player. A master of elemental blues turnarounds and rhythms, he did keep time beautifully, and although a guitar cord pops out of its jack now and then ("Somebody pulled the plug, man"), he makes no mistakes. No, he wasn't in Moore's league as an instrumental artist, but in this intimate setting, his raw scrubbing on the electric guitar provided just what was needed—a sound that brilliantly matched that tough leather outfit he was wearing.

By the time he got to his closing number, "One Night with You," the heat of the live performance had stiffened his spine. He wanted to stand up and howl. Yet, since it was a sit-down segment, no one had brought a guitar strap. Laughing the mistake away, Presley crooned, "No strap for you" before standing, balancing his guitar on his knee, and, with Hodge crouching just under camera shot and holding the microphone aloft, wailing out the full version of the song. It isn't just a riveting rock 'n' roll moment; it would also be the last time Elvis Presley was truly cool.

"I thought it stunk, to tell the truth," says Moore today. "In fact, looking back at it, I wish Elvis hadn't of stood up. I think it would have been even better. And then he was mad because—see, he already took my guitar away from me. He stood up and there wasn't a mic, and you couldn't hear, and it wasn't loud enough. And that's when he took my guitar, 'cause it had my amp. And then I didn't have a strap so he could stand up. So he had to put his foot up on a chair."

Moore's objections notwithstanding, most Presley aficionados agree that the moment was in fact great *because* of all the spontaneous imperfections that surrounded it. By triumphing over a feeble sound setup, inadequate preparation, and a lack of flexible equipment, Presley put all his best qualities on display—humor, passion, and guts. This was the Elvis Presley his public needed to see, and for those few minutes during the middle of the Singer special, they got him.

Yet, just as his picking up Bill Black's electric bass and playing "(You're So Square) Baby I Don't Care" for the bassist had been symbolic of their disintegrating relationship, so was Presley's taking Moore's guitar from him. It was no accident. He did it at both sit-down shows—but never again in any public forum. A man who hated confrontation, the singer was plainly demonstrating that he no longer needed Moore to make great rock 'n' roll music.

Presley seemed to know the overall program would jumpstart his career. "D.J. and I went out and had dinner with him at his house," Moore recalls. "He called us off into another room, which he never did stuff like that; he didn't care who was around, he'd just say what he wanted to say. He asked us if we'd like to do a European tour, and we said sure. Love to. Just give us a little notice. And then he asked me if I still had a studio. And I said yes. And he said, 'What's the chances of getting in and locking up a couple of weeks?' I said, 'Sure, just let me know, give us a little time and I'll block the time for it. I will charge you for it.' [Laughs.] But neither one of the things happened."

Fontana remembers: "He called back later when he got through with all [those movies] and we did that *'68 Special*. We did that, then we went up to the house and he said, 'Let's go back on the road.' We said, 'Well, you book 'em and we'll go.' He said, 'Maybe we can go to Hawaii and Australia, England and Germany.' He wanted to go all over, really. It never did materialize. I don't know what happened. Management again. Colonel wouldn't let nobody do anything, I think that's what kind of queered that deal."

Many writers have suggested that Colonel Parker's status as an illegal alien kept him from booking a European tour. Moore disagrees: "That's a crock of—after Elvis reached the status that he did, they could have gone to some senator somewhere and they could have got all that straightened out. INS let him alone."

The next time Moore and Fontana heard anything about performing live, it was from Tom Diskin in 1969. Diskin wanted to get the group together for live gigs in Las Vegas. "Tom Diskin called everybody," states Moore. "Jordanaires, myself, D.J., Bob Moore, Boots, all the Nashville guys, and said Elvis would like for us to come out and work with him in Vegas. He was going into Vegas for—I remember two weeks, but Gordon of the Jordanaires said he thinks it was three weeks. And you would have to tie another week on there at least for rehearsal, and right then Nashville was at a peak. Everyone was going 'round the clock. What they were offering a week [in] salary, all the guys were making in half a day."

All of the Nashville musicians were better off financially by not doing Vegas with Presley. The Jordanaires, in particular, scored big, with a "Real Thing" commercial for Coca-Cola. "We made more money off of that than working the whole year with Elvis," reveals Gordon Stoker. "We would've missed that had we gone, even though we loved Elvis dearly. Of course he hated that D. J. Fontana, Scotty Moore, all six of us quit at the same time. They were doing sessions here in Nashville, too, and we just didn't want to do the shows in Vegas. That's how come we quit."

Years later, Moore learned that Colonel Parker had deliberately offered a low figure so Presley would be forced to replace everyone. It worked. Once his bandmates turned Presley down, Parker ended up paying James Burton and the rest of the TCB Band far more than what was offered to Moore and Fontana. Initially, the singer's feelings were hurt by his original band's refusal to play Las Vegas, but Fontana remained friendly and cleared the air. "I saw Elvis a little bit later on, after they'd hired everybody else. And I explained it to him. I thought he might be mad but he said, 'Nah, I understand.' He said, 'I don't blame you. You did the right thing. You had a wife and kids and everything.' He said, 'If I could do that, that's what I'd do. I'd stay home.'"

In the world of late-1960s–early-1970s pop, Presley was actually better off without his old gang. It's hard to imagine Moore, Fontana, and the Jordanaires executing some of the material he would hit the charts with over the next few years: "In the Ghetto," "Suspicious Minds," "Kentucky Rain," and others (although Chips Moman would ultimately produce the singer's finest album, *Elvis in Memphis*, which would feature strong contributions from many former members of the Bill Black Combo). Moreover, Moore didn't approve of Presley's new sound. "Well, I don't like it very much," he told *Rockville International* in 1973. "I don't like it in comparison to what we used to do, but it's my personal opinion."

Moore says he never truly lost faith in Elvis Presley, but he was deeply disappointed about the proposed tour falling through. A short time later, he stopped playing guitar altogether. "I just didn't see any future in it, really, at that time," he plainly states. "I just closed the case, I guess. I sold all my guitars. I had a little classical guitar for quite a while and I got rid of it, too. The only thing I kept was the custom-made amplifier that Ray Butts made."

Engineering completely took over the portion of his life that he'd once devoted to guitars.

"I enjoyed the stage with Elvis. It's almost as if our minds were hooked up by a computer, in a way. But then, when I got into engineering, I really enjoyed it, too, because then I could play the whole band. I started doing things like the CMA shows live out of the *Opry* house. It would be about two or sometimes three of us engineering. I would handle the orchestra and vocal group and things like that, and maybe the other guy would handle the stage vocal, or if they had some extra players with them onstage. We'd all work together, and that was fun."

Bit by bit, through the late 1960s and the 1970s, both Moore and Fontana faded into the shadows of the music industry, and for the most part, they liked it that way. Although the drummer made a point of visiting or calling Presley whenever he was in Memphis, Moore simply had no contact with the singer he had discovered. "I figured that he could call me easier than I could call him," Moore truculently states.

Yet the guitarist-turned-engineer knew that something was amiss with Presley's health. "After a few years went by there, I saw where they'd taped one of those live performances, I could see that something was wrong. The man was too vain to let himself get in that kind of shape. And I wasn't in contact with any of the people or anything, so I don't know what the rumors were. I couldn't have been around and not said something. I mean, *loud*. So it was probably just as well that I wasn't around in those days."

Presley died on August 16, 1977. Fontana remembers exactly where he was that day. "I was at Shelby Singleton's out on Belmont Avenue here in town," the drummer soberly recalls. "He had bought Sun out, so I was doing a Sun session, I guess. I don't know who the artist was right off, but Shelby broke in and said, 'Hey, we just heard on the radio that Elvis just died.' I just said, 'No—naw—that can't be.' We had heard rumors about that for the last five years. So I said, 'Oh, I kinda doubt it, Shelby.' It was about four-thirty and we got through at five anyhow, and Shelby said, 'You want to knock the session off anyhow?' I said, 'No, let's just go ahead and finish.' I only lived maybe five minutes away from the studio. 'I'll run home after that and see.'

"I got home and got on the phone and couldn't find a soul that I knew. I tried to call Joe Esposito and Charlie Hodge and George Klein, everybody that I knew. When I couldn't find a soul, I said, 'Something's wrong for all those guys to be out of pocket.' They were all the way in Memphis, too. I called the house, you know, the mansion, and Tom Diskin answered the phone, which was the Colonel's right-hand man. He told me it was true, then I talked to Joe, and I said, 'I'll be down in the morning as quick as I can get down there.' So, I went down there to the funeral."

Out of the national outpouring of grief rose author Gail Brewer-Giorgio's *Is Elvis Alive?* phenomenon. To which Fontana responds, "Well, naturally, I wish he were. I think we all do, but I was at the funeral and I did see him. So I know he's passed away, and there's nothing we can do about it."

Presley's death forced a rare crack in Moore's stoic manner, causing his voice to break as he spoke about it to his fourth wife, Emily. There were too many things left unsaid between them, too many hurts and slights that should have been forgiven. In the years to come, he would bury his conflicting feelings in compulsive hard work and a lot of scotch while avoiding everything that had to do with his days as a musician. When people asked for interviews, he would refuse by simply shaking his head and saying, "Elvis is dead."

The Return of Scotty and D.J.

"D.J. is funny. He has a real subtle sense of humor. . . . One time I called him up and said, 'D.J., what's happening?' He said, 'Nothing, every minute.'"

—Stan Kesler, founder of the Sun Rhythm Section

"Touring with [Scotty Moore] helped me in a lot of ways. . . . When we worked with Scotty, we would slow it down and turn it down, and it would become more his type of thing. He doesn't feel that things swing well if they're played too fast. I definitely got a lot out that experience and came a long way as a singer. . . . Singing with Scotty and D.J. behind you is pretty amazing."

—Lee Rocker, former Stray Cat and
bass slapper extraordinaire

RECORDING BEHIND fellow percussion legend Ringo Starr for his 1970 LP *Beaucoups of Blues* was one of the highlights of D. J. Fontana's Nashville career. "Well, Ringo, he knew everybody who ever cut a record, I think," he says of the former Beatle. "They all do. They keep up with everybody. And we had all the guys that Ringo had ever heard of on his album. We had Jerry Reed, Charlie Daniels, the Jordanaires. That's what he wanted."

Pedal-steel legend Pete Drake produced the all-star sessions. "I had been working for Pete off and on for ten or twelve years," says Fontana. "I did a lot of his sessions, demos, and everything. We even went on the road together; he had a band and we'd go out there and play. That's how that got started. They had been setting it up and setting it up, Apple had; they just had to get all the money straightened out, what studio they were going to use, whatever, and go from there. That was quite a hassle to get all those guys together and get everything done."

"Yeah, I was the engineer on that," Scotty Moore chuckles. "I think the music industry made a big deal out of it, which I'm glad they did. And the little studio—we almost had fifteen-hundred people in there—in the lobby, I think."

Despite the extraordinarily large crowd of musicians, Fontana reports the sessions weren't that different from the normal Nashville recording dates. "Pete was producing, and if something didn't go right he'd say, 'No, no guys, we can't do that. Let's do something else.' That's how a session used to go in this town. Everybody worked together, we'd all think of something to play; we won't play at the same times, and everybody knows what to do."

Fontana and Starr didn't talk much about drumming, but D.J. liked the former Richard Starkey. "Oh yeah, Ringo was as nice as he could be." He also liked the music they laid down, "Yeah, I thought it was good. I don't know if it ever did anything." Starr's album was only a middling success by Beatles standards, reaching number thirty-five on the country charts and number sixty-five on the pop charts. It would be another decade before rockers would completely infiltrate country music.

Fontana was also briefly on-screen as a strip-club drummer in Robert Altman's 1976 film *Nashville.* Years later he would tell Dan Griffin that, between takes in the hot strip club, the riser the little trio played on was lowered and the crew would give him beer. As a result, with each take he became increasingly tipsy (it's noticeable onscreen), though his drumming remained rock steady. Although he was an inveterate drinker, Fontana would give up excessive alcohol consumption and cigarettes by the early 1990s without a whimper. "D.J. has this great force of will," observes Griffin. "If he decides to do something or not do something, that's how it's going to be."

Yet no amount of will power could change the course of Fontana's slowly fading studio career. Although many studio veterans from the fifties and sixties were still working full time, Nashville changed in the 1970s. A new crowd was moving in; more self-contained bands were playing on their own recordings, and they were using new technology that featured click tracks. Fontana didn't enjoy Music City's modern record-production methods, which included using drum machines and building tracks in isolation rather than cutting live. "Once they got into all this electronic stuff," he explains, "it sounded like one drummer was cuttin' everybody's records."

More importantly, he didn't think the up-and-coming acts were truly country. "They're mostly rock 'n' rollers," he remarks. "There's no country guys out there that I know of. I remember listening to Lefty Frizzell, and I miss Willie Nelson, Cash, and all those guys. All the old-timers, they don't play 'em anymore. That's a shame. Haggard? How the hell you going to beat Haggard? He sings better than most! George Jones, he outsings 'em all. They [radio] won't play George."

Fontana's technique, which had never been metronome-like in its precision, slowly fell out of favor with modern producers who had no inkling of the concepts of feel and swing. Work began drying up, and the drummer played at some non-union sessions simply because that's where the next check would come from.

After Elvis Presley's 1977 death, Fontana was often asked to record more rockabilly-oriented material, usually by Shelby Singleton, who had bought the Sun catalog from Sam Phillips in 1969 and rechristened the label Sun International. Singleton immediately began flooding the market with reissued Sun material by Johnny Cash, Carl Perkins, and Charlie Rich, as well as by Jerry Lee Lewis, who enjoyed three top-ten country hits with previously unreleased recordings. The crafty producer/promoter also licensed hundreds of masters and unreleased tracks to the British Charly label, which in effect triggered a worldwide rockabilly revival. One of Singleton's more controversial moves was recording an Elvis Presley soundalike named Jimmy Ellis, putting him in a mask and cape, and redubbing him Orion.

"Oh hey, the guy could sing," reports Fontana. "He's one of the better ones, I'll tell you that. Orion, he didn't wear the jumpsuits or none of that. He'd go out there in a nice-looking jacket and a pair of pants—well, he had the mask. I think that was Shelby Singleton's idea, and it worked for them for a long time. Sure did."

Orion sounded more like the 1970s balladeer Presley than he did the frisky 1950s Hillbilly Cat. That didn't stop Singleton from creating one of the most cynical pieces of exploitation ever foisted on the record-buying public. With

Fontana on drums, Singleton took classic Sun tracks by Jerry Lee Lewis, Johnny Cash, and others and dubbed Orion's uncredited Elvis Presley imitations onto them. Then he allowed a whisper campaign to build; a campaign that proclaimed that both the 1978 album *Trio +* — (an allusion to the Million Dollar Quartet of Cash, Perkins, Lewis, and Presley) and the 1979 *Duets* featured rare recordings by Presley. There is not one Presley performance on either disc. (The *Duets* song most commonly thought to feature Presley, "Am I to Be the One," is actually performed by Jerry Lee Lewis and Charlie Rich.) Still, these projects were strong sellers. *Duets* was a number-thirty-two hit album on the country charts, with a Jerry Lee Lewis remake of the Drifters' "Save the Last Dance for Me" reaching number twenty-six. Incredibly, *Cashbox* voted Ellis's Orion persona one of 1980's three most promising country male vocalists.

Some bought into Orion's act as inspired schlock; the more gullible audience members thought he truly was the King. The latter viewpoint was encouraged by Gail Brewer-Giorgio's novel *Orion* (the title did not refer to Ellis's alter ego), as well as by the specious theories espoused in her "is Elvis alive" books. Both Fontana and the Jordanaires recorded with Orion, and many people at the time took that as a winking validation, by Presley associates who were in the know, that Elvis actually was still alive. In reality, the Orion sessions were just another gig to them.

Eventually, the Presley impersonator would fade farther into the background, recording for the small Aron and Orchid labels, and doing shows with and without his mask. When bookings thinned out, he ran a pawnshop and worked as a bail bondsman. In 1998, while manning a convenience store in Selma, Alabama, Jimmy "Orion" Ellis and his ex-wife were shot and killed during a robbery. "Oh that was terrible," states Fontana. "The guy didn't bother a soul, and he was really just as nice as he could be all the time. You never know what's going to happen to people anymore."

The sad fact remains, however, that Fontana had recorded with a man who was widely perceived as an Elvis imitator. It would not be the last time, and the results would not always be as classy. A major step up from such relationships was Fontana's association with Sonny Burgess, Paul Burlison, Stan Kesler, Smoochy Smith, and Marcus Van Story—also known as the Sun Rhythm Section.

Dying his hair bright red in the 1950s (before Johnny Rotten had even been born) and climbing the walls way before Bono ever did, Albert "Sonny" Burgess was an original punk rocker. Burgess and his group, the Pacers, once enjoyed a reputation as the hottest show band in the mid-South. The raw energy in his cotton-patch blues vocals crackles through such Sun releases as "We Wanna Boogie," "Ain't Got a Thing," and his manic masterpiece, "Sadie's Back in Town." None of the songs were more than regional chart entries, but during the rockabilly revival that was spawned by the death of Elvis Presley, they were regarded as great lost hits. After the Sun era, Burgess played bass for Conway Twitty during the future country superstar's rock 'n' roll days. When the former Harold Jenkins broke up his original band, the Twitty-Birds, for financial reasons, Burgess played weekend gigs and recorded with a group called the King IV. In the early 1960s, the bulk of his income came as a traveling salesman for a St. Louis sewing-supply firm. Occasionally, a European rockabilly fanatic would coax the cult hero back to the studio to cut songs in the old style, but Burgess didn't really renew his commitment to music until he retired from his day job.

The Sun Rhythm Section: Jerry Lee "Smoochy" Smith, Stan Kesler, Sonny Burgess, Marcus Van Story (riding the bass), Paul Burlison, and D. J. Fontana.
Courtesy of Sonny Burgess

Stan Kesler wrote five songs that are associated with Elvis Presley, including "I Forgot to Remember to Forget," the King's longest-running number-one country single. Initially a session pedal-steel player and an engineer, Kesler became a respected producer in Memphis during the 1960s, most notably for Sam the Sham and the Pharaohs, who racked up million-sellers with "Wooly Bully" and "Little Red Riding Hood." At the time Griffin met him, Kesler was working as an engineer and producer for Sam Phillips's studio at 639 Madison Avenue in Memphis.

Not a former Sun artist, Paul Burlison was the guitarist for Johnny & Dorsey Burnette's Rock and Roll Trio; his was the first fuzz-tone guitar used on a white rock 'n' roll record. (Ike Turner's guitarist, Willy Kizart, first employed it on a Sam Phillips–produced blues record, Jackie Brenston's "Rocket 88," in 1951.) Burlison's style would be acknowledged in later decades by Jeff Beck, Los Lobos, Stevie Ray and Jimmy Vaughan, Aerosmith, and a whole slew of neo-rockabillies. Retired from the treadmill of the music business, he had become a building contractor in Mississippi. Jerry Lee "Smoochy" Smith had begun his music career as the fifteen-year-old piano player for the Mar-Keys and cowrote their instrumental hit "Last Night." Marcus Van Story had played bass for Warren Smith, Charlie Feathers, and Jerry Lee Lewis at Sun. In later years the harmonica-playing bassist recorded his own album for the Barrelhouse label.

Kesler remembers how the band came together in 1986. "Well, this guy who worked for the Country Music Hall of Fame, he was connected somehow with the Smithsonian. He called me down here and told me about the Smithsonian Folklore Festival they have. He said, 'They honor a different state every year. This year we're honoring Tennessee.' He asked, 'Do you think you could put together a band? I think it would fit well with the theme of the thing to have a rockabilly band and show how music progressed along.' I said, 'I don't know. There's a few guys around, I suppose we could put together a few guys to go up there.' He said, 'Well, it would be for two weeks. You'll have to work out the pay with the woman from the Smithsonian.'

"Of course Roland was right there, and I talked to him and he said, 'Yeah, we'll get Sonny Burgess.' I said, 'Well, we'll need a slap-bass player, we'll get Marcus [Van Story], and J.M. [Van Eaton] will probably go.' And we thought, 'Paul Burlison would be a good one to put in there. Smoochy Smith on piano.' So, we called this guy back and told him, and he said he'd have the lady call us. In the meantime, Roland backed out on us; he decided he didn't want to go, but we went ahead.

"I was pretty nervous. I hadn't played in so long. My chops were down. But after two or three gigs, man, it just came together. We got pretty tight. [At the festival] they had different tents where the bands would play. It'd be full inside and people standing on the outside. So, that's how we got started. Word got around and we started getting bookings."

Like Roland Janes, J. M. Van Eaton was originally part of Billy Lee Riley's Little Green Men (who were known for such songs as "Red Hot" and "Flying Saucers Rock 'n' Roll"). He had been Sun's house drummer, playing on hits by Jerry Lee Lewis, Charlie Rich, and he'd even been Johnny Cash's first studio drummer. ("The first time I touched the cymbal, he nearly jumped through the roof," laughs the drummer.) A born-again Christian, he had been playing gospel music with a band called the New Seekers when he wasn't working as a bond salesman. "It was a lot of fun," says Van Eaton of his Sun Rhythm Section days. "We were playing outside in these festivals, I enjoyed that, and we began to draw huge crowds. You wouldn't believe how popular that band got! Guys like Bob Dylan and Bruce Springsteen's band were coming to hear us play. So they started booking and we were playing in New York and what have you, and I couldn't keep it up. Number one, they weren't making a lot of money. And they did some stuff I didn't want to do, plus they were traveling a lot, which I didn't want to do."

"J.M., because of his job, he couldn't take off every week," states Kesler. "Sometimes we'd have to leave town on Thursday for these weekend things. I think his boss asked him, 'Do you want to work or do you want to play music?' So, he had to quit. So we got D.J. and asked him if he'd be interested in doing it. He said, 'Yeah.' He finished out the whole thing with us. It had the fire of the fifties rockabilly, and the feel."

By the time he was asked to join in 1988, the drummer was up for touring again, especially with old buddy Sonny Burgess. The band enjoyed an initial spell of popularity before sinking into lower-class bookings. "We were up in Washington, Oregon, all through there a couple of different times. Canada, Vancouver, up through that area," Fontana marvels. "God, we worked Chicago; they had a blues fest up there. They had festivals all over, and we worked 'em for seven or eight years. Just about every weekend we were gone somewhere with the Sun Rhythm Section. Then we went down to North Africa and worked down there about three months. Yeah, we went down to Sudan, Kuwait, Jordan, Tunisia—we was kind of all over the place."

According to Stan Kesler, the Africa tour was actually set up by the U.S. State Department. "We did like a thirty-day tour over there. We played several times in England and played Norway, Sweden—we never did play in France." In Bangladesh, where no one had ever heard an original Sun record, Kesler recalls they went over especially well. "They were out there just dancing around and really getting with it. Each side of the stage had a man with an AK-47. But there was never any problem. Everyone had a good time."

Asked if people in Third World countries recognized any names of artists that the Sun Rhythm Section members had been associated with, Kesler responds, "Yeah, they recognized the name Elvis. Most of 'em did, but it seemed like Bangladesh did particularly, and they were the most backward civilization we were in. That was a *poor* country. There ain't nothin' there but a river that runs through there. The embassy guy took us for a boat ride and took us up the Ganges River. We were riding along there and all of a sudden there was this body just floating down the river. He said, 'Oh, that's nothing. There's nothing to that.' Then over on the other side of the river there's people bathing and washing their clothes and everything. They told us, 'Don't drink the water. Don't even brush your teeth in the water here.' They gave us bottled water to drink and brush our teeth with. Sudan was pretty modern and up-to-date by comparison. I think the hotel there had their own well and own water, and it was good to brush your teeth in, but they said, 'Don't drink it anyway.' They didn't want to take no chances."

State department tours to exotic locales made for colorful band stories, but these types of bookings weren't plentiful or particularly lucrative. The band sorely needed a champion to heighten public awareness and open new vistas for them in the United States.

Enter Dan Griffin.

Griffin has worn many hats in the music business. During the 1970s, he played bass guitar in Southern touring bands. A chance meeting with songwriter/artist Marshall Crenshaw and producer Mitch Easter led to Griffin working in road management, concert promotion, and independent label and personal management in the 1980s and 1990s. Griffin has worked with artists as diverse as 10,000 Maniacs, Alex Chilton, Jackson Browne, Donald Fagen, Leon Redbone and author/radio personality Garrison Keillor. He was voted 1989–90 promoter of the year in upstate New York, and he presented events in Albany, Utica, and Troy, New York; Charlottesville, Virginia; Lenox, Massachusetts; Nashville, Tennessee; and Burlington, Vermont. In 1991 Griffin worked with Columbia Records to produce the first of Canadian artist Bruce Cockburn's worldwide satellite-broadcast Christmas concerts at the Bearsville Theater in Woodstock, New York. He has worked closely with Rounder Records and S.E.S.A.C.'s Nashville office, developing new artists and organizing tour packages. The native Alabaman also toured as a sponsor liaison with the Rolling Stones on the band's 1997–98 *Bridges to Babylon* tour and on some of Elton John's 1998 dates.

Griffin's association with Scotty Moore and D. J. Fontana sprang from a chance phone call. "I received a phone call in the tiny upstairs office of the Joyous Lake, on a nice spring day," says the former Woodstock-area promoter/manager. "A calm-voiced lady, not the typical booking-agent type, asked if the Joyous Lake still booked music in the club. She asked if I would be interested in booking the Sun Rhythm Section, a revue of fifties music by veterans of the legendary label. 'Sorry, we don't do cover stuff here,' was my first answer. Out of curiosity, I asked who was in the band. 'Sonny Burgess, Stan Kesler, Paul Burlison, Smoochy Smith, and D. J. Fontana,' were the names she rolled out. I gulped twice by the time she got to the last, most famous name. I knew that, while they weren't household names, each was a noted artist in the days of Sun Records. They had performed alongside the greats—Elvis, Roy Orbison, Jerry Lee Lewis, and Johnny Cash. These men had created the music when their frontmen were creating the persona."

By 1992 the Sun Rhythm Section was still performing at weekend festivals and playing clubs as fill-in dates during the week. The two nights in Woodstock that Griffin agreed to promote would be during the week, a hard time to draw audiences. While closing the deal, Griffin jokingly asked, "No Scotty Moore, huh?" The booker laughed and said she would be asking a lot more money for the act if he would tour. Fontana had told her that Moore—who had just gone through his second bankruptcy—had recently decided to get a guitar again (after having sold his equipment years earlier), and that he was rumored to be interested in playing music again, but she had no details.

"I contacted all the newspapers in the area and the local NBC affiliate in Kingston to set up press and interviews," recalls Griffin. "Invitations went to local legends the Band, David Johansen (also known as Buster Poindexter), John Sebastian, Donald Fagan, and Graham Parker. The players in the Sun Rhythm Section had worked with the guys in the Band when they were known as the Hawks. If there was a more appropriate show for Woodstock, it had not presented itself in a long time."

The first night sold out quickly. Griffin had no idea what to expect from the band musically, but he figured the material would be standard rockabilly covers. "I had the small, quiet fear that I could be promoting a parody of their former selves," Griffin reflects. "Before moving to Woodstock I had worked with the reconstituted Byrds, and it was a sad sight to witness performances that featured only a few glimpses of their past brilliance. This had the potential to be worse.

"Nervously, I went downstairs and introduced myself. The club owners were not familiar with the artists, but they treated them like royalty, especially since this was our first sold-out show in some time. Our sound man for the night was a celebrity in his own right; Jon Ashton, guitarist from the Psychedelic Furs, begged to work the show. Neither Woodstock nor the Southern gents knew what to expect." They needn't have worried.

Woodstock was treated to music that ran the gamut from the Sun hits to new material. Each member presented himself with the flair of a seasoned professional. Jokes aimed at band members and their histories worked well in the middle of the serious musicianship. Many references to D.J. and Elvis were made by Sonny Burgess, and the crowd cheered at every one.

"It soon became obvious who was star of the show," observes Griffin. "D.J. just played his drums, laughed, and nodded with every poke at his history with Elvis. Sonny loved talking to the audience as much as he did playing. When he played he was like a man on fire." Gray-haired Sonny Burgess played a wireless red Fender Telecaster, ran and jumped through the audience and all over the stage, and sang the forty-year-old songs with the same conviction as he bestowed on his newer material.

Griffin noticed that Burgess and Fontana enjoyed a very special chemistry, playing off each other both musically and personally. "Smoochy liked the campy, comedy aspect of parodying Jerry Lee Lewis and other Sun Records artists," says the coauthor. "He was fun to watch, but had the overbearing persona that kept him from being taken seriously. The group curmudgeon, Stan Kesler, was just solidly holding down the bass lines, quietly smiling, but never saying a word."

Paul Burlison had dropped out of the tour due to his wife's serious illness. "I regretted not having him there," says Griffin, "but the band made references that he was not missed in the ranks. Sonny seemed to have a bit of rivalry going with Paul. D.J. and Sonny talked about Paul's limited style and his trademark licks that he repeated over and over again."

Griffin, sensing he had achieved all he could in the Joyous Lake region, was happy to relocate to Nashville, Tennessee, where he could make fresh music-industry connections and become a hands-on manager, promoter, and producer. Excited by the illustrious background of the Sun Rhythm Section, he threw himself into his work with energy and optimism.

During travels with the band, Griffin often rode, and sometimes roomed, with Fontana. Taking note of this development, Burgess would occasionally grin and ask, "Well, have you seen 'the monster' yet?" Griffin didn't really know what the singer was talking about until a later car trip with Fontana enlightened him. "We were driving along in the middle of nowhere and D.J. said to pull over because he had to take a leak. Well. D.J. just stepped out of the side of the car—leaving the door open—and he faces the inside of the car and pulls his dick out to pee. I swear, I've never seen anything like it. John Holmes or the guy from *Boogie Nights* could not compete with D.J. on that score. After viewing his manhood firsthand, not only did I understand why Scotty referred to him as the Prince of Darkness, but why he had been a favorite of Music Row secretaries from practically every label."

The Sun Rhythm Section was often booked into dives, where they played to indifferent bar owners and patrons who had no interest in their past; not exactly what they had come out of retirement to enjoy. Griffin told Burgess and Fontana they should be doing a real record with new material instead of rehashing the Sun hits they hawked at shows. The Sun Rhythm Section had put out an album on the Chicago-based Flying Fish label, but with old tunes and no promotional budget; the LP was noticed only by die-hard fans. Burgess was set to release the Dave Alvin–produced *Tennessee Border* on Hightone Records, an independent label out of San Francisco. Griffin felt the band could do something bigger. Fontana responded, "You get us a deal and we'll do it!"

"I asked for three months to do something much bigger; something that would not only keep their names alive, but put money in their pockets as well," states Griffin. "They all said yes." But Stan Kesler expressed the first sign of doubt. The band had recently been offered a recording deal through Elektra Records, but that deal came with a budget of thirty thousand dollars. This was a reasonable amount of money to cover recording costs—it was certainly much better than the ten thousand dollars that was usually given by the independent labels—but it would leave nothing for the artists. Even though they came back to the music business out of boredom and a couple of divorces, they still needed money to keep afloat. So far, the music machine had paid them about what it had in the 1950s, not much at all. How would Griffin's plan be different?

"My first response was to detail the plan of asking superstar guests to help out, raising the value of the project," he explains. "In negotiating with a major label, we could expect a recording advance to cover costs of making the record, and I would insist on a signing bonus to be divided between the principle artists: Sonny, D.J., Stan, and Smoochy." It was hoped that a new record would boost show guarantees and that, with a higher band profile, sponsorship deals could cover costs of touring. Fontana was the first to comment, "If anybody can do it, this guy can!"

Scotty Moore had not been a complete recluse, but the behind-the-scenes life suited his temperament and habits. An extramarital affair had resulted in the birth of his daughter Tasha, and his after-hours drinking was a major factor in the end of his third marriage. In his book, *That's Alright, Elvis*, the guitarist-turned-engineer blamed the continuing cycle of financial, work-related, and personal pressures on his escalating alcohol use. Like most hard drinkers, he refused to admit he had serious problem.

As part of a bankruptcy settlement he'd sold his Music City Recorders in 1973, and he'd begun freelancing as an engineer for Monument studios. It was there that he met the most important person of his later life, his girlfriend, manager, and greatest defender, Gail Pollock. As Pollock recalled in a 1996 interview, Scotty Moore had become a master of hiding in plain sight. "One day there was a man sitting in my office who was visiting from Tampa, Florida, and Scotty came in to book some time." Pollock introduced the two men, who chatted for a moment, then Moore booked his time and left. "After he left [the man asked], 'Is that the real Scotty Moore?' I said, 'Well, that's his name.' He says, 'Is that the man that played behind Elvis?' I said, 'No, he's the engineer here in the studio.' The guy did his business and left." It wasn't until she was clued in by one of the studio owners that Pollock realized the engineer's true identity. She was flabbergasted. "That was the first time I knew Scotty played a guitar or had ever played with Elvis. And I was an Elvis fan!"

Monument sold the building to Moore in 1976 and, while still working as a freelance engineer, Moore started the Independent Producers Corporation, a tape duplicating plant. "He had a business duplicating cassettes," remembers Pollack. "I worked for him for twelve years there. He was very private. He didn't take calls about the music industry. He didn't play or do interviews or things like that. We all thought of him as a very private person, the girls who worked in the plant and all. Occasionally, someone would call about an Elvis situation and he wouldn't discuss it. Or somebody would come in and want his autograph, and he wouldn't come out of his back room. So, none of us ever thought of him as famous. We just thought of him as the guy with the funny nose."

Moore hadn't completely divorced himself from playing music. In 1969, he'd contributed some guitar parts to Mother Earth's LP *Tracy Nelson Country*. For Nelson's 1971 solo recording, Moore had assembled the A-list of Nashville session musicians, which was more than Warner's budget allowed for, but each musician had enthusiastically embraced the project and couldn't have cared less about the money. Nelson had even persuaded the retired guitarist to pick up the instrument and re-create his licks for a remake of "That's All Right (Mama)." Nelson's "blues mama" voice was well suited to the Arthur Crudup tune. The entire session had been captured on film by photographer Robert Frank. "The clowning around and fun was enhanced by Tracy's on-screen flirting," chuckles Griffin. "Both Scotty and Tracy joked that they 'nearly' went a bit too far with the friendship, but by holding back they had regretted it ever since."

When Carl Perkins attempted a comeback at Mercury records in 1975, Moore had brought his Ray Butts EchoSonic amp out of storage and played on the single "E.P. Express," a musical tribute cobbled out of Presley's hit song titles. Moore had also played rhythm guitar at several sessions for two of Billy Swan's bestselling albums at Monument, including the session that resulted in the number-one hit "I Can Help." (However, it is former Bill Black Combo guitarist Reggie Young who plays the song's catchy, cascading solo.)

Much of Moore's engineering work during the 1970s and 1980s was for Nashville-based televison shows and specials that featured the likes of Carol Burnett, Perry Como, Johnny Cash. Ann-Margaret, and Dolly Parton. Regarding the Cash show, Griffin was informed that Moore was once asked to join in the musical fun being had by his old comrades, and that he'd flat-out refused.

Moore also helped engineer some awards shows, although he didn't approve of the pretensions foisted upon the ceremonies by the powers that be. "I did a couple of things television-wise," Moore states. "But I won't bring up any other name, but when this CMA started, all your CEOs and record executives and everything—they wanted to love this thing. So [they said], 'Let's do it in black tie.' For what? This is country music! And if they wanted to have a private thing, well let's have a CEOs convention and be done with it. But they want to put on this show for the world, and you don't see what it's really like! I still don't understand it."

Most Nashville people respected Moore's desire for privacy. Some, like Billy Strange, found that, "When you get to know Scotty, he's warm, friendly, and very funny." But if you wanted to know him at all, it took substantial effort.

In 1989, during the Rolling Stones' *Steel Wheels* tour, Keith Richards managed to track down the elusive Scotty Moore through former Memphis Mafia member, then Beach Boys manager, Jerry Schilling. Moore delights in telling the story of sitting at his desk in his Nashville tape-duplication company when his secretary ran in and excitedly announced the call from Richards. Moore, never wanting to be bothered unnecessarily, responded, "Who in the hell is Keith Richards?" The shocked secretary replied, "You don't know Keith Richards from the Rolling Stones?" Moore took the call and, after a few nervous minutes, had a pleasant, laugh-filled conversation that ended with Richards's invitation to fly him to the show in St. Louis the next day.

After the stadium performance, Moore and Richards showed up in Ron Wood's suite with bottles of Johnny Walker Red. There was only one guitar in the room—Wood's—but both music and spirits flowed. As Richards and Moore traded licks on "Mystery Train," Wood asked to grab the guitar and play a bit with Scotty Moore. A jovial but stingy Richards was not about to give up the moment. Wood later told Griffin, "Keith looked at me and said, 'Go away! Get your own guitar!' I said, 'It *is* my guitar!' Then he says, 'Go to your own room!' I said, 'This *is* my room!'" Wood's wife, Josephine, settled the playful argument by dragging the spike-haired guitarist off to bed just before sunrise.

The trip to St. Louis made an impression on Moore. The enormous stage, the audience roar, the lights and the clear sound—all made him think about coming out of musical retirement. Gail Pollock recalls the circumstance that finally made his return a reality. "In 1992, when Carl Perkins was getting over throat cancer, Scotty called Carl a number of times when he was in treatment, and Carl was pretty downhearted about the whole thing." Pollock recalls that Perkins was as afraid of losing his voice as he was of dying. "So Scotty would call and talk to him over a number of different times, and he kept saying, 'We'll do that album that we always talked about once you're well.'

"Well, one day Carl called and he said, 'OK, ready to go. The doctor says I can sing. Let's go down to Sun and do that album.' All of a sudden, Scotty said, 'Man, I haven't played in twenty-four years.' And he was really nervous about it. He had to do a lot of work before he could get back in the studio and play again. He was even more nervous about the crowds, about the people, and about whether anybody cared whether he could play guitar."

The album Moore and Perkins recorded, *706 ReUnion—A Sentimental Journey*, was recorded partly at Sun and partly in Perkins's living room. Fontana, the Jordanaires, Paul Burlison, Marcus Van Storey, Johnny Black, Stan and Greg Perkins, and harmonica master Charlie McCoy played on the sessions. The result was musically disappointing and often unintentionally poignant.

The scripted between-song dialogue and sound effects are contrived and corny. Further, Moore engineered all the life out of the guitar solos, which sound clean and thin—like supermarket intercom music. Rockers and blues shuffles are played in slow motion. Worst of all, Perkins's voice often betrays the aftereffects of his near-fatal illness.

A couple of bright spots do exist. Announcing the instrumental "Black Eyed Suzy Brown" as something "my brother taught me when I was ten years old," Moore leads Perkins into a neatly executed (albeit laid-back) Chet Atkins/Les Paul–style duet. Perkins, always a clever songsmith, enjoyed a fine moment with "Damn Sam," his ode to Sun studio retakes. However, neither this album nor its 1993 follow-up, *Moore Feel Good Music!* (which features Tracy Nelson, who is called "the love of Scotty's life" in the CD's notes), provide compelling examples of Moore's or Perkins's art.

Released on Moore's own Belle Meade label (which was named after the street he lives on) and poorly distributed, the discs were mainly sought out by rockabilly fans, most of whom were completely disappointed by the lack of fire and command demonstrated by the two stars. For his part, Perkins went to his grave believing that these weak-selling discs had made a fortune that Scotty Moore hadn't shared with him. "Because of their past experiences, nearly all the old rockabillies—Carl, Scotty, and even Billy Lee Riley—think everyone is out to screw them," reports Griffin. "The only people I've dealt with from that era who have their heads screwed on straight are Sonny Burgess and Jack Clement." It was through Burgess that the concert producer would first meet the elusive Scotty Moore.

August, 15, 1992, was the day that Griffin learned to love sound checks. "Sonny Burgess invited me to accompany the Sun Rhythm Section to Memphis for a celebration surrounding the fifteenth-year anniversary of Elvis Presley's death," he remembers. "The Sun Rhythm Section was on a bill that included Carl Perkins, the Jordanaires, James Burton, and the first onstage appearance of Scotty Moore in twenty-four years.

"The Sun Rhythm Section would open the show," Griffin recalls, "so their sound check was set for last. With time to kill, Sonny and I went to the building restaurant for a bite to eat. At a table eating was a gray-haired gentleman sitting with a blonde, middle-aged woman. Sonny recognized them and said a quiet hello. After sitting down with our food, I realized, *that's Scotty Moore!* When Scotty got up to leave he said, 'I'll see you up there, Sonny,' and smiled at me as he passed the table." Burgess, who was as reluctant to invade Moore's private space as everyone else at the time, neglected to introduce them.

That night the Sun Rhythm Section played a blistering opening set, running through Sun tunes and choice covers. Backstage, D. J. Fontana made a joking prediction that Moore would not even show up for the memorial concert.

"Carl Perkins had been very ill with throat cancer and this was his first appearance since a major operation nine months earlier," remembers Griffin. Despite warnings from his doctor not to strain his voice, Perkins needed a good rehearsal to help combat his stage fright. After a run-through with his sons, Greg and Stan, Perkins called out to a younger man he had been talking to earlier. James Burton walked out with a red Telecaster and plugged it into an amp. Burton played as a guitarist who kept up with trends, mixing his trademark licks with modern sounds. "James and Carl ran through a few chicken-pickin' style numbers, trying to outdo each other in speed and tricks," Griffin laughs fondly. "It was a draw." Then Perkins looked around and asked someone offstage, "Anybody see Scotty?"

A "Yo!" came from behind the curtains and Scotty Moore appeared with a blonde Gibson Super 400 guitar. He walked to the center of the stage and, after being plugged in by a stagehand, placed himself facing the front of the stage in between Perkins and Burton, who turned inward looking at him. A few mumbled words and a quick strum to check tuning later, and an instrumental of "Love Me Tender" was played by the trio. Each man took a solo turn at the melody while the others play the chords, quietly and distinctly.

In the moments they played together, no sign of rivalry or nervousness appeared. But the long sound check wore out Carl Perkins's voice to the point of hoarseness, and the effort of the rehearsal and evening performance would send the singer/guitarist back to the hospital the next day, forcing the cancellation of his planned tour of England with Moore, Fontana, and the Jordanaires.

"After the lights went down and three thousand Elvis fans filed into the theater, everyone was speculating whether Carl would be able to perform and if Scotty was going on as planned," Griffin recalls. "He had rehearsed a set with D.J., Carl, and Ronnie McDowell, but there were other guitar players on standby in case something drastic happened."

Fortunately for rockabilly buffs, the show went on as scheduled. "Carl acted as emcee and began talking about an old friend who helped him get over his blues when he was nearly knocked down from his illness," says Griffin. "He talked of a man who influenced many, but had chosen to hide away in a regular job in Nashville, shunning the spotlight for twenty-four years." When Perkins announced the name "Scotty Moore!" the place erupted in a standing ovation, with deafening shouts of "Scotty!" heard in accents from all over the world. "Scotty did not perform like someone who had not played a live show in twenty-four years," says Griffin. "He seemed shy but confident as he ran through the Elvis numbers with Carl, Ronnie, and band." For the first time in a quarter of a century, Scotty Moore did not say no to music fans. However, as Griffin would soon learn, he didn't always say yes right away, either. "That is his style—always keep 'em wondering."

After the big show, Griffin once again inquired about Scotty Moore, telling Fontana how much more valuable their project would be if they had the elusive guitarist involved. The drummer bluntly answered that Moore would be retreating to his shell after the Elvis Presley event, as had been his custom for the previous twenty-four years. Griffin felt that having Scotty Moore involved in the Sun Rhythm Section project was imperative.

Shopping for a label for the project, Griffin first called the most obvious choice: RCA. Elvis Presley's catalog was still the company's biggest asset, and a return of his former band members promised to open up new promotional possibilities for projects old and new. "D.J. had warned me not to trust RCA," says Griffin. The musicians had seldom had good experiences with the label. Neither Fontana nor Moore had even received a copy of the recently released boxed set of Presley 1950s material, even though they had been asked to help promote it. When Griffin asked for promotional items for the Woodstock shows, RCA sent only a set of Elvis stickers from the promo kit. "I joked with [RCA honcho] Joe Galante about this," chuckles Griffin, "and the next day a package with five sets, one for each of the guys and one for me, was at my door."

Galante, who had guided RCA's Nashville division to the forefront by overseeing the signing of Clint Black, Alabama, and the Judds, expressed some interest in the project. "Galante put me in touch with Dave Novick, an A&R representative for RCA in New York," recalls Griffin. "When Dave found out I knew Bill Lloyd and planned on working with him as a producer on the project, he suggested we work the record through his connections in the Nashville A&R division, headed by guitarist Josh Leo."

Bill Lloyd, a fine solo singer-songwriter and guitarist who had once been half of the hit-making country duo Foster & Lloyd, was Griffin's first choice as producer. However, Lloyd was busy producing an album with Poco's Rusty Young. Told to wait until Lloyd's project was finished, Griffin tried to get plans moving on another front. The Sun Rhythm Section was asked to look for songs, and songwriters were asked to submit material for consideration. "During this planning period, I made calls to possible guest artists—Bob Dylan, George Harrison, Keith Richards, and John Fogerty. I also reapproached D.J. with the idea of talking Scotty into participating, as a featured artist or premier guest. D.J. turned the situation over to me by giving me Scotty's home phone number."

Surprisingly, the guitarist was receptive. Glad the Sun Rhythm Section was making a real record instead of just rehashing the Sun hits, Moore said he would be happy to help out. Thrilled over the rock pioneer's acceptance of his offer, Griffin enlisted the services of the great rock and blues guitarist Danny Gatton as a second producer. At Bill Lloyd's suggestion, E Street Band bassist Garry Tallent was the third producer approached for the new record. "In my plan," explains Griffin, "the band would record twelve tracks, four each with Gatton, Tallent, and Lloyd behind the board. On the tracks would be a variety of guests, including Carl Perkins, Jerry Lee Lewis, and the superstar special guests. The names would help lock in the critics; the musicianship would surely be there; but the songs had to be right to snare the public and radio.

"One of the more difficult situations came about during a meeting called in Nashville for the band, prospective producers, and myself. When we met at an office in the ASCAP building on Music Row, much to everyone's surprise, Stan Kesler walked in with Paul Burlison. I was glad to finally meet Paul, as were Tallent and Lloyd, but had not figured him into the equation of the deal," says Griffin. "Neither had Sonny, D.J., or Smoochy. D.J. whispered to me that Stan was so cheap, he called Paul just to share the two-hundred-mile ride. I felt Stan wanted to include Burlison because he felt bad that earlier Paul had to drop out to care for his ailing wife."

Burlison had heard about the deal and came back gladly, just like he had never left. "During the meeting, it was surprising how much Paul talked and seemed totally briefed on the outline of the project," remembers Griffin. "I could tell that D.J. and Sonny squirmed every time Paul interjected a statement or question." Jeff Pringle, an agent for the Buddy Lee Agency, seemed interested in taking on the project. However, the core band members felt it was a bit of "too much too soon, but way too late."

Following the tense but fruitful meeting, Burgess and Fontana called Griffin aside. "Just weeks after taking on this group of artists I now considered friends, I was asked to fire one of the pioneers of rock guitar. Sonny told me Paul's style did not match what they were doing; he played too loud and was out of practice; it simply would not work."

Burlison was disappointed, but he understood Griffin's excuse: "We were not aware of his interest in rejoining, and the deal was in process for the four core members. It was not as painful as I figured, but I swore to myself I would do something with Paul at some point. I am glad I got to keep my promise three years later."

During the early planning stages, Scotty Moore and Stan Kesler were the big draw for Keith Richards's attention. His admiration for the pioneers of rock and blues had been well documented. Griffin recalls, "I received a call from Jane Rose, Keith's manager, requesting my address to send a letter to Scotty and Stan. When I received the letter it was one sheet, handwritten to both Scotty and Stan, expressing Keith's appreciation of being asked to participate in the record. Closing with, 'I've always wanted to say this to Stan Kesler and Scotty Moore: I'm right, you're left, she's gone!' A big letter K followed the joking reference to the Elvis tune penned by Kesler."

All the excitement of putting the record together came to a crashing halt when the powers at BMG, the parent company of RCA, decided to reshuffle the executive deck in Nashville. Josh Leo was out, and two songwriter/producers, Garth Fundis (who had guided Don Williams to country-music stardom) and Tom Schyler, were put in his place as heads of the floundering label. All projects being produced or developed under Leo's wing were out on the street. This bloodletting included the Sun Rhythm Section project and Bill Lloyd's band. None of the artists affected by the shift received a call. Rumors flew on Friday, but nothing was confirmed until an article appeared in the Sunday paper.

Griffin made a frantic call to Dave Novick in New York and attended a rushed breakfast meeting with Joe Galante, pleading his case that the proposed

The last days of the Sun Rhythm Section: Sonny Burgess, Smoochy Smith, D. J. Fontana, and Stan Kesler in El Paso, Texas, 1997. COURTESY OF SONNY BURGESS

project was never intended as a country or a Nashville record. His arguments fell on deaf ears. As is usually the case with label heads, the bottom line was the dollar. A week or so later, Griffin was shocked to receive a form letter from Novick's office stating that RCA had no plans to pursue "developing artists" Scotty Moore, D. J. Fontana, or the Sun Rhythm Section.

For all intents and purposes, the Sun Rhythm Section was finished. They played a few more gigs, but they essentially disbanded after 1997. "Well, you know Marcus passed away, and then Paul was having trouble and his wife passed away," explains Stan Kesler. "So, it just got down to where it was me and Smoochy and D.J. and Sonny. We played some like that, but the fire was gone from it. We had been at for eight or nine years. We were all getting older and getting grouchy and decided it was time to just quit."

Meanwhile, Rounder Records had become interested in a Sonny Burgess project following the glowing reviews and constant touring behind his Hightone release. Enlisting the services of Garry Tallent, plans were made for a

Burgess solo record that would bridge the gap between his raw energy and something radio stations would play. The Cambridge, Massachusetts-based label had recently gained crossover clout with bluegrass chanteuse Alison Krauss. The budgets, however, remained low, and company attitudes reflected those of typical do-it-yourself indie labels.

Garry Tallent was prepared to produce the recording at his Nashville studio for a low price tag. He had also recently established an indie label with his engineer, Tim Coates, and local artist manager Ron LaSalle. Their entity, D'Ville Records, was distributed by Rounder-owned DNA Distribution. The estimated fifteen-thousand-dollar cost to produce the recording was more than D'Ville could afford, but it was right in line with Rounder's budgets.

In the days following the RCA debacle, Scotty Moore kept himself busy working on his long-awaited autobiography. Both he and Fontana occasionally played dates with Ronnie McDowell, performing an Elvis set at the conclusion of McDowell's supper club–styled show.

Danny Gatton had been first choice for producer for the Sun Rhythm Section project. When it looked like it might really come together a couple of years later, he was still the one Griffin wanted to call. However, depressed over his failing career, Gatton had shot himself at his Washington, D.C., home. At a fundraiser/tribute show for Gatton's family (who were left with little), Fontana and Burgess played a set together. "Sonny brought the house down with his onstage antics and jumping in the audience, just like Springsteen used to do," recalls a delighted Griffin.

Moore, who respected Gatton's prowess, declined an invitation to play the benefit. Still stage shy, the guitarist's random performances with Ronnie McDowell had not prepared him to step out on his own. Moore wanted to do more in the music business, but he was unsure of how to approach it. Sonny Burgess's 1996 sessions for Rounder helped ease him back into the big time.

Tallent had taken over the reins of Burgess's venture early on, choosing musicians, instrumentation, and arrangements. The Springsteen bassist, who is known as the E Street Band's historian, was a bit of an autocrat in the studio. "When Garry, Sonny Burgess, and I were looking for material," reports Griffin, "it seemed our choices were always being nixed in favor of selections Garry had chosen. Ultimately, Garry's selections worked very well, but it looked a little one-sided early on."

Bruce Springsteen had enlisted Tallent for a week of sessions a month or so before the Burgess recordings, and Tallent remembered an unfinished rock-

Sonny Burgess. Scotty Moore began his recording comeback playing guitar for Burgess's Rounder-released album, *Sonny Burgess*. COURTESY OF ROUNDER RECORDS

abilly number called "Tiger Rose" that the Boss had been tinkering with during the sessions. He thought the track would be perfect for Burgess, and he quickly secured Springsteen's permission to record it. "Bruce had to finish the lyrics and read them into Garry's answering machine when he was satisfied," states Griffin. "Garry worked out the melody, and Sonny played a beautiful guitar figure that made the track his own."

The producer also came up with the song "Bigger than Elvis," which was written by Henry Gross of Sha Na Na, as well as the 1976 hit about a dead dog, "Shannon." Says Griffin: "I knew D.J. would love to be asked to be on ["Bigger than Elvis"] and, at Garry's suggestion, I called the Jordanaires and got their OK. As a major coup to complete the Elvis track, I asked Garry about inviting Scotty.

"Scotty said yes right away," recalls Griffin. But he had his doubts that the guitarist would show. "Finally, on the last day possible, Scotty said he will be there. The Jordanaires and D.J. were prepared to record on that day also. Garry let me know he did not plan on using D.J. on the track, in favor of John Gardner, the drummer on the other sessions. D.J. wondered why he was not asked to play on the entire record, but bought Sonny's explanation that Garry was calling the shots. Showing up expecting to play on the track with his buddies and bandmates, D.J. was visibly hurt when he found Gardner behind the drums."

On the day of the recording of "Bigger than Elvis," a major electrical storm hit Nashville. "On the day we finally get Scotty there, we have no power," exclaims Griffin. "We had all heard the stories, totally untrue, of Scotty leaving the studio if all the elements were not right or if he could not get the right sound from his amp."

When Moore arrived, the power was still flickering out, but it stayed on for an extended time while he got his setup ready. In a very good mood, he laid down his tracks in an hour, painlessly working out the parts after hearing the song for the first time. Tallent, who had been pacing the floor, became less nervous and even suggested a couple of changes to his hero. All went well, and Moore seemed truly in his element.

During a break Griffin blurted out an idea he had for a project to both Moore and Fontana. "I wanted to make a pared-down version of our RCA project, this time just featuring Scotty and D.J. as the artists. 'Why don't you guys let me put together a record for you like this?' A pause that seemed like forever was followed by Scotty looking off in the distance and saying, 'Well, if you think you can get somebody interested, go ahead and try.'"

The next day Griffin presented Moore a list of seven artists who had agreed to participate in the project. For the first time in their respective careers, Moore and Fontana would have their own album together.

Nearly All the King's Men

"Every guitarist in Milwaukee wanted to be Scotty Moore."

—Kurt Neumann, the BoDeans

"For one night, I got to be a Hillbilly Cat!"

—Keith Richards, the Rolling Stones

ON THE EVENING before the first session for *All the King's Men*, a dinner party was arranged for all of the project's key people. Kurt Neumann, Sam Llanas, and Bob Griffin from the BoDeans; D.J Fontana; and Scotty Moore (along with their respective companions, Karen and Gail); were to be the guests of honor. Garry and Tammy Tallent, Tameron Hedge, and Dan Griffin were hosts. No one but Garry Tallent had met the BoDeans before the dinner. Moore chose not to attend, but D. J. Fontana held court with quips about the food, the Presley phenomena, and the rock 'n' roll life. "D.J. seemed a bit nervous being surrounded by fifteen or so people he did not know," recalls Griffin. "These were the same musicians he would have to prove himself to behind the drums the next day. He made up for his anxiety in the only way he knows how, by talking—a lot."

The drummer played on his "rock star" status for comic relief; it was his way of laughing at the system that had provided his livelihood for more than forty years. Sometimes his rambunctious humor proved embarrassing. "I had shared a memorable meal with the drummer early in our traveling days," says

Griffin. "As the waitress walked away he said, 'I wonder if she knows what it's like to fuck a legend?'" Griffin realized Fontana had to joke about his image to maintain a sense of balance amid the hysteria that still surrounded Elvis Presley.

The BoDeans' frontmen thoroughly enjoyed Fontana's company, but to the younger musicians, Moore was still the mystery man and the key factor in the session. Both the BoDeans and Garry Tallent were nervous about performing with the musical innovator. They were also aware of his long-standing reputation as a recluse and an eccentric. Tallent's limited experience with Scotty was good but tense. "Scotty was not very happy with the song choices for the session and, while he believed me about their relevance to the project, he had never heard of the BoDeans," says Griffin. They had just had a huge radio hit, the television show *Party of Five* theme "Closer to Free." An avid television watcher, Moore knew both the series and the song.

All concerned agreed on using the Sun Records method: listen to the song, work out the parts on the spot, and record it right away. Moore was nervous being the lead man and focal point in the younger musicians' eyes. In early discussions he'd asked to include his local musician friends in order to provide him a level of comfort. This worked for the BoDeans' frontmen, since they preferred to just sing on the track; they didn't care whether or not they played instruments on it. But Garry Tallent, who would play bass in the session, quickly nixed the idea of outside help, especially help from Moore's cronies. The Bo Diddley–influenced number, "Locked Up in the State of Illinois," needed very little in the way of instruments; just guitar, bass, and drums. At Moore's insistence, pianist Little Willie Rainsford joined the session.

Griffin intended to film the sessions for a documentary, but he had trouble getting Moore and Fontana to dress for the cameras: "I knew that Scotty and D.J. would almost certainly show up in their regular dress of Cuban barber shirts, light slacks, and slippers." Moore and Fontana laughed each time someone suggested they use a dresser for the filmed sessions. The idea of being told what to wear brought back memories of being forced to dress in silly outfits for the Presley films they detested. They did not see the importance of looking good just for the film, especially their own film. "I've got nice clothes!" was Scotty's terse reply before a photo shoot. "He did have nice clothes," agrees Dan Griffin. "He just refused to wear them for the sessions."

According to Griffin, Moore employed a consistent modus operandi on every aspect of the project—maintaining control by remaining noncommit-

A particularly elegant Scotty Moore, 1997. Courtesy of Sweetfish Records

tal. This approach allowed him an easy out if things got too harried. Since he had received an advance and had agreed to most of the terms of the contract, Moore planned on seeing it through, but he was wary. The film crew arrived early in the morning to prepare for a downsized production. Says Griffin, "Shooting with only two High-8 video cameras in a closet-sized studio, they came prepared with more people than we expected, a catering setup, and many more lights than planned or needed."

As is his custom, Fontana was the first to arrive. Still smarting from being snubbed on the Sonny Burgess record, he and Garry Tallent exchanged nervous handshakes. Dan Griffin was nervous, too. "I hoped it would not color the mood of the day. It didn't then but raised its ugly head at an even more crucial point a few weeks later." When Moore arrived for the *All the King's Men* sessions at the Moondog Studios, everyone shook his hand "like they were greeting a company president at a cookout." As lights and microphones were adjusted, the reluctant guitarist had the look of a man not sure of what he was undertaking.

Before beginning their chosen song, Kurt Neumann started the riff to Presley's "Trying to Get to You." Moore picked up on it, and the two guitarists played perfectly together. When microphone levels were finally set, "Locked Up in the State of Illinois" took shape. During a break from rehearsing, a sweaty Scotty Moore walked outside, peeked back in the door, and with a seriously displeased look on his face, signaled Dan Griffin to follow him. "Is this it?" Griffin wondered. "Is he pissed to the point of canceling?" Neither assessment was true, but Moore let it be known that the cameras and crew were a problem for him. "Next time we're gonna do things ass backward," the guitarist insisted, "rehearse the song *before* the cameras roll."

The musicians nailed it on the second take, but Tallent called for one more for good measure. In his view, the more takes he had on tape, the more edits and possibilities for perfect segments there would be to choose from in mixing the track. This was not Moore and Fontana's preferred method of recording a song. Moore turned to the producer and tersely warned, "You're gonna take the soul out of it!" Fontana was especially glad for the red flag. "Garry OK'd his drum tracks," recalls Dan Griffin. "Little did I know Garry had other plans for D.J.'s parts. Before the sessions began, I had told Garry I didn't care if D.J.'s timing was not what it used to be; the tracks had to reflect his style. Garry seemed more concerned about D.J. than any other aspect of the project. More than once before the first session, Garry commented on his anticipation of timing edits or computer-generated drum-track repairs."

The BoDeans stayed behind to record vocal tracks, and Moore insisted on recording his lead-guitar tracks in the privacy of his home studio. A couple of hours later Dan Griffin heard music coming from the control room. "Garry saw me enter and, not smiling, walked into the room out of earshot from Kurt and Sam," he remembers. "The bass-playing producer told me we had a problem. Annoyed that D.J. had taken his drums, Garry asked if I could, at the very least, retrieve the snare drum from him. He painfully explained that D.J.'s tracks were not usable, but they could fix the snare by doubling it so it can be edited later or adjusted by computer." Thinking Tallent must be right, Griffin

Mr. D. J. Fontana, 1997. COURTESY OF SWEETFISH RECORDS

called Fontana at home and explained that the producer did not have the snare loud enough and needed to double it for better effect. Fontana's response was succinct and to the point, "I got a solution—turn up the *knob*!"

After years of working with Bruce Springsteen and other perfectionists, Garry Tallent expected the musicians to produce a modern, radio-ready record. He didn't want the looseness that often accompanied the old sound. Listening to Presley's and the Blue Moon Boys' early RCA records, one can hear variances in timing and levels, but often those imperfections added to the recording's spirit.

Had Scotty Moore known how the producer was undermining his friend and partner of forty years, it's likely he would have called an immediate halt to the project. He had always used Fontana on his sessions, even his home demos, and he respected his drumming ability. "My only choice, for the time being," explains Dan Griffin, "was to make an attempt at appeasing both camps. I returned with the drum. Kurt doubled D.J.'s snare track and walked out of the control room with a smile on his face." Neumann then exclaimed, "I'm the happiest guy in the world. I got to play guitar with Scotty Moore and drums with D.J.!"

During one of Dan Griffin's visits with Moore, the guitarist handed him a fax from Scott Chinery, a guitar collector/entrepreneur. Chinery was having a party at his Tom's River, New Jersey, mansion in celebration of a new line of instruments, the Blue Guitars. The invitation had asked if Moore would be a guest of honor at the event. Two names of other guests caught his eye: Tal Farlow and Les Paul. Along with Chet Atkins and Merle Travis, they were Scotty Moore's biggest influences. Moore had always been a jazz and R & B fan; he barely tolerated country music and he played rock by default, because there were so few commercial opportunities to play jazz during his emergence. A chance to meet his hero, Tal Farlow, and to see Les Paul for the first time since the 1950s, piqued his interest.

Chinery arranged for a limo to pick up Griffin and Moore and bring them to the party. The house was an incredible museum of ancient and modern art, displaying a real Egyptian sarcophagus and guitars from every era. The normally party-hating guitarist smiled and signed autographs for the many attendants, all of whom recognized him immediately. "Scotty seemed surprised that so many well-dressed people knew who he was after all these years," recalls Griffin. "Scotty was equally happy to be around serious musicians and people who had less interest in Elvis, the enigma, and more in musicianship."

When Moore learned that Tal Farlow had arrived, his eyes brightened and he quickly calmed his nerves with a couple of drinks before being introduced to the man who'd been responsible for Moore's interest in jazz as a young navy man. Now in his eighties, the tall, lanky jazz guitarist was delighted to meet Moore, although he was a bit surprised that Moore knew of him. "Scotty was just stunned that Tal even knew who he was and admired his work," reports Gail Pollock. Shortly after their conversation began, Moore and Farlow were asked to participate in a fast jam session. They sat on the couch and chatted amiably, holding blue-tinted guitars, when someone commanded, "Scotty, lead us in on 'Mystery Train'!" Moore began the signature Sun-era licks and the others followed. "Later," Griffin recalls, "Moore beamed when Tal Farlow told him he had never played a song in the key of E before that night, and he did it for Scotty!"

An invitation for Scotty to attend Les Paul's eighty-first birthday party at the Iridium club in New York came within days after Moore's return from New Jersey. Moore accepted the invitation. In attendance at the party were Gene Cornish (of the Rascals), Roger McGuinn (of the Byrds), and Clarence "Gatemouth" Brown. By the time Les Paul began his birthday set, Moore had imbibed a couple of cocktails too many. "Les was between numbers when he saw Scotty standing in the door and motioned him to walk onstage," reports Griffin. "Scotty promptly shook his head no and Les persisted, as did second guitarist Lou Pallo. Scotty walked out when Les announced him to the audience. Three sheets to the wind, Scotty Moore found himself on a stool beside Les Paul, and before he knew it—a guitar in his hand. Scotty played the next half hour, following Les's lead with jazz chords and short, less-than-brilliant solos. Scotty still jokes about it, but was visibly embarrassed by his performance."

Scotty Moore and Les Paul at Paul's eighty-first birthday party.
COURTESY OF DAN GRIFFIN

Back in Nashville, Garry Tallent arranged a two-day marathon session at Nashville's famed Woodland Studios. Moore also liked Woodland, not only because of its equipment and size, but also because it was the only recording facility in town that still allowed smoking. Tracy Nelson, Cheap Trick, Joe Ely, and Steve Earle were scheduled to record a track each at four separate sessions, two per day.

Although they seemed an odd choice for the project, Cheap Trick had impressed the former Blue Moon Boys with their eclectic, bagpipe-driven version of "Don't Be Cruel," and both Moore and Fontana lit up at the mention of the band's name. "I love those guys!" Fontana exclaimed, and he spoke of band member Bun E. Carlos as a nice guy and a great drummer.

Moore, always the control freak, wanted to be more involved in the arrangements, and would have preferred that Tallent remain at the recording console and offer suggestions to the musicians, not dictate to them as he had done at the first session. That, however, was not Tallent's style as a producer. "He liked to be actively involved," says Griffin. "Garry was always taking the limitations of budgets and the abilities of the artists in mind, but did not seem to have a positive approach to this record from the beginning." Moore again called in pianist Little Willie Rainsford, and he added his friend Gary Branchaud on bass, effectively knocking Tallent from the player's seat without the producer/bassist's prior knowledge.

The Tracy Nelson track, chosen by Tallent, was a Henry Gross tune called "Is All of This for Me?" Moore liked the demo and believed that the tune's jazzy feel would be great for Nelson's voice, but he suggested something smoother than the demo's lounge shuffle. In contrast, Tallent walked into the studio room after the first run-through and told everyone to stick to the original arrangement and style. Immediately, the tension in the room got thick. Moore was not used to having his creative judgment questioned. After a short standoff, Moore gave in and the others followed suit. Later, a disgruntled Fontana passed Griffin in the hallway and griped, "That boy don't know what the fuck he's doing! Scotty's gonna walk out of here and not come back. I guarantee ya!"

By the time Cheap Trick arrived at the studio, Nelson, Rainsford, and Branchaud were gone. Rick Neilson, Bun E. Carlos, Robin Zander, and Tom Petersson took their places alongside Moore and Fontana in the big studio room. The song "Bad Little Girl," which was written by Zander and Mike Campbell (of Tom Petty's band, the Heartbreakers), was unlike anything the

Blue Moon Boys had played. It was a loud, driving rocker in the vein of the Beatles' "I'm Down," with a drumbeat that was perfect for Fontana and Bun E. Carlos. The primary tracks were finished quickly, and as Fontana packed his things, Carlos asked sheepishly, "D.J., would you mind signing a pair of sticks for me?" Before Fontana could answer or grab a pen, Scotty walked by, looking straight ahead and quipped, "The boy must have a wood-burning stove at home!"

The Stray Cats' upright bassist, Lee Rocker, had a calming effect on both Moore and Fontana that would prove invaluable during the session. (Moore had previously guested on a recording by Rocker's band, Big Blue.) Joe Ely was scheduled for the first session. As the usual discussions about tempo and rhythm pattern began during the song rehearsal, a cloud seemed to drift into the studio. Tallent had envisioned the track as a "Jailhouse Rock" update (quite unlike Ely's demo), and he wanted Fontana to re-create his double snare licks at the start of every verse. "D.J. never liked re-creating his licks from the Elvis records," observed Griffin, "especially when asked by a producer with whom he was not in sync. All the other participants watched the two square off for the inevitable confrontation."

Indeed, a heated altercation over the Joe Ely song resulted in Fontana storming out of the studio, jumping in his car, and speeding away. After the drummer got a few blocks away, he thought twice about what he was doing and returned to play the part the way Tallent wanted. Fontana explained his return to Griffin: "Well, Dan, I had enough of his shit and left. I thought about Lee and Joe coming all this way, so I came back for them. I hated to let them boys down."

When the musicians returned to yet another take of "I'm Gonna Strangle You, Shorty," Fontana politely stated that he did not like the drum pattern and could they *please* try it his way, just once. Frustrated, Ely looked through the control room glass and said, "Hey Garry, can we just do this one straight?" In the cramped control room, Moore's and Fontana's significant others heard Tallent say, out of earshot of the artists, "Yeah, we can do it any way you like, but I'll just go in and fix it later!" He may as well have made the comment into an open talk-back mic.

The tension was somewhat relieved by the appearance of Steve Earle, who had once worked as a delivery boy [whose company made regular deliveries to] Moore's tape-duplicating company. Earle operated in the loose recording method the Blue Moon Boys preferred, and he'd written "Hot Enough for Ya" with Moore and Fontana in mind. In a flash, they ran through it once, recorded it twice, and Earle put down his guitar. "That's as good as I'm gonna get today," he exclaimed. "Garry, call if you need me to fix anything. Have a good evening, boys." As quickly as the troubadour had arrived, he departed. Fontana laughed, "Now *that's* the way a record ought to be made!"

However, everything Moore had feared about modern recording methods had come true. As a result, he wanted control of the situation. Tallent had honestly tried to get him to discuss the songs and situations before heading into the studio. But neither Moore nor Fontana would ever attempt to communicate their feelings with the man until after damage had already been done.

Griffin was faced with a problem. Tallent was in charge of production, but it was Moore's and Fontana's record. To compound matters, Tallent called Griffin the day after the four-session weekend to report that *none* of Fontana's tracks were usable, especially those on the Joe Ely session. Further, he could salvage the Cheap Trick tracks only by wiping Fontana's work from them and using those of Bun E. Carlos alone. Tallent then spoke of bringing in another drummer to overdub the drum parts. "According to Garry," recalls Griffin, "D.J. would never know his original tracks were replaced." Out of respect for the producer, Griffin grudgingly granted him permission to mix in tracks from another source. On further reflection, however, Griffin realized that Scotty Moore would receive raw mixes of the tracks to lay down his parts. As an engineer and producer himself, he was sure to know the difference between what had been recorded in his presence and what he was hearing.

Tallent had delayed giving Moore the BoDeans tracks until the guitarist was leaving the studio after the Joe Ely and Steve Earle sessions. The timing could not have been worse.

The expected phone call came at about nine that evening. "We have a big problem," Moore snapped to Griffin. "I don't know what is going on here, but somebody has fucked with D.J.'s drums, and they ain't gonna get away with it!" This was the breaking point. Griffin had agonized over the decision to wipe Fontana's tracks out, and today he wishes he'd had "the balls to stand up to Scotty rather than jeopardize my friendship with this supremely talented man, [Garry Tallent]." However, the next day over lunch, Griffin fired Garry Tallent from the project. Rather than being angry, the producer actually seemed to take it all in stride. "He seemed relieved when it was over for him."

Once in charge, Moore stripped away Tallent's bass parts and rerecorded each track to his satisfaction. Less vindictive in nature, Fontana would laugh about the trouble with the producer from time to time, but he always added, "Yeah, he's a good old boy; that's just the way they do things in New Jersey!" A few months later, Fontana and Tallent were both booked to play on a Paul Burlison session. At the studio, the drummer and bassist eyed each other nervously and shook hands. Says Griffin, "Both played better and more cohesively than on any of our original sessions. At Burlison's session, they were paid musicians working for someone else. Not partners."

Griffin had been talking with Keith Richards and the Band for some time about doing a track with Moore and Fontana. The Band was still a big concert draw, pulling in thousands a night for the three core members, drummer Levon Helm, bassist Rick Danko, and organist Garth Hudson. When Robbie Robertson left the Band after buying his publishing shares from the other members, it created a rift that could never be repaired. When Griffin approached Robertson in 1996 about the possibility of working with Moore and Fontana, he initially agreed to participate, but begged off the project once he learned his former bandmates were involved.

Jim Weider, Robertson's replacement on guitar, was a key to getting the Keith Richards–Band session together. Equipment needed to be brought into Helm's high-ceilinged home, where many of the sessions took place, but Scott Petito was available to engineer the sessions. Stan Lynch, the former drummer for Tom Petty & the Heartbreakers and a writing/producing partner with the Eagles' Don Henley, was chosen to produce. During meetings with Lynch several months earlier, Fontana had kept Stan in stitches while the two participated in a panel discussion titled "Trailblazers of Rock and Roll." The two percussionists told great road stories that had just the right mix of intelligence, humor, bravado, and humility.

Levon Helm was nowhere in sight, and neither Garth Hudson nor Rick Danko showed up at the start of Moore's and Fontana's sessions for "Deuce and a Quarter." With Moore and Weider on guitars, Fontana and Lynch both playing drums, Paul Burlison sitting in for Danko on bass, and Richard Bell on keyboards, however, the song quickly took shape. After a few run-throughs, Randy Ciarlante, the Band's auxiliary drummer, sang a scratch vocal that would be replaced later by vocals by Helm and Richards. In two takes a fine-sounding basic track was created, but Scotty Moore and D. J. Fontana left the studio that night feeling a bit rejected by their hosts.

After three hours of musical jams, with Hudson playing saxophone instead of keyboards, Levon Helm appeared. "His skin was so pale, eyes dark and tired, like a man ready to collapse," states Griffin. "By the time Levon was ready to hear that night's work, Rick Danko showed up. Rick could hear a song once and lay down a nearly perfect, signature Danko bass line in one pass." In the amount of time it took to get Danko's bass line, the main vocal and high harmonies were perfected. With the central players back at their home, Lynch wanted to get in some post-production work with Hudson.

"Watching Garth Hudson assemble his band of keyboards and modulators is worth a documentary all by itself," observes Griffin. Everything the mild-mannered eccentric did was meticulous and carefully thought out—sometimes to the extreme.

Every minute of watching and listening to Hudson tinker with equipment and fiddle with notes made the late hour increasingly tense for the normally calm Stan Lynch. Scott Petito had engineered the last record for the Band, and he had forewarned all the other musicians that Hudson did not like to record until the studio was vacant, usually after midnight. He also insisted on low light or even candlelight. As time slipped by, Hudson continued to experiment until his keyboard noodling reached nerve-wracking proportions.

At three the next morning, Lynch looked at Griffin and said, "OK, that's enough fooling around. I'm going down and get this show on the road!" Petito had warned everyone that Hudson always let him know when he was ready for a run-through. An hour earlier, the engineer had asked if Hudson was ready and he'd received a subdued, negative reply. Irritated by the seemingly pointless delays, Lynch jumped up from his seat, raced down the stairs, and inquired, "So Garth, think they can lay down a track or two?" An enraged Hudson bellowed his response: "I said I'm *not* ready and the tape won't roll until whenever the fuck I say I am ready, and if it's six in the morning when I'm ready then that's when we'll roll the tape!" To emphasize his point, the eccentric Hudson slammed his hands down on the keyboard.

Lynch came up the stairs as quickly as he had descended them, beet red from anger and embarrassment, saying, "Let's get the hell out of here; I've got better things to do than wait on this shit!" Scott Petito volunteered to stay and get the track. Hudson's prediction was right; it was six in the morning before he was ready to record. However, with speed equal to his partner's, the track was done in two takes and he was out of there.

While Petito was waiting out Hudson, D. J. Fontana had been in the hospital. "D.J. had been in such pain from fluid buildup that he had to have the pressure relieved and a catheter surgically inserted," Griffin recalls. "D.J. was told by the doctors to take it easy and get further exams when he got back to Nashville." Griffin asked the drummer if he wanted to fly home, but Fontana didn't want to miss Keith Richards's arrival. "He really wanted to stick it out, so to speak. D.J. was able to sleep most of the day and felt somewhat better for the evening session. He was hailed a real trooper for coming back to work with something strategically placed in a vicarious position."

Jane Rose called ahead to confirm the arrival of Keith Richards and to request a bottle of Stoli, along with extra Marlboros and a couple of cans of Orange Crush. The soft drink and vodka had replaced Jack Daniels as Richards's favorite refreshment. Richards brought along his eighty-two-year-old father, Burt. When Richards had told his father he was going to play with Elvis Presley's guitarist, the senior Richards said, "You mean *that* guy? Well, I gotta go see this!"

Sporting a cane, a pipe, and a Scottish cap, Burt Richards resembled a short sheepherder. According to Griffin, "He laughed as much as his son, always smiling and ready with a joke. He found his place of comfort upstairs, out of the way of the musicians, and made himself at home on a couch to listen. Burt stayed alert and happy for the entire night, drinking Guinness and smiling at everyone in the control room."

Griffin asked Richards for a few words for the film. Very politely the Stones guitarist replied, "Let's make some music first!" Everyone agreed to suspend shooting until Richards completed "Deuce and a Quarter." While the track was rolling, Keith played around with tones and guitar lines. Then came the short notes he had played on "Brown Sugar." In three quick passes of the tape, he had enough parts for Stan Lynch to later fashion a perfect Keith Richards guitar track.

"By the time vocal overdubs were attempted, Keith had finished the first bottle of Stoli and Orange Crush; Scotty was well into his Johnny Walker," says Griffin. "D.J. was teetotaling due to his ailments." Richards had not listened much to the melody, so he threw out the original phrasing and made his own way around the lyrics. Those familiar with Richards's unorthodox vocal style were pleased with the sound, remembers Griffin. "But Scotty—brave with Johnny Walker—decided to go downstairs and be Keith's vocal coach. Scotty stood beside Keith and called to Stan and Scott Petito to 'Roll the tape!' They pretended to dance together as the track played." Several takes were halted by Richards's disarming fits of laughter over Moore's vocal coaching. "No! No! No! You're not enunciating, Keith! Sing it like *this*." Finally Richards did it Scotty

Moore's way. Griffin laughs, "Many people have since told us it is the first time they understood every word Keith has sung on a track."

The after-session jam was every bit as entertaining. "Scotty and Keith had sat back down with their guitars," states Griffin, "this time to play for themselves and not a record. Jimmy Weider and Paul Burlison on guitars; Richard Bell and a less grumpy Garth Hudson on keyboards. Rick Danko had gone into hiding once again, so Marshall Crenshaw picked up the bass. The all-star jam was complete when Levon and D.J. sat down at the drum."

Stan Lynch, who did not intend to be left out, played tambourine as they ran through a few Elvis Presley Sun selections. Suddenly, Jim Weider yelled out, "Hey Levon, let's do 'Hand Jive.'" Almost immediately the troupe lunged into a thirty-minute version of "Willie and the Hand Jive." "Scotty had already put down his guitar and decided he would direct the many musicians in the room," recalls an awed Griffin. "At one point, he was conducting and Keith sat in a chair in front of him. Scotty bowed to Keith, but like a humble student, Keith stopped playing, put down his guitar and bowed on his knees in return."

Stan Lynch, savoring the moment, looked over at his role models on the drums and said, "Gentlemen, I want to thank you for my job, my house, my car, and my hair!" Levon responded, "Hear hear!"

Fontana quickly jibed, "Hey, don't blame it on us!"

After the festivities ended, Griffin finally got his interview with Keith Richards. He began by asking Richards what it felt like to play with the Blue Moon Boys. Laughing, the British superstar answered, "It's something I just *had* to do. Who could say no? For one night I was a Hillbilly Cat!"

The sessions for *All the King's Men* were well under way when Fontana asked if Griffin had considered Ron Wood, the Rolling Stone with whom he felt most comfortable, for the project. Fontana also requested Charlie Watts, whose work he respected. Ron Wood's estate, Sandy Mount, outside of Dublin, Ireland, houses a home studio that was built in a former horse stable. There, Wood has hosted the likes of Carl Perkins, Jerry Lee Lewis, Eric Clapton, Bob Dylan, Van Morrison, U2, and of course, the Rolling Stones. It was available the first week of December, and Wood suggested that Moore and Fontana come to his studio in Ireland. Further, he offered his studio free of charge and even invited the older rockers to stay at his home for the duration of the sessions. Along with engineer Eoghan McCarron, Wood recorded countless jams and enlisted each guest to play a rendition of a song written for his lovely wife, Josephine.

D. J. Fontana, Ron Wood, and Scotty Moore relax at Sandy Mount (Wood's house), 1996. COURTESY OF DAN GRIFFIN

Jeff Beck had been on Griffin's personal wish list of guests from the beginning. Getting him was another matter. By the time he had hashed out all the details with Beck's manager and label executive, John Kolodner, it was too late to fly the superstar guitarist in for the Nashville sessions. Once the sessions at Wood's home studio were scheduled, the wrangling to secure the former Yardbird's services began anew. When Beck's people learned that Van Morrison was scheduled on the same session with Beck, the guitarist's displeased management suggested that Griffin choose between the two.

Then, before Griffin could absorb the implications of that comment, the phone rang with a request from Morrison's camp to please not schedule him at the same time as Mr. Beck. The message went on to state that the two should not even pass each other on the way to the bathroom. The decision about which performer would record with Moore and Fontana at a later session was then made moot by a call from Leo Green. Morrison had decided he was unavailable for the sessions.

Upon Beck's arrival, Griffin thanked the performer for making the trip, but Beck turned the tables and said, "No! Thank you for inviting me! I couldn't turn this down. What an honor to be asked to play with Scotty and D.J.!" Beck further told Griffin how he had not seen Ron Wood for eight years and, surprisingly, that he had never been to Ireland before.

Wood and Beck warmed up by playing old Presley numbers such as "Blue Moon of Kentucky," "Hound Dog," and "Jailhouse Rock." They got a kick out of playing the songs with the records' original musicians. During the jam, Moore began playing a variation on his classic "Mystery Train" introduction. Beck joined in with a lick that was similar to his noted "Superstition" track with Stevie Wonder, and a totally new song emerged. During another break, Wood and Beck elaborated on the song's theme—a tip of the hat to Carl Perkins—making the new version a tribute to the Blue Moon Boys. Wood quickly created a series of verses about each musician, beginning with Bill Black, then Fontana, and finally Moore. Not once did the lyrics make reference to Elvis Presley. In short order, the song "Unsung Heroes" was born.

Beck and Wood offered cowriting credit to Moore and Fontana, but the two humbly refused, not wanting to seem so cocky as to have cowritten a song that is a paean to themselves. Yet Beck and Wood remained adamant that, while writing credit was theirs, the publishing money would go directly to the surviving Blue Moon Boys.

Later, in his own pub, Wood asked why Griffin had not invited Mick Jagger to join in on the recording. Griffin explained they had three Rolling Stones members for the project; it would have been overkill if they'd asked for the entire band. Wood laughed and said he'd talked to Jagger the week before, and that when he told him that Moore and Fontana were coming to record, the Stones' singer seemed surprised that he wasn't asked as well. When Griffin winced with guilt, Wood said, "Don't worry about it; we'll call him when we take the next break." Back in the studio, both guitarists prepared for guitar overdubs, when Jo Wood announced to her husband over the intercom, "Ronnie, Mick Jagger is on the phone for you."

After a short talk, Wood turned the phone over to Moore and Fontana, and Jagger promptly asked, "So, are you boys having a good time without me?" The chief Stone assured both men that he would like to help out, and he invited them and their entire entourage to his Christmas party at his London estate. Moreover, Wood offered to fly everyone there and provide lodging. The event was set for the night after the track was mixed.

The night segued into revelry in Wood's private pub, with free Guinness and billiards until just before dawn. Moore and Fontana, at ages sixty-six and sixty-seven, respectively, held their own against Wood and the crew. In fact, they were the only ones who recovered sufficiently from the party to perform the last night's work at the studio.

After eight hours of mixing, Moore was satisfied, and he invited Wood outside for a breath of fresh air. Suddenly a startled Eoghan exclaimed, "Oh shit, it's eating the tape!" Worse, Eoghan had cleared the consoles of all the settings while the tape machine was reading the one-time print of the final mix. The mix they had slaved over for so long was lost for good. The choices were to fly the master tape to Nashville and have Moore remix the track alone at a later date, or to continue immediately while the settings were fresh in their minds, missing Jagger's party. They chose the latter. Sometime later, when Moore saw Jagger, he asked, "If we do another one, are you up for it?" The British rock icon was resolute, "I want to be the first one that you call."

At three in the morning, Moore sat down with Eoghan and quickly began to adjust the instruments to their best recollections. Three hours later, they left the studio as the sun began to rise. It had been a long week in Ireland, and the duo had endured as much fun as they could handle. When Griffin checked in on Moore the following day, he barely could speak. He told Griffin that Fontana was in even worse shape. The week of playing music, recording, and partying like a young heavy metal act had finally caught up with them.

Once they returned to Nashville, Moore recorded an offbeat soul track with bluesman Joe Louis Walker and a Presley-ish country ballad with the then-hot Mavericks. However, the guitarist enjoyed a brainstorm. He wanted to honor his late partner by cutting a track, in an updated Bill Black Combo style, with Reggie Young, Ace Cannon, Bobby Emmons, Jerry Arnold, bassist Mike Leech and keyboard whiz Bobby Woods. "Reggie and Bobby Emmons wrote the tune that we did called 'Goin' Back to Memphis," Moore told James V. Roy, who runs Moore's Web site. "The track still has the Bill Black feel, but it's updated just enough to get into the nineties." At the session, Moore recalled, each musician told his favorite story about the late bassist. "It was like that old radio show, *Can You Top This*."

"That was a great evening," testifies Ace Cannon. "All this happened in Nashville. I was the only outsider as far as not being right up there in Nashville where Bobby Wood, Mike Leech, Gene Crisman, and all the ones who called me in to do it [were]. They told me, 'Just come right in there and play whatever you feel.'"

The Bill Black Combo tribute surfaced as the best overall performance on the *All the King's Men* album. Moore and Fontana, who were perfectly at home in a Nashville studio, played with like-minded professionals who knew how to get things done, not big-name stars. Reggie Young's pencil lick created a solid foundation for both Moore's delicate blues fills and fadeout allusion to "Heartbreak Hotel." Cannon's sax took in elements of new-age jazz, and Emmons's scorching work on the Hammond B-3 offered the counterpoint of 1960s rock. "We got all those guys back together and did a hell of a cut on it," says Fontana. "I mean exactly like the Bill Black Combo. It was a lot of fun."

As recordings were being completed, Griffin shopped for a deal with a record label. After some frustrating experiences with the major labels, where he made the rounds and educated twenty-five-year-old executives on the history of these legendary artists, Griffin decided to consider a well-funded, independent label that knew and respected the Blue Moon Boys. "The thought of these tattooed, body-pierced twentysomethings making calls to buyers on behalf of a duo of aging musicians scared me," says Griffin.

Griffin approached Sweetfish Records, which had recently made a deal for Paul Burlison's solo record. The label was owned and operated by Rees Shad, a trust-fund-baby-turned-studio owner and songwriter. (Unlike Moore and Fontana's disc, Burlison's would be owned by Sweetfish, although one of the tracks was cut at the same Woodstock location with Jim Weider. Ultimately, neither disc would set the world on fire, but Griffin feels that the Burlison disc, *Train Kept a-Rollin'*, was the best recording project he has ever been associated with.)

The result of all the tumult and travel surrounding the *All the King's Men* sessions was a rather soulless, uneven album; few listeners can tell who is playing what or why. Rockabilly fans were alienated by it, and classic-rock aficionados regarded it as a little more than a collectible. Neither Moore nor Fontana made distinctive impressions, and only a few of the songs—"Deuce and a Quarter," "Hot Enough for Ya," and "Unsung Heroes"—seemed worth the effort. On the strength of its guest list and the historical importance of the principal players, the set was generously reviewed by major publications. Yet, despite its high-profile guest stars, sales of the CD proved disappointing.

"Goin' to Memphis" (which most reviewers ignored) stood apart because on that song Moore and Fontana were participating in the type of music fans had actually wanted them to be doing all along—basic rock and blues. As a result, the reconstituted Bill Black Combo track was nominated for a 1998 Grammy Award.

Dead Elvis Week

"1954, at the ripe old age of four years old, I was watching the Tommy and Jimmy Dorsey Stage Show. There was a young singer on that night by the name of Elvis Presley. I never will forget it, because this guy came on and pointed at the camera and started singing this song and it was like somebody had poured a big bucket of water over me. It was electrifying and so different. Not only did I notice the singer, but I noticed the guy playing the big upright bass, and he was smiling and laughing, and I noticed the guitar player. Of course, I'm talking about Scotty Moore and Bill Black, who were behind Elvis Presley. So I was watching the whole thing, just being taken in by every bit of it. And from that moment on, I became the world's biggest Elvis Presley, Scotty Moore, and Bill Black fan."

—Ronnie McDowell

"Most of the things I do in the States is with Ronnie McDowell, who is a country artist, who has had some great, great country records way up in number one and stuff. And he's been the official—as far as Priscilla and the estate—the official voice of Elvis for soundtracks and stuff like that. He's not an impersonator and he doesn't dress up, and unless he is doing something for them, he doesn't try to sound like

Elvis. He just has that natural timber in his voice that works. And I enjoy working with him."

—Scotty Moore

AMONG ALL THE rock superstars and legends on the *All the King's Men* disc is Presley-impersonating country singer Ronnie McDowell, who delivers the set's stylistic low point, "Soulmates." Dripping with false sincerity, the tune plays out like a parody of an Elvis Presley 1950s teen ballad.

McDowell burst onto the music scene in mid-August 1977. In the hours following the shocking announcement of Elvis Presley's death, McDowell wrote the song "The King Is Gone," recorded the tracks, pressed promotional copies, and shipped the tribute single to radio stations across the country. Picked up by the Scorpion label, it became a certified gold record and hit number thirteen on both the pop and country charts.

D.J., Scotty, John Fogerty, Ronnie McDowell, and Sam Phillips, 1997.
COURTESY OF RUSTY RUSSELL

McDowell claims not to have mimicked Presley on the recording, that it just came out that way. Yet any impressionist will tell you it takes genuine effort to emulate Presley's voice to the degree that McDowell does. Further, perception of McDowell's talents suffers from what Will Kaufman, the author of *The Comedian as Confidence Man*, refers to as "irony fatigue." Kaufman coined the phrase to describe comedians (such as Lenny Bruce, George Carlin, and Bill Hicks) who wish their message to be taken seriously. It also applies to McDowell, a singer who achieved stardom through his impression of Elvis Presley but who wants to be regarded as someone who creates worthwhile original music. (Moore, Fontana, and the Jordanaires all say that he doesn't deliberately try to sound like their late boss.) Decades after his hero's demise, the Portland, Tennessee, native still imitates Elvis Presley in feature films and television documentaries, whenever RCA does not allow usage of the original tracks. Because he's worked on it for more than thirty years, his impression is superior to that of the average Vegas tribute act, but it lacks the electric drive and emotional passion of the real thing.

After "The King Is Gone," McDowell did not always imitate Presley, but his musical channeling did bring him stardom and has remained a popular part of his live show. Moving from Scorpion to Epic and Curb records, the former commercial sign painter wracked up twenty-nine top-forty country hits from 1977 to 1991; fourteen of them hit the top ten, and two (1981's "Older Women" and 1983's "You're Going to Ruin My Bad Reputation") were number-one records. He is a competent journeyman singer/songwriter whose collected works are less memorable than those of a Presley-influenced pop and country veteran like Billy "Crash" Craddock.

The 1992 Memphis event that brought Scotty Moore out of retirement also introduced him to Ronnie McDowell. By that time, country radio had ignored McDowell's offerings for a couple of years, though he still toured regularly. (Earlier, he'd attempted duet singles with Conway Twitty and Jerry Lee Lewis, but those did little to slow his chart decline.) The singer's offer to join forces and perform Presley material on a semi-regular basis brought Moore back to the music world full time.

More than the chance for Moore to make an easy buck, it was McDowell's personality that bonded Scotty Moore to him. The guitarist truly feels that the singer/impressionist's gracious persona is reminiscent of Presley's early, humble demeanor. Loyal and generous, McDowell is the man Moore often wished Elvis Presley had been.

Over the next few years, Scotty Moore and D. J. Fontana performed with Ronnie McDowell at state fairs, community picnics, and company parties. It wasn't hard work for Moore; he didn't have to invent anything new, just play the same old licks. But often, the two men who'd influenced history's most important rock artist found themselves playing in front of people who needed to be told who they were.

Near the end of his show, McDowell would sit on a stool, a lone spotlight shining on him as he told a story of how his sister called him in to see something on television, and how he was taken by the image of Presley and his band as they performed on *The Ed Sullivan Show* in 1956. At this point, McDowell would tell of meeting the Blue Moon Boys in Memphis. Then the lights would come up, revealing Moore and Fontana at the ready, and they would begin playing "That's All Right (Mama)" or "Blue Moon of Kentucky." Invariably, McDowell also threw in a tune that did not belong in the Hillbilly Cat era, such as "Viva Las Vegas," "Burning Love," or "Hurt."

Moore usually avoids the usual, "What was Elvis really like?" questions by talking about McDowell. He seems truly taken by the singer's Presley-like charisma, and many times he's told Dan Griffin that "he was amazed at the similarities between Ronnie and Elvis." Yet Griffin noticed that, at any Presley-related event in the United States, the audience seemed more interested in McDowell than in Moore and Fontana. If the two Presley sidemen ever noticed, they never let on. McDowell has used his Moore and Fontana connection to legitimize his existence in the eyes of Elvis Presley fans. However, he has also been a tireless friend to both men. In the vast scheme of things, that is more important to Scotty Moore than worrying about whether the singer is hip or unhip.

After the RCA debacle, Moore and Fontana were approached by Graceland in 1994 to perform at an all-star Elvis tribute in Memphis. The pay-per-view and cable special, by Warner-Avalon Productions, was scheduled to mix modern acts like the Judds, Billy Joel, Bruce Springsteen, Bob Dylan, Dwight Yoakum, the Mavericks, Melissa Etheridge, and Chris Isaak with offerings by such Presley contemporaries as Carl Perkins, Johnny Cash, and Jerry Lee Lewis. All were asked to present classic Presley songs in their own styles.

"When Scotty was contacted about the event, he told them his suggestion of appearing with Ronnie and his band," recalls Griffin. "They would give Ronnie a segment for the show, but they wanted Scotty and D.J. there for a major part of the performances. Scotty agreed."

The afternoon of the broadcast, McDowell's manager, Joe Meador, received a call informing him that his singer would most likely be cut from the show, or that his segment would be placed at the opening, used for the pre-broadcast run through, or taped but not shown. "It became apparent that the producers never intended to use Ronnie for anything other than getting Scotty to commit to the event," reflects Griffin.

Meador called McDowell, who had been a great help to the technical crew during sound and camera tests, and the angry singer promptly hopped on a plane back to Nashville. He had canceled two paying engagements, opting instead to reimburse promoters' deposits, and he'd paid his band to rehearse with the other artists on the bill. Now the producers wanted to use his band behind the stars while cutting his portion of the show. Moore called the producers and expressed his displeasure, but it was too late.

McDowell's troubles were a precursor to the show's eventual failure. Many of the artists announced to appear did not show up, and several that did never received payment. The pay-per-view, cable, and network follow-ups were unsuccessful. After many contractual disputes, Polygram pulled the audio recording from the shelves with little regret. Embittered, Moore told Griffin that the show's musical director, Don Was, "couldn't produce himself out of a pair of shoes." The pay-per-view event did serve a purpose; it demonstrated to Moore that he could hold his own with younger artists, and it bolstered his confidence regarding new projects. However, McDowell's inclusion in events continued to be a sticking point between the guitarist and others.

The first time that Dan Griffin sat with Moore to discuss the possibility of making the *All the King's Men* album and a documentary film, the guitarist had said he wanted to include Ronnie McDowell. At the early stage it was a suggestion, not a demand. "Garry had no intention whatsoever of using McDowell," reports Griffin. So, it was only after Tallent left the project, and Moore took charge of the music production, that it became a major problem.

After all but two tracks were cut for the record, Moore told Griffin he wanted to schedule a session with McDowell and his band. Griffin compromised. He arranged for the Jordanaires, Millie Kirkham (whose high soprano was used to such great effect on Presley's recording of "Blue Christmas"), and Nashville "a-team" guitarist Harold Bradley to perform on the track so that it would seem to have a more logical connection to Elvis Presley. Griffin reports: "If at any time I had said, 'There will not be a Ronnie McDowell track on the record no matter what,' Scotty would have quit the project. . . . When the time came for Ronnie to sing the vocals," says Griffin, "Scotty had him do it in his 'Elvis voice.' The manager/producer looked on with fear and amazement, but today he adds, "It did make Scotty happy."

For their live shows together, McDowell recruited Moore and Fontana to re-create their tracks from their days with Presley. Moore diligently worked on his tunes, with the requirement that McDowell do them in Elvis's original keys. According to Moore, this proviso provoked a good deal of humor during their popular live appearances together. "We have a lot of fun onstage, kidding him about the key. I say, 'You want to do so-and-so and I say you gotta do it in the original key.' And he says, 'It's tearing my throat up.' And then he gets a standing ovation and I said, 'Elvis wanted to sing, and they wanted to see him bleed, and he knew it. Why do you think he did "Jailhouse Rock" the way he did? People loved it, but God, he's gonna die [vocally] any minute!'"

Inspired by their chemistry on stage, McDowell sought to provide a nostalgic treat for fans of his Presley impersonation by recording an album with the King's original surviving musicians. Something McDowell probably didn't take into account was how rusty the former Blue Moon Boys were. During the early 1990s Moore and Fontana had guested on a Christmas single for the Royal Court of China, a Nashville alternative band, but McDowell's *A Tribute to the King* project was their first foray into recording a full album together since Moore's *The Guitar That Changed the World.*

McDowell was barred from releasing *A Tribute to the King* and other self-financed projects by his label, Curb Records. The singer requested a release from Curb and signed a deal with Intersound to put out *A Tribute to the King* in 1997. The original twenty-song set quite naturally highlights McDowell's facile vocal impersonations on a variety of Elvis Presley's hits. Overall, the production is fey and sterile. The rock tunes lack grit, and the ballads gush unconvincingly. The Jordanaires—who also like McDowell as a person—aren't particularly used well. Fontana plays his late boss's old hits with genuine kick, but Moore's work is thin and tentative. Despite his clear love of Presley's music, McDowell and the Hillbilly Cat's original collaborators generate no chemistry together in the studio. That said, the disc (which was recently rereleased with a few more tracks added to it) has been enormously popular with McDowell's fans down through the years.

Publicist Lance Cowan was told by talent bookers, "No Ronnie!" Lee Rocker and the English bands Moore played with overseas also blanched at the idea of McDowell's Presley imitations undermining the legitimacy of their gigs.

Yet time and time again when he brought offers of gigs to Moore, Griffin was forced to face what he calls the "Ronnie McFactor." The only way Griffin could persuade the guitarist to do a live date without McDowell was to make sure the country star/Presley-tribute artist had already been booked elsewhere. This applied to national television shows such as *The Tonight Show with Jay Leno* and *Late Night with Conan O'Brien.*

Dan Griffin says: "I came to see Ronnie's desperation at keeping a presence in the music business when he tried to enlist my help in climbing on another celebrity-death bandwagon. In the days following the death of Princess Diana, Ronnie wrote a song in praise of the tragic tabloid star. On the Friday afternoon before the funeral of the princess, while on vacation from the music business, I received a frantic call from McDowell and Steve Shepherd. Ronnie wanted me to call Europe to research the possibility of digitally transferring the tune to radio stations all over the continent. He was convinced it would be a repeat of his Elvis tribute, 'The King Is Gone.' After Diana was buried and fodder for the papers, the subject was dropped. Ronnie must have decided to wait for the next major demise of a public figure."

Each year during the week of August 9 through 16, as many as eighty thousand Elvis Presley fans from every part of the world flock to Memphis to commemorate the death of the King of Rock 'n' Roll. The event that Dan Griffin calls "Dead Elvis Week" has grown by leaps and bounds since the 1992 fifteenth-anniversary celebration that brought Scotty Moore out of retirement. No one ever mentions, at least publicly, how strange it is to hold the biggest celebrations of Presley on the anniversaries of his death. Some writers have opined that the celebration is perfectly in line with the Southern tradition of honoring dead heroes. After all, in his 1988 hit "If the South Woulda Won," no less a figure than Hank Williams, Jr., sang, "The day Elvis passed away would be our national holiday," like that would somehow be a good thing. The fact is, the Elvis Week celebrations are held in August for very sound financial reasons. Presley's birthday, which also attracts fans the world over, occurs just after the Christmas holidays have depleted their potential customers' spending cash. Despite the hot, humid weather, no other major spending holiday occurs in August, and the festivities are held during the last gasp of most American vacation schedules.

August 1997, the twentieth anniversary, was the biggest event until that time and a very important milestone for Scotty Moore, whose autobiography (as told to James Dickerson), *That's Alright, Elvis*, hit the shelves the last week of July 1997. The CD release of *All the King's Men* had been scheduled for June of that year, but it was delayed until the first week of August. Unlike Fontana, Moore had always found "Dead Elvis Week" distasteful if not downright morbid. However, with two items of new material and lots of photos to hawk, Moore and Fontana returned to Memphis to sell their wares.

The most noteworthy event was *Virtual Elvis*, a Graceland-sponsored concert held at the twelve-thousand-seat Memphis Coliseum. The organizers contracted all surviving Presley band members, from the Blue Moon Boys to the Vegas-era TCB Band, the Jordanaires, J. D. Sumner & the Stamps, and the Sweet Inspirations, to perform alongside Elvis Presley's image, which was projected onto a giant video screen. Ads promised to present songs from all phases of his career, with the original musicians performing on the stage beneath the screen. Initially Moore had said, "Absolutely not!" Fontana followed suit out of respect for his partner, despite the large guarantee that was offered to each of them. Moore then countered with the offer that he would appear only if the Blue Moon Boys performed with Ronnie McDowell, his band, and the Jordanaires. Demonstrating great integrity, he refused to perform if the screen featured Elvis Presley singing to their live music. This plan, he insisted, would give a bit of authenticity to the program. The offer was accepted. But Graceland's producers had planned on using big-screen clips of Presley and the Blue Moon Boys from the Ed Sullivan and Steve Allen shows, culminating with clips from the *'68 Comeback Special.* They kept the footage prepared in case Moore reconsidered at the last minute. To his credit, he never did.

The show began as planned, with the entrance of the police and a limo. As the sound system blared the theme from *2001: A Space Odyssey*, the timpani rolled and a sequined, jumpsuited image of Elvis Presley appeared on screen. The Vegas-era TCB Band, performing "See See Rider" below the screen, was drowned out by the roar of the crowd. Dan Griffin called the spectacle "a ridiculous concept on paper that turned out to be the ultimate celebrity grave robbing. Aside from that, it was quite impressive technically."

Moore and Fontana had known all the TCB Band members—James Burton, Jerry Scheff, Ron Tutt, and Glen D. Hardin—although there had never been much interaction between the two camps. The TCB Band members were all consummate musicians, but their approach was strikingly different from that of the Blue Moon Boys. The Sun material, as performed by the TCB Band, was always crammed together in a corny throwaway medley. That night, as they played the slick, lackluster 1970s material, the audience leapt to their feet and looked adoringly at the screen image of an overweight, sweating Elvis Presley.

The Blue Moon Boys, with Ronnie McDowell and band, were given an energetic welcome from twelve thousand fans who'd each paid seventy-five dollars to see the show. They performed a tasteful set of Sun-era tunes that began with "Blue Moon of Kentucky" and ended with "That's All Right (Mama)." Moore, Fontana, and the Jordanaires played with fervor. However, Moore's unwillingness to play with a projected illusion of Elvis Presley resulted in a polite, yet decidedly underwhelming, audience response. Moore's hope of adding authenticity to the show was lost on a crowd that longed to revel in recycled images of the late King.

It was Presley's daughter, Lisa Marie, who truly brought the house down, with a stunt patterned after the electronically engineered Nat King Cole–Natalie Cole duet. When the screen came down, the audience was treated to flickering images of Elvis Presley with his then-newborn baby as his unmistakable voice crooned the melancholy "Don't Cry, Daddy." Joined on the chorus by the grown-up Lisa Marie, who showed off a surprisingly good voice, the duet moved many in the audience to tears.

Griffin later learned that Lisa Marie and the concert's producer had worked night and day, overdubbing and pitch-bending the original master tape to ensure a natural-sounding presentation. Jack Soden, a Presley executive, told Fontana that RCA would never allow the master to be used for a recorded release of the duet, and the label granted permission for the master to be used only for a one-time performance.

Far from being a burden during Elvis Week, Ronnie McDowell not only proved popular with fans, but he was also often the key to getting a reluctant Scotty Moore to do promotional appearances. Dan Griffin recalls one particular incident when McDowell saved the day. The Graceland-owned Elvis Café on Beale Street had scheduled a live CNN interview with and performance by both Moore and Fontana in the afternoon, along with in-store appearances to promote Moore's book and the *All the King's Men* CD that evening. "D.J. had woken up early with chest pains and rushed off to the emergency room," remembers Griffin. "The doctors had ordered him home for rest or he would have a repeat of his heart attack from the past spring."

Moore made it through the book and CD signings, but he'd balked at the CNN/Elvis Café appearance, where Lauren Sidney of *Showbiz Today* was set to interview him. According to Griffin, "Scotty insisted that, instead of sitting alone with a guitar and playing some licks from Elvis's Sun tunes, that he play a short set with Ronnie McDowell and his band. The producer's reluctant acquiescence did little to relieve Moore's foul mood. "He seemed determined not to have a good time without D.J.," observes Griffin.

The street outside the Elvis Café was inundated with fans. Inside, Moore was told that the interview would not be held in a private room as planned, but before a live audience on the main dining room's performance stage. "Scotty went ballistic and retreated to the dressing room," reports Griffin. "A couple of quick Johnny Walkers and he calmed down a bit, but still refused to go on." With the broadcast in danger of being canceled, Ronnie McDowell sat with Moore and pleaded with him, emphasizing that the broadcast would be a boost to both of their careers. "Scotty reluctantly agreed," says Griffin, "facing enormous confusion between being pressured into something he did not want to do and the feeling that he was somehow being hoodwinked."

During the CNN interview, Moore truculently referred most of the questions to McDowell. The onstage portion of the show was better. Running through "Baby, Let's Play House," Moore, McDowell, and George Grantham, on drums in place of the ailing Fontana, rocked the joint. The audience had expected to hear loud Presley music piped in over the plates of overpriced hamburgers. What they got was an authentic link to Presley and a strong live performance from his chief imitator.

After a week of witnessing the madness of the Presley cult, Moore proclaimed it all an abomination to the singer's memory. He told Griffin that Presley retreated from the fans not out of rudeness, but because he didn't feel he was equal to their adoration. The guitarist had long said, "Elvis hated to be referred to as 'the King,'" and, "Elvis would never have approved of the way his image had been sold, even by his own family." Moore strongly disliked being a part of it, especially this late in life. For financial reasons—and because it was often the right thing to do for the fans—he had to play the "Elvis game." But he didn't have to like it.

Moore was genuinely annoyed to learn that he was booked into a hotel that was hosting a Presley-imitator convention. After viewing more "Elvi" than should be legally allowed, the guitarist hid in his room between shows and steadfastly avoided the press.

In stark contrast, whether he played major concert venues or casinos with Presley-tribute acts, Fontana viewed his gigs as "just another job." To the outgoing drummer, something like Elvis Week was a little easier for him than most gigs. So what if he had to talk about Elvis Presley to earn his check? He'd *liked* the late singer, and he liked telling stories. Throughout the years he developed the knack of speaking to each interviewer in a way that convinces them they are hearing something new. Moreover, Fontana's personal warmth and self-deprecating humor allowed him to connect with fans in a way that the shyer Scotty Moore could not. As a result, while the guitarist is clearly more appreciated by historians and fellow musicians, Fontana remains more popular with fans.

Moore would have never participated in anything like 1998's *Rock 'n' Roll Graffiti*. The video, which featured reminiscences by Fontana, sold via late-night television infomercials, features music and road stories by artists from the golden age of rock 'n' roll. "Everybody was there—Frankie Ford, Dee Dee Sharp, all the doo-wop groups," Fontana recalls. "Man, I've never seen the likes of all these artists in all my life. Mary Wells was there. Otis Williams, the guy from the Diamonds. Hey, I got a kick out of listening to those guys. They've got a lot of good stories, too." Fontana was also pleased that the music still worked. "Man, I was shocked! These guys could sing as well as they ever did. They were just absolutely thrilled they were so good. They had a rehearsed band already sitting there, they knew all the songs, and had all the charts written out."

Moore's personality was the polar opposite of Fontana's. Although warm and friendly to fellow performers (particularly his contemporaries) offstage, the guitarist was just too emotionally reticent to participate in the dog-and-pony show of constant personal promotion that Fontana seemed to revel in. That's why Griffin was so surprised that Moore, after surviving "Dead Elvis Week," still wanted to do a cross-country promotional tour behind the *All the King's Men* CD and his autobiography, *That's Alright, Elvis*. But Moore knew that if he wanted his wares to sell, he had to promote them.

Like most autobiographies in the modern age, *That's Alright, Elvis* was part memoir, part personal public relations. Dictating to author James Dickerson (whose supplemental research is rock solid), Moore never truly revealed himself. From the start, he asked that the book not be written in first person so he could seem the reluctant hero, not the bragging protagonist. The result is a dry and cold reading experience. "It was a very dull book," admits Griffin. "That's only because Scotty was in control. I mean, Scotty wasn't going to tell any stories that would make him look bad—or even remotely interesting. Jim Dickerson thought he was really getting a hot deal by getting the Scotty Moore biography, but Scotty only put in there exactly what he wanted to put in there."

In the book, which sold roughly fifteen-thousand copies upon initial release, Moore backs away from discussing the Presley-Parker–related bitterness that caused Moore to put down his guitar, and he tells very little about his interpersonal dealings with Bill Black and D. J. Fontana. Further, the most colorful Presley recollections come from his ex-wives Bobbie and Emily, while the guitarist himself practices the art of selective memory. The guitarist states that he made just $30,123.72 with the rock king during their fourteen-year association. But he seems to be forgetting the Presley organization's yearly Christmas bonuses—especially a ten-thousand-dollar check that Joe Esposito issued to both Moore and Fontana. (Fontana recalls it clearly.) Esposito isn't even mentioned. Nor are any of the Memphis Mafia, save for a fleeting allusion to Red West. Further, Dan Griffin is briefly quoted, but Moore never gives him credit for getting the ball rolling on either the *All the King's Men* project or the proposed documentary film. Coming off as distant and unemotional, Moore ultimately proved that a man can hide in plain sight, even in his own autobiography.

For the book and CD promo tour, Moore suggested packing in as many promotional stops as possible, as long as the routing suited his preferred schedule of sleeping late and sticking to the speed limit. During the early days, Elvis Presley and the Blue Moon Boys wore out several cars traveling to radio stations and meeting the record-buying public. "Scotty remembered the power of the handshake," states Griffin. "Elvis and his band had done it this way. So, forty-one years later, the process of signing books, CDs, photographs, and everything the fans had in their possession seemed like a good idea—on the surface."

The tour began in Nashville with an induction into the L.A.-based Guitar Center's Walk of Fame. In addition to Scotty, James Burton, Chet Atkins, and Duane Eddy were also inducted, and each man was asked to place his handprints in cement plaques during a ceremony at the Country Music Hall of Fame. On hand were Hank Garland, Reggie Young, and the comparatively youthful Peter Frampton, who seemed out of place.

When the guitarists casually made the prints, Frampton walked up to Moore—who had no idea who Frampton was—and asked if he could assist Elvis Presley's guitarist clean the baby oil and cement off his hands. A bit embarrassed, Moore laughed, "Sure, go ahead, just don't get yourself dirty!" Frampton, whose double LP *Frampton Comes Alive!* is still the biggest-selling concert album of all time, beamed with pride as he helped wipe and dry Moore's hands.

Usually, a Presley-styled "thank you very much" was all the audience ever received from a Scotty Moore acceptance speech. This day he also introduced one of his personal guitar heroes, Chet Atkins, who was recovering from successful brain surgery. "Scotty spoke of Chet giving him a guitar in 1990 after Atkins learned Scotty did not even own one anymore," reminisces Griffin. "When Chet brought Mark Knopfler by Scotty's tape-duplicating company, [the Dire Straits leader] noticed an old RCA ribbon microphone being used as a paperweight on Scotty's desk. Scotty offered it to Mark and, in return, Chet sent over a beautiful Gibson guitar that Scotty uses more than any other instrument." Atkins and Moore had remained friends over the years and enjoyed a lasting, mutual respect. Indeed, the man who was synonymous with guitar excellence told Monument producer Jim Malloy (who repeated it to Jack Clement), "Scotty Moore is the best guitar player I've ever heard."

A radio interview in Little Rock, Arkansas, resulted in the very first "Spinal Tap meets National Public Radio" experience. Griffin peeked through the glass to see a man in a colorful outfit, wearing a hat with balloons stuck on it and sporting a handlebar mustache that drooped into the microphone. "The clown-dressed disc jockey was not the interviewer," Griffin laughs, "but he was talking to a rough-looking bunch of militant rappers being quizzed in the slot before us. The radio guy had just arrived and had just been informed he was talking to Scotty and D.J. He had vague recollection of them from rock-history documentaries, but thought they were dead." The idea of having a prime-time interview on a station with a three-state coverage kept Moore and Fontana from canceling the interview. Griffin recalls, "Mr. NPR did a good job making an impromptu introduction, but then the guy blew his cover when he asked why Bill Black did not join them on the tour." After exchanging confused looks and a bit of silence, the men informed the ill-prepared host of Black's demise in 1965. "There were no calls," sighs Griffin. "Just dead silence."

An appearance with a radio station in Houston, another public service outlet, proved a more fulfilling experience. Well informed and very supportive of the new project, the organization raised more funding in the hour that Moore and Fontana were on air than during any other segment the whole weekend. The Houston signing provided them their first encounter with the "record collector 'gurm'" (Fontana's term for a breed of fan that always follows him around the country). "They are consistently white guys with dyed, jet-black hair; somewhat overweight, and have a glazed look in their eyes," explains Griffin, "especially when locating a 78 rpm, mint condition Sun recording. The gurms always carry a stack of original Sun memorabilia and records, especially bootlegs, and pass through the line more than once with an endless supply of material for autographs."

Quiet and usually uninterested in a photo op with the celebrities they are stalking, the gurms generally asked that items be signed without a personal name attached. The autographed, anonymous items are more valuable for resale than a record signed, "To Brenda." These bozos tend to be dealers who go from record show to record show, selling the autographed product for inflated amounts. To combat the problem, many store managers have instigated a "purchase only" policy.

The promotional tour through Texas was great one day, disappointing the next. Austin, however, was a triumph. Not only did radio host Jody Denberg invite Ian McLagan, the former keyboard player for Rod Stewart and Ron Wood's band the Faces, to meet Moore and Fontana, but the two were mobbed by the area's knowledgeable music lovers. Griffin recalls that fans were lined up three hours early and decked out in "every type of rockabilly-style dress: jet-black hair in pompadours, tattoos in all shapes. There were people just off work in business attire and college radio junkies with goatees and flannel shirts." In the middle of the autograph session, an undercover detective dressed in casual clothes and sporting a day's growth of beard, unkempt hair, and scars on his face burst through the line. He then pointed to a badge on his belt and whispered sternly to Griffin, "Cap'n Martin said I could come down and have my picture taken." Griffin quickly told him to go around the counter to where his clients were sitting and, without saying a word to Moore and Fontana, the detective handed his camera to a customer, jumped between the men, and put his arms around them both. The two musicians just grinned for the camera and made the rough cop's day.

Occasionally, Moore used the tour to deal with unfinished business. The guitarist had Griffin set up a visit to the Dallas Hard Rock Café for a very good reason. For years the establishment had displayed a Gibson Super 400 guitar that had allegedly been owned by Elvis Presley, and another instrument that had supposedly belonged to Moore. The latter, while valuable, had never been owned by the Presley guitarist. "Scotty had been asked to autograph it in 1969 for a fan," explains Griffin. "He was determined to get the management to change the plaques and get a free meal in the meantime."

The Hard Rock's management treated the Blue Moon Boys like rock royalty, playing their tunes, showing film clips, and introducing them to overjoyed patrons. Moore got a free dinner. "We finished the meal and Scotty then brought up the subject of the guitars," continues Griffin. "The primary guitar in question was one that Elvis grabbed from Scotty during the filming of the

'68 Comeback Special. A photo of Elvis and the guitar from that taping was used on the cover of a live album from the International Hotel. On the plaque beside the guitar was a statement declaring the mounted instrument belonged to Elvis and was used on the Las Vegas live recording. Neither statement was true."

The Hard Rock had paid a large, undisclosed, sum of money for the guitar, which Moore had sold in 1969 for ten thousand dollars. Its value today would be ten times that amount. The company had also purchased the Gibson guitar, which Moore had not owned, but had signed and dated. Moore wanted the plaques changed to reflect his original ownership of the guitar that Elvis Presley played and, on the one about the guitar he'd signed, to "like the one played by Scotty Moore." The Hard Rock's manager remained friendly and calm, but showed no interest in changing the plaques. "Scotty laughed it off, " says Griffin, "but it still bothers him that his prized instrument will forever be attributed to belonging to Elvis."

"D.J. started complaining about his overall condition after the dinner at the Hard Rock," recalls Griffin. "He brought up his backache, pains in his arm from signings, and his indigestion." Griffin had no reason to doubt him; the ride in the tour RV was not the most comfortable of situations. But the drummer managed to charm Wal-Mart buyers and Sweetfish Records personnel at an important meet-and-greet luncheon. "D.J. seemed in good spirits," jokes Griffin. "As with many retired, aging gents in the South, Wal-Mart was one of his daily stops in his off-road life in Nashville." The visit with Presley's former band convinced the buyers to place a sizable order of both the CD and the book for their stores. For the time being, both Fontana and the label were happy.

The breaking point came in Los Angeles during events surrounding B. B. King's induction into the Blues Foundation. Fontana and Griffin checked into the Hyatt Regency on Sunset Boulevard, the hotel of choice for touring musicians. Fellow hotel guests included Goth rocker Marilyn Manson and the punk band Porno for Pyros. Playing a concert nearby, the makeup and cloak-wearing musicians had brought a similarly dressed following who waited for the musicians' entrances and exits at the hotel. The older rockers mixed like oil and water with the predominantly Goth crowd. "It was quite the spectacle," laughs Griffin, "even for a Saturday night in Los Angeles." The scene outside was alive with even more strangely clad individuals. "D.J. did not flinch when passers-by, dressed for shock value, glared at his conservative appearance," reports Griffin. "He had seen it all before."

Moore hawking his CD in Los Angeles, 1997. COURTESY OF DAN GRIFFIN

Following a meal at Mel's Diner, Griffin and Fontana began the three- or four-block walk back to the Hyatt. Suddenly, the drummer's arm hurt and he was short of breath. Panicked, Fontana instructed Griffin, "Dan, get me on a flight back home—tomorrow morning." Moore would have preferred to attend the B. B. King ceremony with his partner in tow, but it was on his agenda to be a force on the scene, with Fontana or without him.

The Blues Foundation event boasted a who's who of blues stars ranging from the twenty-year-old Kenny Wayne Shepherd to the ninety-year-old John Lee Hooker. Bonnie Raitt, Buddy Guy, Dr. John, Rufus Thomas, Ruth Brown,

Billy Gibbons, B. B. King, Scotty Moore, and Lee Rocker at the B. B. King Tribute Concert. COURTESY OF DAN GRIFFIN

Ike Turner, and B. B. King performed and socialized. Impromptu sets between artists who had not appeared together in years, if ever, made the event more special.

Moore traded solos with bluesman Joe Louis Walker on a solid rendition of Jackie Brenston's 1952 R & B hit "Rocket 88," which had featured a young Ike Turner playing impressive piano boogie. Although Moore dreaded the planned informal jam, he played with finesse and fire. The likes of Elvin Bishop, Lee Rocker, and Billy Gibbons of ZZ Top watched in amazement as the legends clowned over licks and guitar settings.

Backstage before the performance, Moore noticed a tuxedo-wearing John Fogerty talking to Dr. John. Two weeks earlier, at a Hard Rock Café presentation in Nashville, Fogerty had jokingly thanked Moore for not suing him for stealing the "Mystery Train" licks used in Creedence Clearwater Revival's 1969 hit "Bad Moon Rising." In a moment of great playfulness, Moore walked up behind the younger guitarist, grabbed him by the neck and jibed, "Gimme back my licks, John!" Fogerty immediately knew that it was Moore. They hugged each other as Fogerty warned, "Don't squeeze too hard, Scotty; I gotta pee really bad and can't find the bathroom!"

Scotty Moore left the event happier than Griffin had seen him since the recording sessions in Dublin. After years of shunning the cult of celebrity, he now enjoyed the company of artists who had his respect. For the first time in his life, he felt comfortable in the spotlight. The next day Moore spoke with Fontana on the phone. The drummer's Nashville doctor had given him a clean bill of health. Much to Scotty's chagrin, Fontana said he probably should have stayed, and he added, "Hell! I might have had a good time!" "Scotty didn't want to hear it," recalls Griffin, "but said nothing as usual, except to brag about the fun he'd had."

Yet Moore encountered a dilemma that many legendary musicians before him had faced. It was one thing to be feted by the great stars of rock and blues; it was quite another thing to make a meaningful living. The positive reviews generated by *All the King's Men* and *That's Alright, Elvis* had not put a lot of money in his pockets. Further, the rock 'n' roll era had given way to the age of hip-hop. Once the nation's most dominant commercial music, the true rock 'n' roll that Moore and Fontana had created now enjoyed only pockets of support in America. If he wanted to finally earn some decent paychecks, he would have to do what Elvis Presley himself never did—tour Europe.

The Graying of Rock 'n' Roll

"Lee Rocker plays with Scotty quite a bit, and I went down to see them and I got up with Scotty. I kind of didn't want to play. I was in the front row enjoying listening to Scotty Moore, and then they called me up and I was like, 'Gee, I'd rather just kind of listen to him.'"

—Brian Setzer

"To me, it's like getting on a ten-million-dollar horse or something. You have to give that horse a lot of respect. D.J. gets a lot of respect from me, so when I play with him I'm on my best behavior."

—Alvin Lee

ASLEEP AT THE Wheel, Chet Atkins and Tommy Emmanuel, Alison Krauss & Union Station, and Lee Roy Parnell were Scotty Moore, D. J. Fontana, and the reconstituted Bill Black Combo's competition for the 1997 Grammy Award for Best Country Instrumental Performance. The category wasn't exactly appropriate for the rockin' blues sound of "Goin' Back to Memphis," and their chances against three established stars and a genre icon weren't good. Yet Moore, Fontana, the Combo, and Dan Griffin just felt in their bones that the award would be theirs.

Front row: Dan Griffin, Scotty Moore, D.J. Fontana, Tameron Hedge. Back row: Bobby Emmons, Ace Cannon, Mike Leech, Gail Pollock, Reggie Young, Jerry "Satch" Arnold, Bobby Wood, and Karen Fontana backstage at the 1997 Grammy Awards show. COURTESY OF RUSTY RUSSELL

"Tameron Hedge called me up and said, 'May I speak to the Grammy-nominated producer, Dan Griffin?' I said, 'Yeah, right.' She said, 'No really, they just announced the Grammys and we got nominated." Moore and Fontana had already heard the news and they were thrilled. Griffin thought the Grammy voters would be sympathetic to Moore and Fontana's cause because, "They know that Scotty and D.J. have gotten the short shrift on everything—plus, how ironic was it that they were nominated with the Bill Black Combo?"

Each of the nominated artists received two complimentary tickets to the ceremony. Since Moore planned to attend with Gail Pollock, and Fontana would take his second wife, Karen, Griffin shelled out seven hundred dollars for his own ticket. Once again, the circumstances implied something good to Griffin. "The lady who sold the tickets to us said, 'Oh, I really love that record.

D. J. Fontana and Scotty Moore looking quite natty while expecting to win at the 1997 Grammy Awards. COURTESY OF DAN GRIFFIN

I'll make sure you get really good tickets.' We were in the eighth row from the front. We were in a perfect spot. So, in the back of my mind I'm thinking, because they put us in such good seats, that we must've won."

Moore, Fontana, Reggie Young, Ace Cannon, and Jerry "Satch" Arnold sat together inside New York's Radio City Music Hall and anxiously awaited the results. Their *All the King's Men* disc needed a Grammy win if it was going to have any commercial future. A UPS strike had kept Sweetfish from capitalizing on feature articles in the *New York Times*, the *Washington Post*, and *Guitar Player* magazine and all the radio and television interviews that had praised the return of Moore and Fontana. As a result, the star-studded CD had been an unexpectedly weak seller. A Grammy victory would not only boost sales, but would also provide Elvis Presley's former musicians validation as viable modern artists.

During the long wait, Moore—anticipating a win—asked Griffin to make his acceptance speech for him. It was a rare acknowledgment of the manager/

producer's hard work and their times together. While Griffin was going over in his mind what he would say and whom he would thank, the name of their category's winner was announced: Alison Krauss. The neo-bluegrass queen had won for her rendition of "Little Liza Jane," which was featured on her *So Long So Wrong* album.

Disappointed, Fontana, and the Combo members felt like they had been kicked in the gut. Moore, as usual, tried to hide his feelings. "He just got up and left," states Griffin. "I think he went and got drunk with Lee Roy Parnell." They were all welcome to stick around for the evening festivities; Griffin, Fontana, and Combo did, but Moore would not. "It was a once-in-a-lifetime event, but Scotty could've cared less. He was totally deflated by the loss."

Fontana, however, remained hopeful, saying later, "I'd like to try to do another. Maybe it would win a Grammy next time."

The remaining party had a wonderful time hobnobbing with music-industry stars, and Griffin believed the Blue Moon Boys were making career progress. "Despite poor sales, I still felt we accomplished our goal of making a record that would be an appropriate career bookend for these men. I had no intention of letting Scotty lie dormant until the end."

Sweetfish Records did not share Griffin's outlook.

Burdened by unexpected travel and promotional expenses, *All the King's Men* was too deep in the red for Sweetfish to recoup what they had paid out. The record industry in general was hemorrhaging cash, and even the most brilliant independent labels were going out of business at an alarming rate. (Sweetfish itself would close shop in 2001.)

The label had helped pick up part of the tab for Griffin's documentary on the Blue Moon Boys in exchange for a piece of the action. Griffin hoped the label would continue to finance Moore and Fontana as a recording act. Subsequently, he was shocked when Sweetfish withdrew its support for a high-profile project at a critical time.

Lee Rocker had planted the idea for an all-star performance at New York City's Bottom Line club. Griffin wanted to invite guest vocalists who had appeared on the CD and bring in such superstars as Bruce Springsteen, Carly Simon, and Billy Joel to sing their favorite Elvis Presley songs with his original band. According to Griffin, the guest list would have included such luminaries as Keith Richards, Charlie Watts, Ron Wood, and the Max Weinberg 7 from Conan O'Brien's late-night NBC show. "Max was one of D.J.'s favorites," reveals Griffin. The feeling from Weinberg was mutual. When asked to set up

Scotty Moore, Max Weinberg, and D. J. Fontana on the set of *Late Night with Conan O'Brien*, 1998. COURTESY OF DAN GRIFFIN

and play right next to Fontana, the E Street band percussionist asked, "Why do you need two drummers? You already have the best!"

Griffin planned to offer the Blue Moon Boys a guarantee and points for the audio and video portions of the shows, and to include the various guest stars in the profits as well. "Each guest would also have ownership of their performance for future use," explains Griffin. Besides being a lucrative gig requiring four sets over two nights, the publicity potential would have been enormous. The Bottom Line had already advertised the shows, and tough-to-please *Village Voice* critic Robert Christgau had made it his "Pick of the Week."

The event never took place. Although he had raised most of the money from other sources, Griffin still needed cash from Sweetfish, as well as their official OK. It was not forthcoming. "Both [label head] Eric Krohel and Sweetfish had come to the ends of their ropes with me, Scotty, and D.J.," Griffin reveals. "Eric sent a fax that hit home with me on many counts. I had received expense money, used my portion of advances on making the documentary, and always had my hand out for more. Scotty and D.J. never seemed satisfied with the food, hotels, and flights offered in return for a promotion. By being difficult to deal with, there was no love lost for the two at the record label." Moore and Fontana's option for another album with the label was summarily dropped.

Griffin tried in vain to resuscitate the project, rationalizing that he could gather historically important film and audio performances. However, one week to the day before the event, he canceled the shows at the Bottom Line. Later, as part of a deal to take ownership of his still-incomplete documentary, Griffin sold his interests in *All the King's Men* to Sweetfish.

Initially, Griffin and Sweetfish shopped around the notion of an album containing Elvis Presley's gospel tunes done in collaboration with R & B pioneer Ruth Brown. Another idea was a disc called *All the Queen's Men*, featuring appearances with British stars. None of them came to fruition. In the meantime, Fontana publicly fumed about Griffin's dealmaking abilities. "D.J. was not aware that I had heard many tales of his grumbling over the balance in payment of his record advance," explains Griffin. "While on tour with Sonny Burgess in Europe, D.J made loud and rude comments to [German promoter] Horst Fascher and Sonny about my 'incompetence' and the fact that I owed him money."

Fontana saw Griffin as one of a long line of users and abusers even after he'd been paid what he was owed. "D.J. never put in perspective the inflated fee I negotiated for his advance; the completion bonus to guarantee they made it through the project; and Sweetfish's payments for promoting the CD," sighs Griffin.

Much of Fontana's irascibility stemmed from poor health, which he had previously cited as a reason to cancel out on several events at the last moment. Neither Griffin nor Moore were sure they could count on him for a proposed 1999 tour of Europe. Pete Pritchard, the bassist on an ill-fated 1992 U.K. tour, wanted to put together a great local band to perform a tasteful revue of songs from the Elvis Presley catalog. Moore's take for fifteen shows—the longest tour he had played since his days with Presley—was twenty-five thousand dollars.

Heading off Moore's request, Griffin got around the dreaded "Ronnie McFactor" by informing the guitarist that McDowell's fee would make it impossible for him to receive his desired $2,500-per-night-minimum. The guitarist got a measure of revenge when he insisted that the lineup of Presley tunes largely consist of the same ones McDowell uses. Fontana was another problem. "Scotty seemed to think it would be much easier having D.J. than getting used to another drummer," recalls Griffin. "D.J.'s ability to talk to reporters and the fans was also a bigger advantage in having him along."

Lest he unexpectedly canceled, which would have forced Griffin to refund deposits, Fontana's name was not included in the contracts, and he was paid as a band member, not as a featured artist. The ads proclaimed, "Scotty Moore & Friends" or "The Scotty Moore Band," with the second line reading "featuring D. J. Fontana." Griffin offered the drummer twice what the other band members were making and one-fifth of Moore's projected take. "I can honestly say, I hoped he would refuse. He did not."

Fontana had already toured Europe with the Sun Rhythm Section for several years and had witnessed Europeans' startling devotion to the heroes of rock 'n' roll. "They know everything we've ever done for the last forty years, and they respect that," reports an amazed Fontana. "They come out to see you and we play all the Elvis tunes. And they know every lick that you could play; they know every vocal, and they sing 'em all. They play 'em all in their own minds, the kids out there. I watch them all the time. I see a lot of kids out there now. They know all the stuff about us."

While on tour, Moore and Fontana were invited by Keith Richards and Ron Wood to fly to Germany to be with the Stones on a huge outdoor date. Delighted, both Blue Moon Boys jammed with Mick Jagger, Richards, Wood, and Charlie Watts in the rehearsal room. They all had such a good time that Wood invited Moore onstage at the end of the show. "Scotty was a bit stunned when Ron introduced him to the ninety thousand German fans," chuckles Griffin. "He smiled, made a mock bow, and joined the Stones for an impromptu number." After the show, the two guitar-playing Stones and the aging Blue Moon Boys partied for the next week.

During the overseas gigs, Griffin noticed that Gail Pollock had to rub Moore's arthritic hands, and sometimes his feet, for the better part of an hour, or else the guitarist couldn't take the stage. Many dismissed Moore's pain as a condition of advancing age, but it was a symptom of bigger problems.

During the middle of the tour, Moore returned to the United States to play some weekend dates with McDowell. Just before McDowell's show, Moore had trouble catching his breath; his feet had swollen to the point that he wasn't able to wear shoes, and he was sweating profusely. Overhearing Moore's predicament, a doctor in the audience asked to see the guitarist. After a quick exam, the concert-going physician informed the guitarist that he was having a heart attack.

Sporting a strong aversion to hospitals (he hadn't even been born in one) Moore refused to go into Nashville's Baptist Hospital until six days after his first attack. Once he was there there, doctors told him he needed open heart surgery. Three main arteries were blocked, and he had developed diabetes, which, they concluded, had brought on the heart attack. Moore informed them he wanted to go home and think about the surgery option. The doctor in charge sternly told him that, should he leave the hospital without the surgery, he would be coming back in a hearse.

Five hours after the doctors performed the surgery, Scotty Moore was a new man. Not entirely by choice. He was forbidden from smoking his usual two packs a day or from partaking of his favorite scotch, Johnny Walker Red, or fried foods. By the time Griffin got to Nashville at Christmastime, Moore had lost forty-seven pounds.

Moore asked that Griffin reschedule the canceled tour dates "sooner rather than later." Bookings fell into place for April and May. The interim proved to be a long, hard one for Moore. "The postoperative depression and change in lifestyle nearly did him in," confides Griffin, "but at least he had the trip to the U.K. to look forward to."

Backing Moore and Fontana were keyboardist Liam Grundy, Pritchard on acoustic bass, and guitarist Peter Davenport. The vocalist was the multitalented Ian Conningham, who made his living as an actor in London's West End theater district and who had recently been featured in the Buddy Holly play, *Buddy!* Conningham doubled on drums with Fontana and played rhythm acoustic guitar alongside Moore. "Conningham had a great voice that did not try to mimic Elvis," remembers Griffin. "Yet he hit every note and nuance. Ian displayed confidence, but never tried to overshadow the backing musicians who, for the first time, were really out front."

Still in some pain, Moore had warned Griffin ahead of time that his plan included "smiling a lot" and playing as little guitar as he could get away with. Despite this unpromising attitude, rehearsals in Scotland went well—until Moore insisted that, among the twenty Elvis Presley songs they would play each night, the sacred ditty "How Great Thou Art" be included.

After a few seconds of embarrassed silence, the band said that they did not know the song. Griffin remembers, "They seemed relieved when Scotty yelled, 'Next!'"

Later, Moore cornered Griffin in their tour van and said, "Call down to RCA in London and see if they can get us a cassette of 'How Great thou Art.'" The guitarist believed that the U.K. fans would appreciate hearing "Elvis's favorite song." Subsequently, Moore kept insisting the show include "How

Great Thou Art." The band panicked. The four rockabilly purists believed the song selection should stick to the Sun era and early RCA years, and that the band use the original arrangements whenever possible. They were adamantly opposed to performing a tune so out of context with the rest of the material. It was up to Griffin to smooth things out.

"Scotty," Griffin began, "the song just does not fit the rest of the material in the show, and the band is not comfortable with doing it. Besides, Ian has never heard it." After a moment of deadly silence, Moore looked at Griffin and smirked, "See, it is just like I expected." Not explaining what he meant, the guitarist didn't mention the song again, although he quietly brooded about it for the rest of the tour.

For the most part, the shows went well. A classic Elvis Presley song elicited an amazing response from fans who had never gotten the chance to see the real thing—Presley and the Blue Moon Boys. "When we arrived at the venue, the usual rockabilly-clad guys were waiting with records and guitars in hand for signatures," says Griffin. "The Scottish fans were always polite but persistent, some waiting for hours for just a handshake." Five years earlier, Prestwick Airport (located just outside of Ayr) had presented Moore and Fontana with a plaque commemorating the only place where Presley had touched ground on British soil. (At the end of his army stint, in 1960, Presley's U.S. Army plane had landed to refuel on the way from Germany to the United States.) The Blue Moon Boys were ushered into the Graceland Lounge and shown photos of Presley in 1960 and of themselves in 1992. It was a rare tourist experience for the two hardened pros, and one of the few happy moments of the tour.

In Aberdeen, Fontana's anger over the billing of the show seemed to explode out of nowhere. The club owner had inadvertently shown him a flier that listed all the names of the band—except his. The drummer had already been informed why he was listed as a guest and not as a featured artist, but he did not like it. He would have liked it even less had he known the difference in pay scale. At the peak of his ire, Fontana demanded that Griffin book a flight back to the States right away. Quietly, Moore began asking around for a replacement. The tumult was all for naught. "In typical Fontana fashion, the old drummer played better than the first three shows and joked with the band while onstage," states Griffin. "By the time we returned to the hotel, without a word to me, he told the band he would finish the tour. But we had two other drummers lined up just in case."

The London show at the Mean Fiddler was oversold, and Griffin recalls, "People were hanging from the rafters. Scotty and D.J. had done a lot of radio and TV interviews, so the people who could not get tickets would come to the venues to catch them arriving and departing, hoping for a photo or autograph. When we left the London club Saturday night, it was almost like the Elvis days, with people chasing them, flashing cameras in their faces." However, the best was yet to come.

Dan Griffin remembers the following with great affection. "Back at the hotel I had a message that Scotty and D.J. had an invitation for dinner on our first night off in several days. The gentleman was calling for a friend—George Harrison! A large black car picked us up and drove us to a beautiful little English town on the Thames. We pulled to the front of the most amazing house I had ever seen. It was once a monastery, and when it was restored they left the religious motif. Just as we were getting out of the car, a golf cart pulled around the side of the house and a beaming Beatle George waved.

Dan Griffin (front), Scotty Moore, D. J. Fontana, and George Harrison at Friar Park, Henley On Thames, England, 1999. COURTESY OF DAN GRIFFIN

"George took us into the house and asked if we wanted coffee—and *he* made the coffee! He asked about their recent health problems and told us about his throat cancer, which he had beaten. He then brought out a birthday gift that his wife, Olivia, bought for him in L.A.—an eight-by-ten photo of Scotty, Elvis, and Bill Black taken in 1954—signed by all three! Scotty was surprised to see one in such great condition and authenticated it for Mr. Harrison's peace of mind. He offered to show us around the property, but Scotty was unable to walk very far due to his problems with his feet from diabetes. Instead, we sat in his music room and he played disc jockey, putting on great old records.

"He played his favorite record, 'Barnacle Bill the Sailor' by a cast of dozens including Hoagy Carmichael, Bix Biderbecke, Benny Goodman, and others. He talked about his friendship with Carl Perkins and our relationship with him. He made sure that everyone was comfortable and happy in the big room with lots of wood. If you remember the video for 'Got My Mind Set on You,' this was where it was filmed. His neighbor and friend, Alvin Lee of Ten Years After, arrived, and George's lovely wife, Olivia, came down and took us to the dining room.

"When dinner was over, he took us to his guitar room and he grabbed a digital camera and directed us upstairs. He had hundreds of guitars in a room with a beautiful grand piano. George took them down and told us the history of each one. He had his Beatle Gretsch and Rickenbacker guitars used during every phase of their career, and guitars that were gifts from Bob Dylan, John Lennon, and others.

"George made few fleeting references to his old bandmates. When he asked if Scotty remembered a certain Elvis song and the guitarist meekly replied, 'No,' Harrison replied, 'That's OK, I can't remember how to play "A Hard Day's Night."'

"He asked Scotty to play certain Elvis songs and asked how the old gentleman had made diminished chords fit in songs where they did not belong. He also pointed out Beatles songs where they swiped Scotty's ideas. It was quite a sight to see and hear. George would jump into a song and would sing with the recognizable voice of a Beatle and the melody of Elvis Presley. Olivia whispered to me that she had not seen him act like this since the night he last saw Roy Orbison perform live."

Harrison's wife also said they would like to come to the last show of the tour in Birmingham. Led Zeppelin front man Robert Plant had a front-and-

Scotty Moore, D. J. Fontana, George Harrison, pioneer British rocker Joe Brown, and Alvin Lee jamming at Harrison's home, 1999. COURTESY OF DAN GRIFFIN

center table for the show, and Griffin made a call to him to ask if the Harrisons could be added to his table. Griffin laughs, "When Robert heard that he laughed and said, 'Can he not afford his own bloody table?'"

Moore and Fontana returned to London in July at the behest of Gibson Guitars, which presented Moore with its Lifetime Achievement Award and the first of a limited-edition, signature-series Gibson electric guitar, an exact replica of the one he'd used on Elvis Presley's hits. Hosted by legendary Beatles producer Sir George Martin at his Air Studio, the event had been planned on short notice, but a litany of rock gods had RSVP'd immediately. Led Zepplin's Jimmy Page had promised Gibson he would show up and give Moore the award, and former Cream bassist Jack Bruce had called ahead to say he would be bringing his favorite instruments.

Griffin recalls the details of the magic night. "Later in the afternoon, we arrived at Air Studio to greet our U.K. band for a sound check. Scotty was happy to be onstage once again and even looked forward to playing his signa-

Robert Plant (front), Dan Griffin, Scotty Moore, and D. J. Fontana in Birmingham, England, 1999. COURTESY OF DAN GRIFFIN

ture licks for the invited pop stars. The band was aware that guest vocalists, guitarists, and bassists would want to join in.

"After three numbers from the band, Scotty and D.J. took the stage to rounds of applause. After a half hour of early Elvis hits . . . I passed a note to the singer to start bringing up the guests. Alvin Lee from Ten Years After was the first to jump up with the guest of honor. Scotty liked Alvin personally, and later told Gail that Alvin inspired him by his gutsy playing and singing of 'Rip It Up' during an impromptu Elvis medley.

"Steve Howe from Yes was next up and a big surprise. Steve was the art-rock guitar king of the 1970s, but played beautiful licks that complemented Scotty's playing. Jack Bruce raced to the stage and pulled out a fretless bass. He was joined by Thin Lizzy guitarist Gary Moore, and the pair ripped into a ferocious version of 'Hound Dog.' Jimmy Page and Jeff Beck arrived—two hours late. Jimmy was asked to come onstage and he flatly refused, telling me, 'I told Gibson I would show up for the guitar, not work for it!' "

Through it all, Moore and Fontana reveled in the attention, but advancing years and declining health robbed them of their stamina. "He and D.J. had us call for a cab to secretly take them back to the hotel, before the press pursued them for more questions," Griffin reminisces. "Scotty has since told me it was the best evening of his life."

During October 1999 Griffin put together three dates in Paris, Finland, and Amsterdam. In Paris, Moore and Fontana appeared with Pete Pritchard, Ian Conningham, and Peter Davenport, and the show boasted more than two thousand cheering fans. Says Griffin: "In fact, the audience was so enthusiastic, they had to repeat songs and even did a blues jam. The only time I ever witnessed Scotty Moore performing a free-form blues, something he hates to do nearly as much as play an acoustic guitar."

In Finland, the Blue Moon Boys participated in an event that Moore had always sworn he wouldn't do—a re-creation of the sit-down portion of Elvis's *'68 Comeback Special.* The rock veterans performed an hour of Presley's music for Finland Public Television with one of the country's most popular bands, the Agents. The television show won the equivalent of a Scandinavian Emmy, sold well on DVD, and was eventually made into a live CD that went platinum in Finland (requiring 50,000 units sold). Griffin fondly recalls, "Later, when the band came to the U.S. for recording in Nashville and Memphis, they presented Scotty, D.J., Gail, and me with beautiful award plaques, which included a Finnish Medal of Honor, all for keeping Elvis alive in Finland."

Moore and Fontana were travel weary by the time they arrived in Amsterdam. "I could always tell when Scotty was not into performing; he does not change into his suit and tie, preferring to perform in his street clothes," says Griffin. Overall, the tour was a success, and it resulted in sales of more merchandise, books, CDs, and photographs than the entire U.S. tour had done. "Little did I know these would be the last dates I would arrange for them," says Griffin. "Scotty was slowly going back into his shell, and I was getting tired of devoting so much time to their projects and not getting paid—although Scotty gave me a five-hundred-dollar 'bonus' after the show in Paris since he had made ten thousand dollars on the show and sales."

Although Griffin arranged and vetted business deals for Moore and Fontana, neither musician would publicly refer to him as his manager. However, the Blue Moon Boys certainly saddled him with management responsibilities. "Every time some oldies band called D.J. with an offer to play with an Elvis imitator he always told them, 'Check it out with Dan first.' When someone would call Scotty about an interview, he'd have them run it by me first." It was in his capacity as manager, and as a budding filmmaker hoping to get his documentary back on track, that Griffin proposed the documentary *Good Rockin' Tonight: The Legacy of Sun Records*.

A New York independent film company called the Shooting Gallery (which had scored a critical and commercial hit with *Sling Blade)* had been thinking of a project along the same lines and asked Griffin to sign on as a producer along with Susan Lacy, the executive producer of the critically acclaimed PBS series *American Masters*. Working with director Bruce Sinofsky, they lined up as many former Sun artists as they could reach, paired them with younger artists, and planned to record an all-star album for Atlantic. Besides his desire to highlight the forgotten rockabillies of the Sun Records era, Griffin had an ulterior motive. "I envisioned it as a way to get another film project underway that would interest people in my film of the comeback of Scotty and D.J."

"My first job as producer was to accompany Bruce to Memphis and Nashville to personally introduce him to the artists who were suspicious of anything and everything," reports Griffin. "Even Scotty was less hesitant about being a part of it since I had negotiated a $2,500-apiece fee for each track he and D.J. performed on for the soundtrack. For the first time, I asked both of them for a 15 percent commission, since I was only getting $7,500 and a producer's credit for nearly a year's worth of work. Also, they stood to make a substantial amount of money from the CD, since the executive producer, Phil Carson, anticipated them playing on twelve to sixteen tracks with special guests."

However, Carson ran into problems with some of the artists who's been asked to appear. While voicing deep respect for Moore and Fontana, many preferred to use their own bands and studios, and sometime even their own producers, opting out of working with Atlantic's Ahmet Ertegun. According to Griffin, this turn of events especially frustrated Moore. "He had anticipated a thirty-thousand-dollar paycheck for the CD, and now it looked as if they would get about half that and would have to pay me my commission on top of that. D.J. even commented, when I asked him to give me a check, 'Oh, did you mean for this project? I thought you meant for everything *after* this!' The sad thing was, he was serious." However, both paid up promptly and, while they were disappointed about not playing on every session, they agreed to continue working on the film.

The film—a star-studded tribute to Moore and Fontana's comeback—would prove to be a matter of contention between the Blue Moon Boys and

Griffin for years to come. Moore and Fontana claimed Griffin owed them a hefty fee. Griffin maintains that Moore truculently ignored the contract he himself had dictated and signed, which said they would be paid out of profits. As of this writing, Susan Graham, executive producer of Night Glare Films in association with Dornasus Productions, has brokered a deal with Moore and Fontana, clearing the way for the documentary's release. Moore has countered that he doesn't want Griffin's name on the film, which may halt the process again. Griffin has often gibed, "If it doesn't get released it'll be the most expensive home movie ever made." Sadly, it appears that joke may come true.

Phil Carson lined up three days of sessions at Abbey Road Studios in London for the next film and recording segment. Bryan Ferry, Jools Holland, Mark Knopfler, Italian superstar Zucchero, and Led Zeppelin bassist John Paul Jones recorded with the pair. A surprise session with Queen guitarist Brian May yielded a remake of an obscure early Sun track, "Teasin' Around." Griffin explains: "When Van Morrison was a no-show, Brian stepped to the plate and performed the great track after we dug through a Sun box set and found it. He learned the song in five minutes and they recorded it in one take. His vocal performance was incredible. At the end of the session I asked him why he never sang like that in Queen and he told me, 'There was someone in the band who wouldn't let me!'"

Unfortunately, the track, along with Mark Knopler's fine version of "Rock and Roll Ruby," was relegated to the Japanese version of the CD and not heard in this country. Zucchero performed a strong version of Charlie Rich's "Who Will the Next Fool Be" that was later replaced by a weaker rendition from Sheryl Crow. After the session, Griffin would not see Moore again for more than a year.

In 2000, the following year, Moore became the first sideman inducted into the Rock 'n' Roll Hall of Fame. Although he was flattered, the sideman caveat continues to rile the guitarist. "I have mixed feelings about the Hall of Fame," Moore explained, "but I do understand, being associated, engineering-wise, with the CMA for a lot of years, I know how political these things are. I still think that we should have went in as a group; whether we [should have gone] in with Elvis at the very beginning or not, I don't know, but the Blue Moon Boys and Elvis were a *group*. But, on the other hand, being the first to go in with a new category, hopefully this would open things up for a bunch of well-deserved players. Jeff Beck, as an example. He's got the damndest way of handling the darn whammy bar in the world. I mean just does things with it that—I don't know how to explain it."

Asked if he'd like to be inducted into the Rock 'n' Roll Hall of Fame, Fontana responds, "Yeah, I'd like to be, but I think it's basically politics, man. They kept saying, 'Aw, we've got to have a band.' We said, 'Well, what were we, man—chopped liver?' We had a *band!*"

Fontana chose not to attend Moore's induction and instead stayed in his room at the Astoria. He allowed Griffin to give his passes to Carson and Sinofsky. "A good time was had by all," says Griffin, "especially Scotty, who had fallen off the wagon some months earlier and began drinking more than he did before his heart attack. He chose not to perform in the all-star jam of the inductees for the conclusion of the event, and went to the Waldorf bar and continued drinking."

The remaining Blue Moon Boys are particularly worried about the legacy of their late partner, Bill Black. Moore had been a consultant for the underrated ABC series *Elvis: The Early Years*. He told Griffin that Jerry Schilling and Priscilla Presley listened to his advice, but, while he enjoyed the attention and the money, he was ultimately distressed about inaccuracies in the script and story line. The show included glaring mistakes and portrayed Black as the bad guy and troublemaker. Schilling placed the blame for "dramatic license" on the network and said it was out of his control. Moore accepted the explanation, but one of his reasons for participating in Griffin's documentary was to enlighten modern audiences about his friend Bill Black. A new generation of neo-rockabilly bass slappers worldwide try to emulate his licks and want to know more about him. So does the most famous rock bassist of our time.

The day after Moore was inducted into the Rock 'n' Roll Hall of Fame, he found himself in an upstate New York studio with Fontana and Sir Paul McCartney. The former Beatle had been on hand to help induct James Taylor and now wanted to play with Presley's original band. The ex-Beatle sang and played his Hofner electric bass as they recorded a fresh version of "That's All Right (Mama)" for the soundtrack to *Good Rockin' Tonight: The Legacy of Sun Records*.

"We got to the studio early, and Paul arrived shortly after with only one assistant and his Hofner Beatle bass, the very one he used on most all the Beatles sessions," recalls Griffin. Cutting live in the studio, the British superstar interjected some lyrics Presley had originally omitted as he imbued the performance with a pleasing touch of English skiffle. After three false starts and one flub from each of the musicians, the track was complete. On listening to the playback, Moore felt that Bill Black's slap bass was noticeably absent.

Paul McCartney, D. J. Fontana, and Scotty Moore at a recording session for the soundtrack of *Good Rockin' Tonight*, 2000. Courtesy of Dan Griffin

McCartney decided to overdub knee slapping, hambone style, to replicate the effect. (That section ended up being the clip for the closing credits of the film.)

During casual conversation, an elated McCartney mentioned that his wife, Linda, had bought Bill Black's original stand-up bass and given it to him. "It must have some old leaves in it or something," he complained mildly. "It's always rattling when I pick it up." Moore and Fontana just smiled and told McCartney that the sound wasn't coming from accumulated debris. "Bill used to change Elvis's guitar strings," Moore laughed, "and he always put the old ones inside the F-hole of his bass." McCartney, his connection to the singer he idolized as a teen now more vibrant than ever, was quite simply blown away. "Once again," notes Griffin, "Scotty dreaded something intensely and walks away having the time of his life."

Moore, however, grew increasingly unhappy with Griffin as events surrounding the Sun documentary progressed. The manager/producer had staged and filmed the show featuring Burgess, Riley, Jack Clement, Ace Cannon, and

Barbara Pittman at Bob King's in Swifton, Arkansas. Both Moore and Fontana snubbed the event.

Griffin, while still working on the Sun film, began a recording project with Billy Lee Riley. "Billy had recently asked me to manage him and I had agreed," he recalls. "Little did I know this would be the final straw, or near-final straw, between me and Scotty."

A two-day session at Jack Clement's home studio, Clementvision, was planned to record five tracks with Riley and a track with Ben Folds Five for the Sun CD and film. While at the hotel, Griffin got a call from Moore, "Which unfortunately was after happy hour."

"He was pissed and shouting about me taking money away from him—not him and D.J.—just him," remembers Griffin sadly. "He figured the more of the Sun artists I got to be in the film and on the CD, the less he would be able to participate, therefore, I was taking money from him. I didn't feel like arguing with him, but I had to point out that he was a Sun musician and Jack, Billy, Sonny, Rufus Thomas, and others were artists who deserved to be there. He quickly hung up the phone. When Bruce Sinofsky called him later, Scotty informed him that he would no longer participate in the project."

Later, Sinofsky arranged for a Sun Records reunion to take place at the original studio. Almost everyone was there, including Sam Phillips. It was the last event for several of the artists. Ray Harris, Malcolm Yelvington, Johnny Bragg of the Prisonaires, Rufus Thomas, and even Phillips would be soon be gone. Moore, rightly figuring it would be the last time he would see a lot of these people, gave in to the director's request that he attend. However, he proposed one caveat. "Perhaps the sharpest blow was when Scotty told Bruce he did not want me there for the session," reveals Griffin. "In fact, it was the film and record company that he should have been angry at, not me. But as is his style, he chose to take it out on those closest to him. I had decided that was the last I would have to do with him."

Eventually, financial troubles would plague the *Good Rockin' Tonight* film. Although Susan Lacy managed to untangle the legal problems for its 2001 PBS broadcast release on DVD, neither the DVD nor the soundtrack album on Atlantic Records sold in the expected quantities. Further, hardcore rockabillies resented that such artists as Matchbox 20, Live, and Kid Rock were screwing around with the classic anthems of Sun Records.

While working on *Good Rockin' Tonight*, Griffin was diagnosed with leukemia. Too sick to deal with the constant stress of deal making and show-

Billy Lee Riley and Scotty Moore at the Sun studio, 1996.
COURTESY OF THE TOMMIE WIX COLLECTION

biz egos, he retired from personal management. "I have had some real adventures with these two men," says the manager/producer of his days with the Blue Moon Boys. "I have gone to the Grammys, traveled to Ireland and around the country. I've met and become friends with many of the people I have purchased records by. I have also gotten to know Scotty and D.J. more intimately than most people ever have, including—and especially—Elvis Presley."

There were also little moments of compensation for all the hard work. "I accompanied Scotty on a trip to Memphis to film yet another interview for the BBC. The interview was set to take place in the Sun studio and with Moore and Billy Lee Riley. During one of the down times in filming, as camera angles were changed, I walked behind Moore and Riley, who were talking in the control room where Sam Phillips once stood. I overheard him tell Riley, 'I'm having the time of my life now, better than I ever did back here.'"

Since then, Moore's and Fontana's health have had their respective ups and downs as well. On December 5, 2003, the guitarist underwent a brain operation to relieve the pressure of a subdural hematoma. Many thought Moore would, or should, retire from the music business after such a scare, but he rebounded, and in 2004 he made his first important musical contribution since *All the King's Men*.

"Well, I had to go to the masters to get that," says Alvin Lee of the strong rockabilly groove found on his Rainman album *In Tennessee*. "I could have tried forever to do that in England or anywhere else in the world. But you have to go where it is done best."

Now living in Spain, Lee had envisioned working with the duo from the moment they first met. "Yeah, it was from meeting Scotty, first in 1995," explains Lee. "I met him as a fan; I had a camera and I got his autograph. I asked him how he played the second guitar solo in 'Hound Dog.' Then I met him again in 1999 with Dan Griffin and D.J. over at George Harrison's house. George had invited them down, and I think they had done a radio interview with my friend [pioneer English rocker] Joe Brown in England. So, we basically all went down to pay homage to Scotty and D.J., and we had dinner and then went up to the studio.

"Then, rather uncoolly, but what the hell, I grabbed a guitar and thrust it at Scotty and said, 'Show me how you play the intro to "That's All Right (Mama)."' That turned out to be the icebreaker, because everybody suddenly gathered around and guitars came out and we had a session with the master.

"I then was invited to this jam session in London, and it was in aid of the Scotty Moore guitar being put out by Gibson. He was there with his band and Pete Pritchard on bass and I got up and jammed with them. Jeff Beck was there. Jimmy Page was there. Jack Bruce was there, and a lot of people paying homage to the maestro. That was just a blast. I enjoyed it so much. I just said, 'Any chance I can get you guys in the studio?'"

The play-it-off-the-floor-in-one-take feel is what Lee hoped to rediscover by going to Scotty Moore's Blueberry Hill Studios. "Absolutely! It's the only way to go," exclaims Lee. "The studio is Scotty's house, basically. It's a kitchen, a bedroom, and an adjoining studio—which is great. I called him up and said, 'Where's the best place to record, Scotty? Any engineers you would prefer to use?' He said, 'Well, let's do it at my place' That was like a dream come true to me—icing on the cake."

Lee was amazed by the seventy-three-year-old Fontana's work on the drums. "He whacks them, too. It surprised me. I thought maybe he played them quite lightly. He knows where the groove is—he knows where the *roll* in rock 'n' roll is. That's why I did this album. I like the roll more than the rock. The roll is what gives it the magic, to me."

Although Moore played on only three of the disc's eleven tunes—"Let's Get It On," "Something's Gonna Get You," and "Take My Time"—his no-nonsense production style proved quite rewarding. "I booked three weeks to record in Nashville, and it took two days and we were done," Lee boasts cheerfully. "That's how good those guys are."

In addition to choosing double-bass slapper Pritchard and country pianist Willie Rainsford for the sessions, Moore reigned in some of Lee's hard-rock instincts and offered some technical advice for the man once dubbed the Fastest Guitar Alive. "He told me to take the funny, distorted sound off of my guitar, and not play so fast," laughs Lee. "He said, 'Alvin, you always play faster than I can listen.' I said, 'What about that solo you did on "Shake, Rattle and Roll?"' He just grinned and said, 'Oh—that was a long time ago.' But he told me off and said 'you've got to find the pocket.'"

From the start, Lee recognized that Moore respected his abilities. "Scotty, working with me, I think he gave me a bit more reign had he done if it were his own session," he explained. Moore also displayed sense enough to let Alvin Lee be Alvin Lee, and he allowed for some extended jams that showed off the English guitarist's trademark musical energy and invention. Further, Lee had never used a stand-up bass before and was mightily impressed. Subsequently, he hired Pritchard for his own touring band. "Live, it works out fantastic. It's a unique sound, which I am actually getting off on at the moment."

"You know what Scotty said?" asks Lee with glowing pride. "He said, 'If you play this album for someone and they don't tap their feet, you'd better bury them, because they're dead.'"

While Moore seems to have found his groove as a producer, his arthritis has made him spotty as a picker. During another "final tour," English writers noticed that Moore did not attempt much lead guitar, but then quickly added, "But it was great to see him." That attitude prevailed at the *50th Year of Rock 'n' Roll—The Legends* show held at the Cannon Center in Memphis on August 13, 2004.

Staged by Donald Lamm during "Dead Elvis Week," the show was a doubleheader. The late evening show starred Presley's group from the 1970s, the TCB Band, with James Burton on guitar. But it was the early show featuring Moore, Fontana, Ronnie McDowell, Lee Rocker, Stan Perkins, bass legend Bob Moore, tribute artist Eddie Miles, and the Jordanaires that was most eagerly anticipated.

The night before, Fontana, looking trimmer and healthier than he had in ages, sat in on a live show at the Marriot with Sonny Burgess and the Pacers, but he had trouble getting his beat on track. At the Cannon Center, playing with McDowell's band—and with an extra drummer below his riser—he quickly found the groove and drummed with youthful flair the whole night.

Dressed to match his jet-black hair, McDowell's portion of the show was larded with gushy sentiment and cloying humor, but his smartly chosen Presley repertoire totally enraptured the audience.

However, it was Billy Swan and Boots Randolph who stole the show. After clearly enjoying Scotty Moore's classic solo during "Heartbreak Hotel," Swan sang a rendition of "I Was the One" that caused several Europeans surrounding this writer to cry out, "Oh, he's *good*!" Best of all was Swan's duet with Boots Randolph on "Reconsider Baby." While Swan sassily sang the grinding plea from *Elvis Is Back*, the saxophonist replicated his nasty blues solo from the record with such scorch and verve that patrons leapt to their feet in approval. At events such as these, audiences wildly applaud any geriatric performer who can execute with competence. However, the seventy-seven-year-old "Yakety Sax" man wasn't merely competent that night; he was brilliant.

Moore was another story. His skin appeared waxy white, and while cheerfully speaking with Griffin, his memory didn't seem intact. Yet his handshake was firm and he was pleasant and upbeat. Onstage, his guitar work slipped in and out. He was note-for-note perfect on "That's All Right (Mama)." ("He could probably do that song in his sleep," remarks Griffin.) But his chops were tentative to nonexistent on "Baby, Let's Play House." Partway through some numbers, he would motion to McDowell's guitarist to take the lead solos.

The most revealing moment occurred with Carl Perkins's son Stan came out to sing his father's "Blue Suede Shoes." A skinny, bearded lookalike who even sounds like his dad when he speaks, Stan Perkins lit into the number with manic rockabilly zeal. A sharp lead guitarist in his own right, he yelled for Moore to take a solo. A few muffled notes and silence ensued. Suddenly Perkins declared happily, "Boy, he ain't lost a lick, has he?" Those in attendance cheered in agreement.

It was evident to both authors that Moore had muffed the solo and that he can no longer consistently play. That said, Perkins and the audience wanted to *believe* that he still could. It was not pity. It was compassion for a man who'd gotten so little in return for helping the most beloved musical figure of the twentieth century find his true path. In their way, they were offering the declining guitarist the same unconditional love they once gave Elvis Presley.

APPENDIX

Those Pesky Elvis Influences

Too many knowledgeable people conveniently forget that Elvis Presley only discovered his unique style in collaboration with Scotty Moore, Bill Black, and Sam Phillips. ("Well, we just stumbled upon it," he told Frank Page during his first appearance on the *Louisiana Hayride*.) The singer's love of gospel, R & B and country certainly provided the tools, but it took an extraordinary amount of patience from the Blue Moon Boys and the Sun Records founder to bring the sound that shook the world to fruition.

However, after Presley's 1977 demise, people began stepping out of the shadows to take some credit for the King of Rock 'n' Roll's success. By then, neither Presley—who had always credited gospel and R & B as his chief influences—nor Bill Black were alive to contradict these claims. Moore, a profoundly uncommunicative individual, simply made himself unavailable for comment. Neither he nor Phillips came forward with their versions of events until after certain stories became part of the grand Presley myth. Some of these claims have more than a grain of truth in them and deserve examination.

One of the rumors that has gained credence within the rockabilly cult is that Johnny and Dorsey Burnette were major influences on Presley's style. Paul Burlison, a white boy who jammed behind the curtain at black music venues for bluesman Howlin' Wolf, also played electric guitar for the Burnette Brothers and had a nodding acquaintance with Presley. In the years before his death, Burlison claimed that Presley had actually first performed rock 'n' roll at an early Burnette Brothers gig, singing the double-entendre blues ditty "Keep Your Hands Off of It" (also known as "The Birthday Cake Song": "Ma and Pa went down to the cellar. I don't know what happened but I heard Ma beller, 'Keep your hands off of it, it don't belong to you'"). If you take into account childhood friend Lee Denson's description of Presley as pathologically shy, and the singer's own early predilection for sincere ballads, this bawdy song choice seems unlikely.

On the plus side, young Elvis certainly knew the Burnettes and had heard them sing around the Lauderdale Courts, the low-income housing project where they lived. Billy Burnette, the son of Dorsey, has heard tales about Presley, his father, and uncle. "I heard stories that my dad used to run Elvis off. Lee [Denson] told me that one time my dad said, 'If you don't get out of here, I'm going to break this sled over your head.' Meaning the guitar. But later on they were nice to him. But he was just hanging out all the time. That was the first kind of rock band he had ever heard that was doing that type of music. From all I know, [the Burnette Brothers] were the first doing that. Everybody that was there tells me the same thing. Elvis kind of wanted to be in their deal."

Also, the Burnettes and Burlison had worked at Crown Electric before Presley. Construction electricians were in big demand during the postwar construction boom, and the job seemed a safe fall-back career for blue collar musicians. They all shared an environment rich in musical diversity and they all knew the same songs that were popular with their peers—the Dominoes, the Clyde McPhatter version of the Drifters, the Clovers, and others.

Yet, it's important to note that Sam Phillips, who openly encouraged Presley to sing the blues, turned the Burnettes down. Their 1953 debut on the small Von label was closer in execution to Johnnie & Jack than was their later work for Coral. Most tellingly, they and literally dozens of other performers of the same age and circumstance who claim to predate Presley didn't start rocking on record until after "That's All Right (Mama)" was around to show them how. Further, Johnny Burnette's passionate, yelping delivery, which makes "Train Kept a-Rollin'" and "Tear It Up" such delightful cult favorites today (they weren't hits) is in no way emulated by Presley during any phase of his career.

Another proclaimed influence is the late Charlie Feathers, and here things get problematic. Feathers, who made his assertions long before Presley died, began recording for Sun Records in 1953. Backed by Memphis music veterans Quinton Claunch and Bill Cantrell, he released a pair of unsuccessful, pure hillbilly singles, the first on Sun's subsidiary label Flip, the second on Sun. His greatest fame at Sun came via his listing, with Stan Kesler, as the cowriter of Elvis Presley's first number-one country hit, "I Forgot to Remember to Forget." However, Kesler told Ace Collins, the author of *The Stories Behind Country Music's All-Time Greatest 100 Songs*, that he had written the entire song and that he'd given Feathers a half share as payment for making the demonstration recording (a standard practice at the time). The song spent thirty-nine weeks on the country charts, but Feathers was disappointed in the financial returns and sold his half share back to Kesler a few years later.

The irony of Feathers's legacy is that he was a functional illiterate who was made famous by great writers. England's "Breathless" Dan Coffey rediscovered him during the late 1960s and wrote at length about his work. Greil Marcus included a wonderful tribute to Feathers's best-loved King recording, "One Hand Loose," in his 1975 masterpiece *Mystery Train*. But it was Peter Guralnick's 1971 book *Lost Highway* that first focused national attention on Feathers's more sensational claims about rockabilly music and his alleged role in Presley's success. Although Guralnick warned his readers about men who "speak with more tongue than truth," he never challenged Feathers's assertions that he'd arranged all of Presley's Sun material and had cut some really hot stuff with him at an Arkansas radio station, or that he'd given Jerry Lee Lewis the idea for his "pumpin' piano" sound. In later years, Feathers would expand his claims, telling various writers that he had cut a demo of "Blue Moon of Kentucky" that Elvis, Scotty, and Bill copied note for note.

The unintended consequences of these claims is that they demean the roles of all involved in the creation of Elvis Presley's music. As such, they demand exploration.

Feathers's strongest verification is offered by his wife Rosemary, who has related clear memories of the early days to her daughter Wanda Vanzant. "We were living on Pauline Street here in Memphis, and Elvis would come by in an old black pickup truck and pick my dad up, and they would go to the studio and stay all day," reports Vanzant. "We did not have a car and my mother had to catch the bus to go to her job downtown, and she would always catch the bus back and get off in front of the studio at 9:00 P.M. just about every night and she and my dad would walk home together. Sometimes she would have to wait on him to finish whatever they were doing in the studio. Sometimes when [Elvis] would pick my dad up they would go to the fan club house. Shirley, president of my dad's fan club, has told me that Elvis had a little crush on a girl that was living across from them."

More testimony pops up in the liner notes for *Uh Huh Honey*, a Feathers compilation issued by Norton Records. No less a figure than Johnny Cash recalls Feathers running the board during Presley's "Baby, Let's Play House" session. Former Sun artist Billy Lee Riley never saw Feathers in the studio, but he believes his claims are true because, "I know how things worked in those days." Ronnie Smith, a friend to both Presley and Feathers, never saw them together at the studio but, "I'd see Charlie right after and he'd say, 'I was down at Sam's yesterday and Elvis was in there.' One particular session was 'Train Arrived' ['Mystery Train'] and Charlie was in the studio and he said later, 'I kept telling Elvis, on the end of it do a falsetto when you're going out. Then Elvis kind of rared back and done it. You should have seen it, he fell up against the corner and he nailed it.'"

More controversially, in his book *Rockabilly: A Forty Year Journey*, author/superfan Billy Poore claims that he has heard Feathers's private collection of Sun session tapes, which feature the distinct voices of Feathers, Presley, and Sam Phillips working together in the studio. Inexplicably, Poore expressed the hope that his friend "has buried them really deep somewhere." (This, of course, makes no sense. Not only would such tapes validate Feathers, but RCA would've paid a nice sum to get their hands on them; money his family could've used during his final, health-challenged years.) However, Wanda Vanzant reports that no Sun studio tapes exist in her late father's extensive archives.

A mountain of testimony seems to discredit Feathers. Stan Kesler, who played on dozens of Sun sessions, said of Feathers, "I never saw him work in the studio with Elvis at all. I really don't think that's true, to tell you the truth." But he grudgingly allowed, "He might've worked with him when I wasn't looking."

During his time at Sun, Jack Clement seldom saw Feathers at the studio. In addition, he is absolutely certain that it was Sam Phillips who created the "and his Pumpin' Piano" tag line for Jerry Lee Lewis. In a 1970s Lewis fan club newsletter, Jud Phillips—Sam's brother, occasional Sun promotion man, and partner—takes credit for the line, and Jerry Lee's sister Linda Gail Lewis concurs. Sax player Martin Willis, one of Billy Lee Riley's Little Green Men and a perennial Sun session man, echoes Clement's statement and adds, "I never saw anybody at the board but Sam if it wasn't Jack."

In Craig Morrison's book *Go Cat Go: Rockabilly Music and Its Makers*, Scotty Moore himself states that Feathers was constantly in and out of the studio but was not a factor on Presley's sessions. In the booklet notes to Revenent's excellent Feathers retrospective *Get With It: Essential Recordings 1954–69*, Moore responded to Feathers's assertion that he'd cut a "Blue Moon of Kentucky" demo for Presley by diplomatically saying, "If he did, I honestly don't recall." However, Louis Black, who never heard his dad Bill mention Charlie Feathers, vouches for Moore's memory, saying, "If Scotty doesn't remember it, it didn't happen."

D. J. Fontana, asked if Elvis ever talked about Feathers during their many long hours on the road together, was emphatic: "He never mentioned him one time—at no time," adding, "If his name had come up I would've remembered it, because I was familiar with him and a lot of other guys. I never heard Elvis say anything about learning from anybody. He just sang what he felt like singing and that was the end of it."

Both drummer J. M. Van Eaton and guitarist Roland Janes arrived at Sun after Feathers had left, but they played on all of Jerry Lee Lewis's most important sessions. As with everyone else who was contacted, they admire Feathers's talent but are hesitant to believe his claims. "He's probably told that lie so much that he probably believed it," Van Eaton speculates. "He knew rockabilly, and he knew who was rockabilly and who wasn't. But he told so much other bull that it was hard to filter out what was true and not true. For example, he was sitting here and telling me, 'Aw man, I go to these beer joints and play shuffleboard and I make a thousand dollars a night doing that.' I said, 'Well Charlie, that's $365,000 a year, man.' But he believed that. So, I would kind of take some of the things he has said with a grain of salt. But I also appreciated the rawness in his music style. I like that. He was fun to be around. He had one of these characteristics, sort of like Jerry Lee Lewis really, where you didn't know if he was kidding or not."

Barbara Pittman, who passed away before this project was completed, recalled the early Sun days quite well. Pittman said that Feathers never ran the board at Sun: "Sam didn't trust anyone but Jack Clement with his baby." She further related that Feathers worked with Phillips only on remote broadcasts around town, where he carried equipment and spools of wire. Asked if Presley ever mentioned hanging out with Feathers or if Feathers had anything to do with Presley's sessions, Pittman stated unequivocally, "No!"

It's also important to note that Peter Guralnick barely referred to Feathers in his exhaustively researched, best-selling biographies on the life of Elvis Presley.

So, was Charlie Feathers a true rockabilly pioneer or a bald-faced liar?

"This is America," quips *Blue Suede News* publisher Marc Bristol. "Why can't he be both?" The roots music writer/musician adds that the Mississippi-born singer might have been putting us all on: "I always found it a bit amusing that he would pull the Europeans' chains with some of his claims. But since he actually came up learning some of his music from [bluesman] Junior Kimbrough, there's no doubt he's the real deal."

Aye, there is the rub.

Charlie Feathers was the goods.

After he left Sun, Feathers cut sides with Jody Chastain and Jerry Huffman for Meteor ("Tongue Tied Jill") and King ("One Hand Loose," "Bottle to the Baby," "Everybody Lovin' My Baby," and others) that made him a true rockabilly cult hero. His voice embraced cotton-patch blues, wry hillbilly, humor, and soul. Few could match the rhythmic zeal of his bluesy stutters or falsetto hiccups. Further, he was one of rockabilly's greatest champions.

Although he never scored with anything remotely resembling a hit record, Feathers refused to lose faith in the music. When not working day jobs, he continued to record for such labels as Kay, Walmay, Philwood, Holiday Inn, Redneck, Renegade, Barrelhouse, Rollin' Rock, Elektra, Sundazed, and his own Feathers' Records. "A month before my dad passed away," recalled Vanzant, "he told my mother, 'You know, I probably never could read or write, but I sure could sing.'" It's because of that passion and dedication that rockabilly fans loved him and supported his work. Few cared about his supposed Elvis Presley connection. So, why did he keep embroidering the truth?

The most reasonable conclusion comes from Quinton Claunch, who worked with Feathers on his first two singles. "He could feel a song, but man, putting up with him was something else," he told John Floyd for his book *For the Record: Sun Records—An Oral History*. "It was insecurity. He's got it in his mind that he created rockabilly. He taught Elvis how to sing, to hear him tell it. He didn't do anything, aside from writing that song with Stan Kesler that Elvis recorded, and he was there when Elvis was recording. He might have been on speaking terms back before Elvis got big, when he was getting started. I don't know. I guess he resented that Elvis came in there and started doing some things that maybe he had in mind to do himself. He just couldn't handle it."

So, why *did* Presley hang out with Feathers for a short time? Take into account this story from Tillman Franks, who managed Johnny Horton when he wasn't running the Artists Service Bureau for the *Louisiana Hayride*. "He liked Johnny Horton," says Franks of Presley. "He'd get Johnny to do 'Old Blind Barnabas' and some of them gospel songs where you'd jerk the words out. Elvis would pick up some of them licks from Johnny, the way he'd jerk them words out. He liked Johnny because he could put lots of feelin' in his songs. He could do 'Frankie and Johnny,' 'Rock Island Line.' He taught that song to Johnny Cash, too, but Elvis would get Johnny in the dressing room sometimes and get him to sing some of them songs to him. On some of those beat numbers, the way Johnny held some of those low notes, I think Elvis learned that from him."

There are stories like that from nearly every phase of Presley's career. On a TNT television special, Jerry Lee Lewis told George Klein that Presley had sent for him in 1962 because he wanted the Killer to teach him the words to the old Clyde McPhatter hit "Come What May." Lewis remembered playing the song all afternoon. "He knew the words all right, George," Lewis told Klein. "He just wanted to hear me sing it."(Presley released a version that was nothing like Lewis's in 1966.) Later, Presley would request similar favors from Fats Domino, Roy Hamilton, and Tom Jones.

A true "audiodidact," Presley liked to grab a singer he admired and make him sing a song over and over until he understood something that intrigued him about their phrasing, breath control, or tone. (Sometimes it was just because he liked the song.) Then, when it suited him, he would feed back what he'd learned into a different piece of material. "Elvis could imitate anybody," said Presley's old friend Barbara Pitman. "He could do Hank Snow, Dean Martin, Mario Lanza, Eddy Arnold, the Ink Spots, anybody. Only when he did them, they all came out as Elvis." This facility is really the key to the artist's growth, from a singer whose work was mainly based on feel and enthusiasm to one of pop music's finest contemporary vocalists.

Conclusion? Feathers briefly knew Presley. A surviving poster shows that they were on the bill together at the Overton Park Shell. He probably did pitch a few suggestions at young Elvis, but the novice singer was too dependent on Moore, Black, and "Mr. Phillips" to ever betray them by cutting outside sessions with him. More importantly, as outtakes suggest, all the arrangements came together spontaneously through painstaking retake after retake. It was all between the band members and the label honcho. Charlie Feathers was not the man behind the man, just a colorful and talented performer whose inferiority complex demanded that he run his mouth and take pleasure in the shock and awe his statements inspired. Yet, deep down inside, one suspects he knew the truth.

A short time before he died, neo-rockabilly Cari Lee Merritt and her husband, Steve, visited Feathers at his home, where they began talking about rockabilly. At one point Feathers grinned and proclaimed, "You know, the only real rockabilly music was made by Elvis, Scotty, and Bill at Sun. Everything else is crap."

INDEX

Bold page numbers denote photographs.

C

D

E

N

O

P

R

W

Y

Z